I0810199

The Art of Richard Mayhew

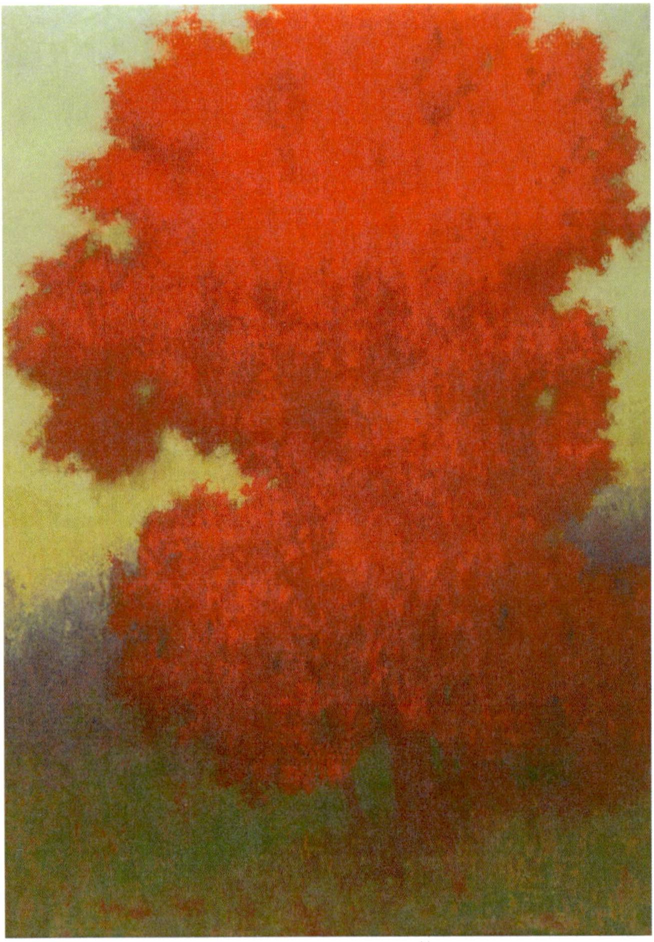

The Art of Richard Mayhew

A Critical Analysis with Interviews

JANET BERRY HESS

McFarland & Company, Inc., Publishers
Jefferson, North Carolina

Also of Interest: *Art and Architecture in Postcolonial Africa*, by Janet Berry Hess (McFarland, 2006).

All images courtesy of Richard Mayhew

Portions of Chapter One appeared in "The Art of Richard Mayhew" in *NKA: Journal of Contemporary African Art* 29 (Fall 2011): 100–109. Copyright © 2012 NKA Publications. All rights reserved. Reprinted by permission of Duke University Press.

Frontispiece: *Untitled (Red Bush)*, 1990s. Oil on canvas.

Library of Congress Cataloguing-in-Publication Data

Hess, Janet Berry.
The art of Richard Mayhew : a critical analysis with interviews / Janet Berry Hess.
p. cm.
Includes bibliographical references and index.

ISBN 978-0-7864-6050-2 (softcover : acid free paper) ∞
ISBN 978-1-4766-0242-4 (ebook)

1. Mayhew, Richard, 1934– —Criticism and interpretation. 2. Mayhew, Richard, 1934– —Interviews. 3. African American painters—Interviews. 4. Indian painters—Interviews. 5. Art and race. I. Title.
ND237.M41137H47 2014
759.13—dc23 2014010655

British Library cataloguing data are available

© 2014 Janet Berry Hess. All rights reserved

No part of this book may be reproduced or transmitted in any form or by any means, electronic or mechanical, including photocopying or recording, or by any information storage and retrieval system, without permission in writing from the publisher.

On the cover: Richard Mayhew, *Love Bush*. 2000. Oil on canvas. 47" × 51".

Printed in the United States of America

McFarland & Company, Inc., Publishers
Box 611, Jefferson, North Carolina 28640
www.mcfarlandpub.com

For my daddy, the most dedicated
and brilliant artist.
And always for Asa.

Acknowledgments

I would like to thank Michelle Manley-Everson, without whom nothing would be possible.

I am grateful to Greg, Amanda, Amber, Gary, Ronnie, Diva, and Nacho Everson for making me a part of their loving family. I will be forever thankful to Mark Protiva, Nancy Scruggs, Wendy Ghiringhelli, Ron Lopez, Bill Sullivan, Dana Mintzer Leman, Jamian Wetlaufer, Jordan O'Halloran, Tammie Richards, Emily Schramm, Annette Abel, Ali Arshi, Ianthe Brautigan Swenson, Valerie Foote, Carla Betti, Stephanie Dyer, Eric McGuckin, Nick Creary, Patience Foster, and Maris Talaugon, for their warmth, understanding, and constant support. I thank Nicole Heggen, Andrea and Curtis Molina, Ariel and Anne Heggen, Suzanne Blier, Dennis Burgen, Roger Hinck, Jerry Adamowicz, David Pouncey, Kathryn Atwood, Sue Foley, Michelle Jones, Tom Duffy, Tonya Moore, Theresa Blue, Conrad Wells, Marty Berk, and Brian Goff for their loving friendship. I am most grateful for the generosity and assistance of Edward Littlejohn, and the blessings and love of Pbanchai Tallman and Robert Farris Thompson.

My dearest students, thank you for enriching my life. I hold close to my heart memories of Cara Franke, Heather Ricks, Nicole Antoinette Fucalaro, Niki Franklin, Monicka Darling, Clayton Thurmond, Emily Byrne, Hazel Chadwick, Audrey Jarvis, Chelsea Rose Gascon, Lisa Slater, Nicole Fletcher, Elizabeth Campbell, Taryn Hernandez, Hannah Hayden, Shavon Lanice Marie Starks, Wrynn Valentine, Kionna Crosby, Angela Washington Thibodeaux, Molly Isbell, Jamie Carlson, Shoshanna Amen, Kristen Sampson, Jackie Robyn, Eva Oliver, Leslie Gibson, Jie Zheng, Margo Tyack, Keegan Finley, Maire McCann, Jenise Gott, Courtney Harkins, Daniel Lanza, Gabrielle Marie, Kelsie Liebert, Joy Young, Katherine Summer Ellis, Aimee Otterson, Tina Marie Tempesta, Melissa Bader, Rebecca Reynoso, Stephanie Evans, Olivia Rold, Kim Liaz, Julie Anne Lockwood, Heather Rosenlund, Sarah Borenstein, Justine Leveille, Katie Rainey, Lauren Allison, Whitney Boggs Gerhard, Pam Murray, Katie Linderme, Kendall Fedor, Cassie Pendleton, Rachel Feller, Marty LaJoie, Ashley Shanks, Rachel Ehrlich, Angela del Grande, Rachel Jackson, Megan Moore, Kelley Isenberg, Danielle Swift, Emily Kerns, Kaley Mounts, Kelsey Pyoree, Cecily Stevens, Abi Chapman, Kinsey Nicole, Marissa Jane Harris, Sharilyn Smyth, Sarah Vasky, Samantha Thurston, William Harrison, Sage Sutphen, Adrienne Buordreaux, Jodi Ortiz, Brandi Robinson, Maytal Leah Orevi, Emily Hutchins, Katie Suffridge, Tyler Gray, Maddie Lewis, Jasmine Elizabeth Grace, Emily Hanson, Melaney Mayne, Jovanna Ayala, Jocelyn and Meg York, Samantha Bereman, and Sarah Wilkerson.

To the Five Sisters Ranch, and particularly to Lori Jean Glass, Lisa Boyd Brashear, Tina Jenne Styres, and Kelley, thank you for saving my life.

Table of Contents

Preface

The African- and Native American artist Richard Mayhew was a pivotal member of the artistic response to the Civil Rights Movement organized by Romare Bearden. This movement, Spiral, was made up of many of the most important African American artists of the Civil Rights and Abstract Expressionist eras. Mayhew associated with Jackson Pollock, Robert Motherwell, Hans Hoffman, and Bearden, and studied with Max Beckman and Edwin Dickinson. He formed alliances with prominent African American artists, including Faith Ringgold, Norman Lewis, Ed Clark, Reggie Gammon, and Emma Amos; his art engaged, and yet existed in tension with, the Social Realism and Black Arts Movements. Mayhew's work is exhibited in major collections and museums throughout the world. Yet despite these historical associations, and the brilliance of his art, his contribution is largely overlooked in art historical and critical analysis.

Richard Mayhew attended a lecture by Faith Ringgold I arranged at the University of Santa Cruz in 2000. My first book, *Art and Architecture in Africa*, discusses the African American diaspora and the topic of Civil Rights, and in that context I discussed Mayhew's art. I conducted extensive interviews with the artist from 2003 to 2012. There are no books on this pivotal figure in the Civil Rights era. Virtually all of the texts that address modern and/or African American art omit discussion of his work, although Romare Bearden's text contains a short chapter addressing Mayhew's art. The latter chapter, however, was hastily assembled by Henderson immediately before Bearden died, and contains inaccuracies in its brief synopsis of his life. Most strikingly, American Indian art history omits Mayhew's contribution altogether. Mayhew has been critically neglected because of his dual ethnicity, and because critical and public expectations categorize African and Native American art as overtly historical, narrative, or activist, in striking juxtaposition to Mayhew's subtle and spiritual art. As one of the last living members of Bearden's association, and as a brilliant landscape artist addressing the spiritual implications of the land from both an African American and Native American perspective, Mayhew stands alone as a pivotal figure in the history of modern American, African American, and Native American art.

Introduction

Astonishing, dreamlike, brilliant in hue, Richard Mayhew's art evokes at once the abstract landscapes of Monet and the color field paintings of the Abstract Expressionist era. Committed, along with Romare Bearden and other prominent African American artists, to constructing a visual response to the Civil Rights Movement, Mayhew continues to produce images that are not overtly political; proud of and emphatically claiming his American Indian heritage, Mayhew is most frequently identified by galleries as African American; dedicated to observing nature and recording its impressions, the artist's career is inextricable from community activism. While Mayhew was exposed to the teaching of Hans Hoffman and Max Beckmann, he has consistently been described as following the Hudson River School, or as visually aligned with Corot or Courbet; although he attended gatherings at the Cedar Bar with Jackson Pollock and other Abstract Expressionists lionized by art historical critics, his affection for fellow Spiral members, such as Norman Lewis, Benny Andrews, and Hale Woodruff dominates his reminiscences. Identified with fellow artists from New York, Mayhew lives in Soquel, California, and his sensuous, color-soaked canvases seem to emerge from another world. Yet despite these contradictions, what remains constant in Mayhew is both the meditative lyricism of his art and his philosophical opposition to the Abstract Expressionist notion of an artist alienated from the community. The questions Mayhew poses to others, in interviews and in life, are far from abstract or rhetorical: "How relevant is what you are doing to the struggles of black people? And how honest is what you are doing? How do you survive as an artist or human being in a society that denies your existence?"[1]

This text will explore the political resonance of Mayhew's art, but also the cultural and historical landscape his art evokes, a vision inspired by his African and Native American heritage, his experience as a musician and artist in New York City, and his extensive work and travel throughout Europe and America. In the first chapter of the text, I explore the biographical underpinning for the dialectic Mayhew creates between the representation of culture and landscape, his artistic narrative of political and spiritual commitments and ideals, and the connection of his work to African and diasporic art. In the second chapter, I examine Romare Bearden and Harry Henderson's claim that Richard Mayhew's work bridges the gap between the representational, socially oriented art of the WPA era and Abstract Expressionism,[2] comparing this notion with critics and historians who align his work with the philosophy of Social Realism and "visionary" American art.[3] The third chapter of the text examines "moments of recognition"[4] in Mayhew's life as an African and Native American, the academic and institutional exclusion and omission of African and Native American art, and how these circumstances shaped his social and philosophical commitments and his art. In the fourth chapter Mayhew's major collector, Ed Littlejohn, and two of his students, Gayle Fulton Ross and Posoon Park Sung, share perspectives on his work and his life.

Over the past ten years I have come to know Richard Mayhew well, conducting 12 taped interviews with him from 2003 to 2008, and a final interview in 2012. The closing section of this book includes a transcription of selected portions of this archive, presenting in Mayhew's own words the intersection of critical perspectives on postwar African American and American Indian art, and his experience of that art. The challenge of constructing a critical and historical framework for Mayhew's experiences, and of discussing the dialectic between political advocacy and abstraction in his art, is evident in these interviews. It is not easy to interview Richard Mayhew. His kindness, humor, and passion for art, and his defiance of social norms and critical expectations shine through, as does his wealth of friendship with major artists of his time, his advocacy for others, his involvement across creative disciplines, and his sense of dignity — as well as his deeply spiritual nature and sheer joy in creation.

He is reluctant, however, to definitively explicate the meanings of specific works of art, and it is only after knowing Mayhew for many years that one can understand the meanings he attaches to such terms as "sensitivity," "spirituality" and "mystique." The interviews nonetheless reveal the flexibility and innovative quality of his technique, the relationship of landscape to Mayhew's cultural heritage, and the use of color and form in his work to comment on social and internal, personal concerns. The interviews also reveal the sheer exuberance and joy of his artistic sensibility, and his expansive definition of art.

Although this text examines Mayhew's biography and artistic influences — his childhood in Long Island; his exposure to artists influenced by the Hudson River School; his instruction by Edwin Dickinson and Reuben Tam; his career as a jazz performer; his interest in community production and advocacy; and his artistic career as a professor, instructor of creative survival, and artist throughout the country — the primary focus of the text is Mayhew's negotiation of the artistic movements of American "visionary" painting, Social Realism, and Abstract Expressionism; his response to the marginalization of African and Native American artists; and his meditative and abstracted, although experientially specific, aesthetic. Mayhew has discussed his 40-year experience as an artist, the "forty thousand treaties broken" with Native America, and his 2003 "Forty Acres" exhibition as a mnemonic reiteration of societal neglect: "You don't come to the end of that until it's fulfilled … forty, forty, forty."[5] Mayhew's philosophy centers upon these cultural and political concerns, but their formal and abstracted expression emerges as the driving force behind his art.

Mayhew has long refused to eradicate from his paintings the physical indicators of African and Native American experience. In an interview in 2006, he maintained that modernist abstraction "avoid[ed] the mystique of the foliage, and the feeling of the shadows in the trees.… I went to a plantation in the South, and I was looking at the foliage in the trees around the place, and I said, 'I wonder what happened in that spot over there.'"[6] This text will address the need for a critical and historical framework for such experiences and perspectives, and examine the agendas and tensions exemplified in critical and historical analysis of Mayhew's art.

Part I

The Life and Art

Chapter One

Origins, Influence and Diaspora

In 1963, the African- and Native American artist Richard Mayhew joined Romare Bearden, Hale Woodruff, and other prominent African American artists to form Spiral, an artistic alliance that represented African American artists in the March on Washington, and that sought to formulate an ongoing artistic response to the Civil Rights Movement. The significance of the abstracted landscapes of Richard Mayhew — with their saturated color and allied message of suppression and denial — lies, according to Romare Bearden's survey of African American art, in the bridge they construct between the communal African American sensibility of WPA-era representation and Abstract Expressionism.[1] Mayhew insisted, in opposition to an Abstract Expressionist sensibility, that representation had an inherent aesthetic value: as he stated in an interview with me in 2003, "The figure was important during the Civil Rights movement — the figure which had been denied and omitted."[2]

Yet, despite Mayhew's association with painters and critics like Hans Hoffman, Max Beckmann and Clement Greenberg, his involvement in Harlem and Greenwich Village as a jazz performer, and his assistance in shaping Spiral, his work has received scant historical attention. Although African American artists like Norman Lewis, Romare Bearden and Richard Mayhew were in the vanguard of the postwar avant garde, the history of Abstract Expressionism has largely expunged their contribution, instead canonizing the work of such artists as Jackson Pollock and Mark Rothko. As Erika Doss suggests, this exclusion "relates to postwar ideas regarding race, gender, and artistic intentionality."[3] Although the perspectives of such critics as Clement Greenberg, and subsequently Roland Barthes and Michel Foucault, aimed at "suppressing the intentionality, subjectivity, and biography of the artist,"[4] both the personal feelings and the biographical reflections of artists like Pollock and Rothko — and their distinctive artistic styles — were accommodated. The "institutional apartheid" and racism Doss describes[5] were manifested at the level of the exclusion of the artist, but were also demonstrated in a climate of the privileging of the individual heroicism of the artist over the communal advocacy, production and performance that is characteristic of African and African American art.[6]

Mayhew's legacy is complicated by his allusion to landscape and his artistic narrative of cultural "spiritual" commitments and ideals, his commitment to creating works with "symbolic religious meaning," as Bearden states.[7] Robert Motherwell's phallic allusion in the "Elegies to the Spanish Republic" series, and the recurrent image of women in Willem de Kooning's "Woman" series — even Pollock's return to figuration in his late work — suggest an engagement with the issue of representation among Abstract Expressionists. Critical and popular expectations, however, have consigned representation in the work of African American artists to the genre of vernacular depiction, what Mayhew has described as "illustrational" or "storytelling" art, or, more disparagingly, "primitivism."[8] These critical, public and institutional perceptions — combined with Mayhew's philosophical alignment with community performance (in part derived from Spiral's attention to African paradigms), as well as his disdain for promotional narratives of agonized heroicism or "individuality" — have exiled Mayhew to the critical shadows. This book seeks to address these issues within the context of the overriding challenge confronted by Spiral: "How do you survive as an artist or human being in a society that denies your existence?"[9]

Discussions of Mayhew's work invariably center on its relationship to "American atmospheric-romantic" painters of the 19th century and to postwar Abstract Expressionism. The influence of Color Field painters is evident in his abstracted landscapes; yet, as Amy Collins argues, "Mayhew celebrates what others find to be the 'impurities' of abstraction; he has happily resigned himself to the impossibility of suppressing references to land- and skyscapes within the general context of large color-field abstractions."[10] A review in 1989 suggested that Mayhew was engaged in updating 19th century luminism "with a rich sense of color and abstract composition."[11] Yet his trees, individual and fiercely identifiable, flout such categories, displaying their individuality explosively and tenderly, as in his 2000 *Love Bush.* A dialectic between the abstract and the representational is revealed in Mayhew's art, gently and effortlessly expressed, but a social dialectic is also evident, a juxtaposition between the American tradition of landscape painting expressing dominant political ideologies — manifest destiny and expansionist democracy, for example[12] — and the explicit claim in many of Mayhew's landscapes, evident in the titles of the works and exhibitions, for land as an American Indian and African American space, concept or entitlement. The suggestion that Mayhew's landscapes "exhibit a very American feeling for nature," as some commentators have suggested,[13] must therefore be considered critically.

Steve Turner states that "part of the beauty of Mayhew's work is its singularity. Once you become familiar with his work, you cannot mistake it for that of any other artist. Fresh and original, heartfelt and principled, Richard Mayhew's work indeed reflects his singular vision."[14] The singular beauty of Mayhew's art manifests and bridges the dialectics described, but it seems, more than the work of his peers, to float free and cohere independently of the juxtaposition of formal and social positions. Despite his involvement in community advocacy, social activism, and the political and social engagement initiated by Spiral, Mayhew's art remains personal, a characteristic that has contributed to the relative critical neglect of his art. Mayhew's paintings and watercolors do not insist upon the primacy of a formal relationship between figure and ground, or upon the ramifications of landscape in ideological or art historical terms; his work appears effortless and improvisational, an expression of what he describes as a spiritual and intensely personal experience.

Figure and Ground

Mayhew's work is often discussed in the context of the Hudson River School and luminist artists, as well as such "atmospheric-romantic" artists as James McNeill Whistler and George Inness.[15] Romare Bearden and Harry Henderson also suggest the alignment of Mayhew's work, in its "fleeting, illusory light," with the art of Henry Ossawa Tanner, Winslow Homer and Thomas Eakins.[16] Half a century ago, critic Sidney Tillum stated that while these artists "may be of some assistance in locating the elegiac remoteness of Mayhew's landscapes.... Mayhew is not nearly so dexterous with detail, striving instead for the radicals of a flat conception while modulating his color values and considering his shapes for amicability to an implied depth."[17] Mayhew's "dexterity" of detail is quite evident in his quill-pen drawings and other illustrations, but Tillum aptly describes the evocativeness of Mayhew's work, and the strength of his approach to abstraction.

The abstraction of Mayhew's paintings and watercolors, as well as their explosive color, suggest to some critics a conscious alignment with Abstract Expressionism. Mayhew acknowledges his friendship with and appreciation for the charismatic figures of the Abstract Expressionist era, speaking bemusedly of shaking hands with Jackson Pollock at the Cedar Bar as Pollock gazed over his shoulder in search of "important" people,[18] and describing a conversation with Robert Motherwell while both were teaching at Hunter College. Motherwell jokingly inquired of Mayhew, "What are you doing — copying me?" to which Mayhew responded, "No, you are copying me."[19] Yet Mayhew turns aside critical efforts to align him with Abstract Expressionist art, emphasizing his fidelity to observed landscape. An interview with Mayhew in Santa Cruz in 2003 is illustrative:

Hess: *What would you say if someone said, because of the color in your landscape, they're so evocative in abstraction and color.... I would put you more with Mark Rothko and color field painters than say, oh, he's an African American artist?*

Mayhew: (Laughs) Oh, it has to do with Native American and

African American artists heavily involved in the beauty of color, feeling, mood — but also, someone said to me, says, what do you see as purple and this kind of blue? So I took him out in the landscape and said, look.[20]

Mayhew's insistent refusal of abstraction as an end in itself is reiterated in his response to questions about the critical dialogue on representation in the Abstract Expressionist era.

Mayhew: The figure was important in the sense of during the Civil Rights movement, showing the figure which has been denied and omitted, and not doing the African American image ... many of the Western painters were not involved with doing an image — and not showing African American images in a lot of European painting. So it's how much one wanted to see their own image, or were involved with their own kind of cultural identity ... instead of just painting. And also I didn't want to just paint the figure for political reasons, I wanted to paint for the uniqueness of multicultural sensitivity. And this is what Romare Bearden did, even though he was involved with mimicking and responding to the cultural activity of Harlem, and also from the South, where he came. But he was also very concerned about that, too. He didn't want to just make figures for making a comment about the Civil Rights thing — he wanted to make some kind of documentary sensitivity in relationship to his cultural feelings and sensitivity. So I felt the landscape was a part of the forty acres and a mule, there was the whole thing about African Americans not receiving the land they deserved, and also the Native Americans, since that is a part of my culture.... I don't want to get away from things like the image or the figure.[21]

It is an elusive line that Mayhew draws between abstraction and representation, between an emotional fidelity to the image and the evocative nature of abstraction. In an interview with Lizzetta Lefalle-Collins, Mayhew suggested that, whenever viewers ask where the figure can be found in one of his paintings, he informs them, "You're the figure."[22] While many of his works allude to specific sites or regions, it is the sensation of space he attempts to evoke, rather than its replication:

> Many of my so-called landscapes are very abstract because they are very free-form; I am involved with the spiritual feeling of space. Just to work with figures would be very limiting because that would identify a particular place or situation. The paintings look like landscapes but that is not necessarily my preoccupation in painting.[23]

Landscape Painting and Political Ideology

Richard Mayhew reveals in his work the tender exploration of nuances of color that characterizes American landscape painting. As Mary Schmidt Campbell wrote of Mayhew's work in 1978, "Color, sometimes subtle and muted, sometimes emblazoned and intense, maps out terrains, where depth, perspective, and atmosphere create complex environments."[24] From Abstract Expressionism as well as American landscape, Mayhew draws his dedication to the intense effects of color: "Viewers are astounded by Mayhew's sense of color — from the atmospheric qualities enhanced by his exposure to the Hudson River School to the tonalities learned from the Impressionists to the large bright splashes of color influenced by the color field painters."[25] Color functions in Mayhew's art to establish both personal and philosophical themes and specific locales:

> [Mayhew's] works are emotional abstractions of physical existence, characterized by subtle tonalities that bring harmony to the elements of the landscape so that they seem to merge into one another. Diffused forms, particularly trees, are recognizable, although abstracted, allowing the viewer to connect them with places they have seen or wish to experience.[26]

Many of Mayhew's works feature a narrow or uneven path, often brilliant in hue, with unexpected pinks, reds, blues and violets. These shimmering, vivid landscapes seem to evoke a contrast between darkness and illumination, between an uncertain and inevitable way. This philosophical orientation is accompanied by a dedication to reproducing the aura of specific landscapes:

> Color captures not only various moods, but also the characteristic palettes of different American locales. The lush greens and deep purplish-blues of "woodside" suggest the cool shadowy forests of the north-

> eastern U.S., while the powdery, cosmetic shades of pink, peach and lilac in "Desert Serenade" evoke the uncultivated wastelands of the Far West. In the latter, the tints are so delicate they appear to tremble, as if we're viewing the scene through rising waves of heat. "Big Sur Pass" ... [emphasizes] a striking palette of near-complementaries — violets, sands, greens and corals.[27]

While Mayhew's art has been aligned with the lyricism and metaphorical engagement with nature characteristic of American landscape tradition, the ideologies driving the respective traditions are markedly divergent. American painting of the 19th century employed landscape as a "vehicle for moral imperatives ... and didactic messages"; in Sharon Patton's view, landscape painting advanced "[w]ilderness pride, new political order, the regenerative powers of the 'New World' and futurity"; landscape signified "a political ideology of 'Manifest Destiny'" and the individualism of American democracy.[28] Mayhew clearly views his work as reflective of a deeper spiritual significance: "I paint the essence of nature, always seeking the unique spiritual mood of the landscape"[29]— but his objectives diverge from the goals of 19th century American landscape. In the catalogue for Mayhew's 1978 Studio Museum retrospective, Mary Schmidt Campbell writes that Mayhew "personally and individually acknowledge[s] his African-American past in his paintings without a breach of his aesthetics."[30] Mayhew perceives his work in both personal and political terms, but his commitment to landscape is grounded in his experience and heritage as an American Indian and African-American artist.

On the most intimate level, Mayhew describes his paintings as "internalized experiences on canvas." He does not paint directly from nature, feeling "trapped" by immediate response: "It's better to go back to my studio and reflect on the essence of the subject."[31] Mayhew's love for travel is reflected in art that emerges after reflection on experience; his work "takes on a lot of the sensitivity of the particular spot. Or the whole feeling of going through a particular region ... [the work] becomes a place. It becomes [the] essence, [the] suggestion of a place."[32] He is pleased that his representations of internalized experience speak to the viewer, happily revisiting the story of two viewers standing in front of his paintings. According to Mayhew, one viewer said, "That's Oregon." The other viewer responded, "That is certainly the central part of Ireland."[33] For Mayhew, art represents "how I feel inside. Not so much a certain place in nature as a state of being."[34]

The "being" that Mayhew depicts, however, also reflects specific personal and political experiences. In an interview in Santa Cruz, California, in 2003, Mayhew described his art in the context of "how much one's ambition was always denied, and so as a result they're only half accomplishments, never arriving at the great accomplishments that one had desired. I know my father was like that. And then my brother and myself. He saw himself in terms of the accomplishment that he never made, that we're making.... He felt very proud and strong ... that the heritage was carried on to the ambition that he had always wanted to achieve."[35] The personal experience that the artist expresses in his work is a richly inflected one, encompassing private convictions, the influence of social and political forces on personal experience, and an overt and conscious identification between the physical environment and his cultural identity. Mayhew believes that it is in his nature, and human nature, to create,[36] and in interviews his engagement with landscape is relentlessly brought back and ascribed to his African and Native American heritage: "It's a dual commitment to nature. The land is very important to both cultures, in terms of stimulation and spiritual sensitivity, and it's very important to me."[37]

Biography

Mayhew's commitment to his heritage, and to the expressiveness of landscape, is an extension of his childhood experience. Mayhew was born in 1924 in Amityville, New York, on the south shore of Long Island. His father, Alvin, was African American and Shinnecock Native American; his mother, Lillian Goldman Mayhew, was African American and Cherokee-Lumbee (a North Carolina nation). "Both of them are actually two-thirds Indian, one third Black. So that kind of makes me fifty-fifty."[38]

Mayhew describes his grandmother Sarah Steele Mayhue (the family's last name was later changed to Mayhew) as a pivotal figure in his life who taught him aspects of American Indian culture that influenced his view of the natural world.[39] The experience of navigating a dual heritage, and racism, was clearly profound for Mayhew, if infrequently articulated; he consistently invests in a narrative related to multicultural advantage. Mayhew recounts, for example, an alliance between his African American and Native American ancestors: the Shinnecock ferried African Americans running to Canada across Long Island Sound into Connecticut.[40] Other biographers embrace this narrative, describing Mayhew's experiences fishing with his brother Alvern and ahis father as deepening his "spiritual regard for earth, water, light and sky."[41]

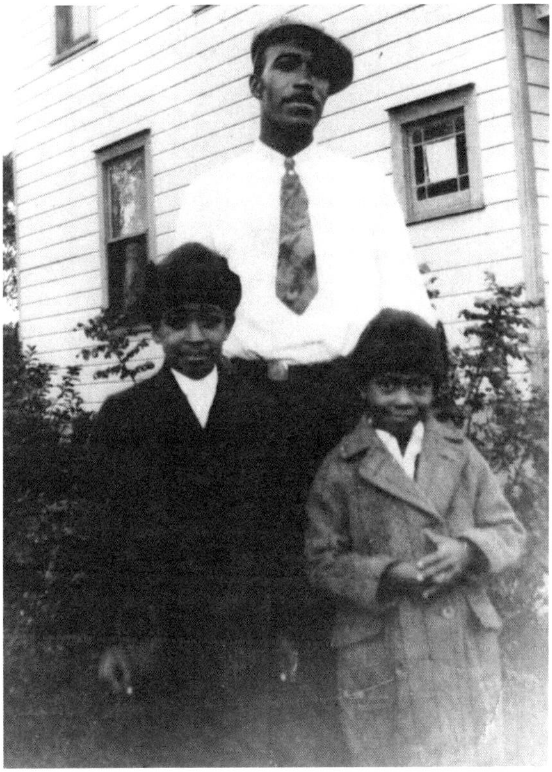

Alvin Mayhew (center), Richard's father; Richard (right) and his brother, Alvin, ca. 1930s.

A pivotal aspect of Mayhew's artistic development was his experience with itinerant artists, many influenced by the Hudson River School, in the Sound. Mayhew describes Amityville as a summer resort where artists took refuge from the city. He often repeats in interviews an anecdote about artists arriving in the Sound and setting up easels in the sand near

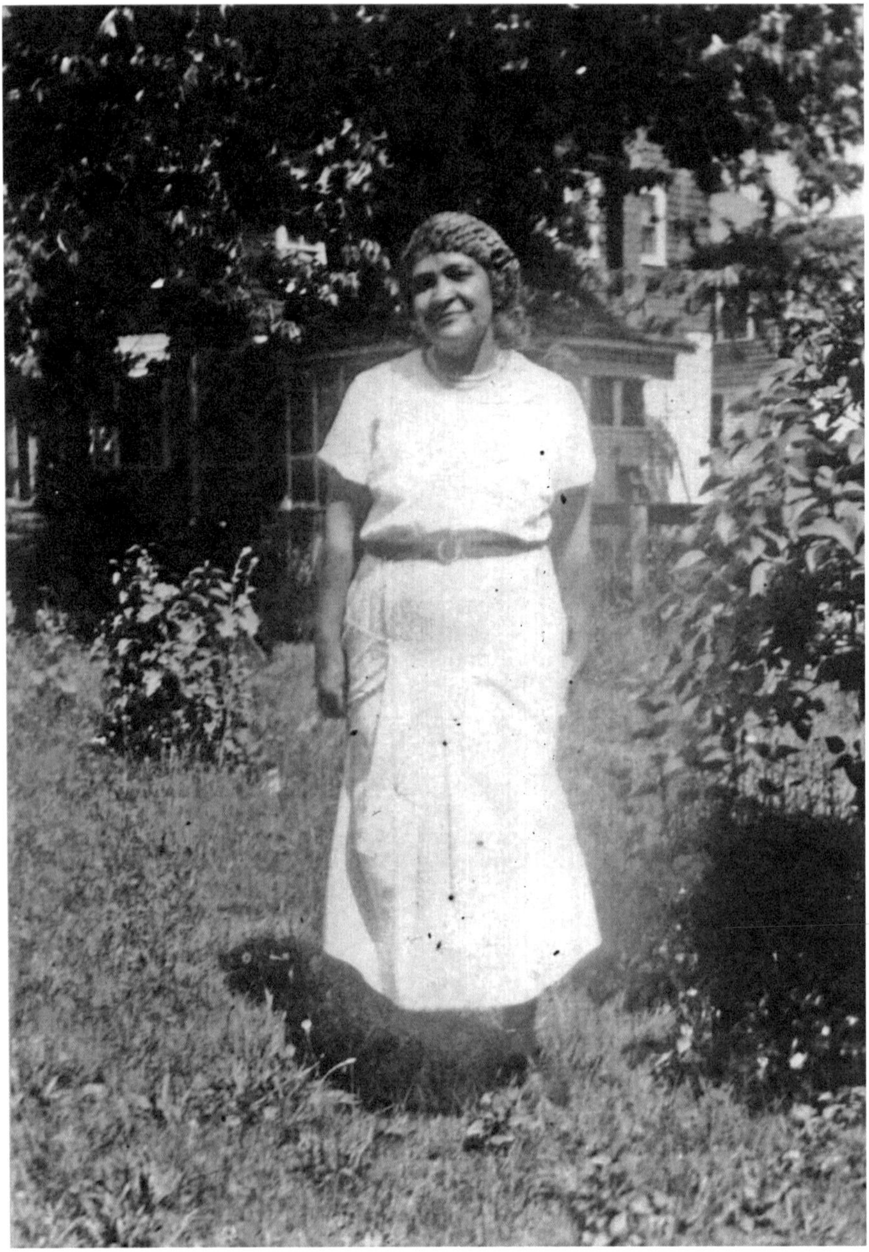

Richard's grandmother Sarah Mayhue.

his home. In particular, he recalls the day when one of the artists asked him to demonstrate his artistic talent:

> Mayhew remembers a moment when he was twelve years old: he was watching a cluster of seaside painters at work, as was his habit, when one of them [James Wilson Peale] turned to him and said, "Let me see what you can do, young man." "So I took the brush from him and I started painting on his canvas," Mayhew recounts. "He looked at me, and he looked at one of the other artists, and he said, "This is a natural talent. This is a talented young painter." Mayhew tells this, now, with a great smile — still delighting in the moment.[42]

Peale became a mentor to Mayhew over the course of three summers, beginning in 1938, teaching him how to stretch canvas, mix paint, clean brushes, and how to draw. As Mayhew states, "By the time I went to school, I could draw upside down and backwards."[43] The artist describes observing the brushes of Peale and others as "magic wands." Visiting artists, he relates, would "dip their brushes in the paint, and pictures would come out of the ends."[44]

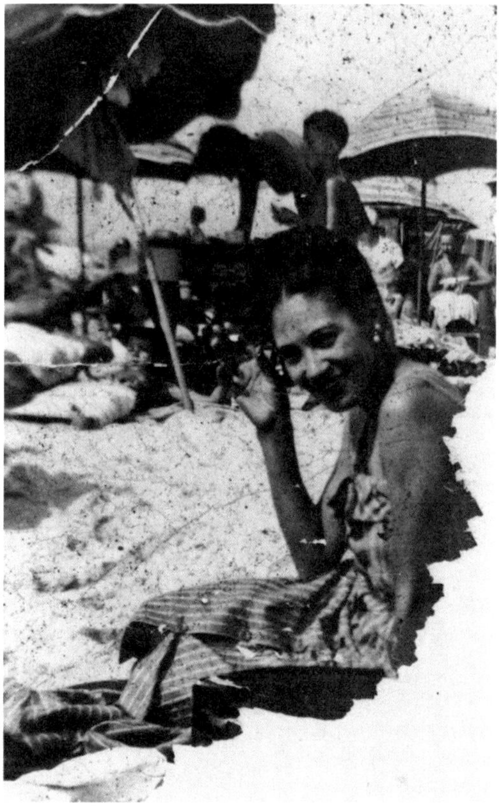

Richard Mayhew's mother, Lillian, ca. 1940 (original is damaged).

Mayhew's father painted houses and signs for a living, and Richard secretly began using his father's materials: "[My father was] a contract painter — a house painter. And also a letterer; he used to do lettering on glass office

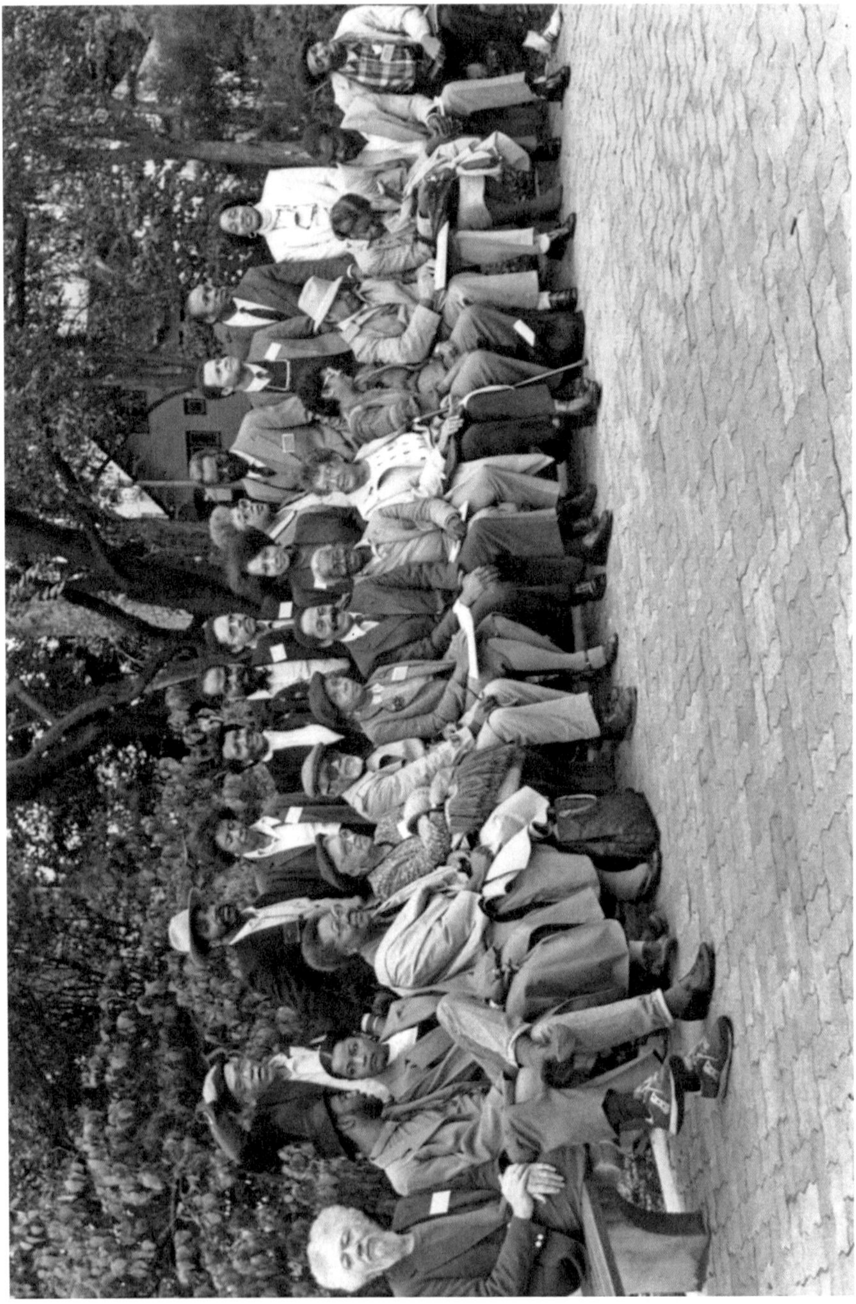

doors. And signs, he painted signs. I used to pick up his house paints and do some painting."[45] An early seascape painted by his father, which hung in the family home, was also an inspiration.[46] Mayhew learned about painting from looking at copies of *Apollo* magazine and other "parlor magazines, arts and antiques magazines from a house in which [his mother] worked as a domestic."[47] According to Lefalle-Collins, "He retreated often to the attic, where the magazines were stored, to shirk chores and to while away hours immersed in a world of art and antiques."[48] Mayhew also read about "all the prominent artists of that time [the 1930s and '40s], the collections of all the museums, what was going on in Paris."[49] As a teenager, he took trips to New York City to visit galleries and museums; on one occasion he visited the Brooklyn Museum, and was drawn to the works of Rembrandt and Inness in the Metropolitan Museum of Art.[50] Mayhew visited the Babcock Gallery, located about a mile north of the Met, to see an exhibition of American landscapes by George Inness, whose Tonalist paintings made a lasting impression on him. As a young boy, Mayhew also visited galleries to see the French Impressionists, whom he greatly admired.[51]

From a young age, Mayhew was drawn to produce art inspired by nature. Early in his life, he traveled along the coast of Vermont, Massachusetts, and Maine, painting and sketching from nature; he later did the same in Ohio, Pennsylvania, and Indiana.[52] As a mature artist, he traveled the breadth of the continent six times ("six times over and six times back," as he states proudly). Schmidt Campbell, writing about Mayhew, argues that

***Opposite*: Artists and art historians attending the Pennsylvania University conference, "Since the Harlem Renaissance," organized by Richard Mayhew at Mayhew's home, 1985. Standing, from left: Reginald Gammon, Curtis Brown, unidentified, Grace Hampton, Barry Gaither, Michael Chisholm, unidentified, Lowery Stokes Sims, Sam Gillian, and three unidentified. Sitting, from left: Benny Andrews, unidentified, unidentified, unidentified, unidentified, Paul Keene, Margaret Burroughs, Richard Mayhew, Ernie Crichlow, Elizabeth Catlett, Betty Blayton Taylor, Francisco "Pancho" Mora, unidentified, unidentified, unidentified.**

> finding landscapes in a society as overdeveloped as American society requires an aggressive effort and reflects a real need to turn away from urbanization ... the quest for the natural scene goes further than a realization of personal history; it suggests an intense dissatisfaction with the quality of life in urban communities.[53]

This notion of dissatisfaction with urban life and retreat to a quieter existence conforms with Mayhew's interpretation of his existence as chosen, but separate and withdrawn: "Really, it's kind of distressing at times to become a famous artist. It's very lonely. Because it means that you're on a ... plateau somewhere. You're put in another echelon."[54]

In 1946, Mayhew moved to New York City and found work illustrating medical journals, working as a commercial ceramic decorator, producing portrait commissions, working as a courtroom artist, and, ultimately, working and performing in the Catskills. "I was an itinerant portrait painter, traveling around with my easel on my back," he laughs.[55] Mayhew visited art museums and studied anatomy in order to replicate tissues and organs in illustrations; he visited the New York Academy of Medicine, for example, to study the anatomical drawings of Leonardo da Vinci and Vesalius.[56] Mayhew and James Wilson Peale illustrated a medical encyclopedia together, and Mayhew designed a text discussing capillaries and arteries[57]; he illustrated children's books, published between 1960 and 1962, including *The First Book of Tools* (1960), *Galileo and Experimental Science* (1961), and *Let's Find Out About Water* (1962).[58] He also illustrated a book on the circulatory system based on his studies in the Medical Library in New York, a book on the opera *Tristan and Isolde*, and a small text on Michaelangelo.[59]

Mayhew received art education from exposure to four seemingly disparate instructors while in New York City—Edwin Dickinson, Reuben Tam, Max Beckman, and Hans Hoffman. In 1951, Mayhew began taking courses at the Brooklyn Museum of Art, where he studied with Dickinson, Tam, Beckman and Gregorio Prestopino. When Dickinson moved to the Art Students League of New York, Mayhew followed; he took classes at Pratt Institute and received a degree in art history from Columbia University.[60] While living in the Bedford-Stuyvesant neighborhood in Brooklyn, Mayhew "also became part of the community of Social Realist and Abstract Expressionist artists on the Lower East Side," and established "the professional foundations of his artistic style as a young man."[61]

After a series of presentations in group shows, Mayhew was given his first solo exhibition at the Brooklyn Museum in 1955; his second one-man show was held in 1957 at the Morris Gallery in Greenwich Village. According to Lefalle-Collins, "His debut was well received; his evocative use of color, light and form caused critics to make comparisons with French impressionist Claude Monet and with the American painter Winslow Homer."[62] Mayhew's next show was at the Isaacson Gallery in New York, and in 1961 he was included in the Whitney Museum's Annual Exhibition of Contemporary American painting.

In 1958, Mayhew was awarded a fellowship at the MacDowell Colony, a community structured especially for creative output. "Whereas he had spent his early years as a loner developing an aesthetic out of his personal history, his love of music and the study of color, his experience at MacDowell alerted Mayhew to the benefits of working in a community."[63] In the same year, Mayhew received a John Hay Whitney Fellowship, which enabled him to continue his studies for two years in Europe. As historians have noted, many African American authors and artists — Romare Bearden, Beauford Delaney, James Baldwin, Albert Murray and Samuel Allen, among others — went to Europe, where they found a more supportive environment for their art. Between 1959 and 1961, Mayhew traveled to and examined archives in the Academia Firenze — staying at the Penzioni Bartollini, next to the Arno, in "A Room With A View" — the Louvre, the Museo del Prado in Madrid, and the Rijksmuseum in Amsterdam.[64] A particular focus of the artist was the study of optics and color theory: "He came to realize that the eye is directed by grids, which the European masters subtly underpainted onto their works."[65] According to Judith Maloney,

> To understand the scientific basis of color effects, Mayhew read books on "the structure of the eye and how it sees and how that affects the nervous system." He read about "how the eye focuses and how long it takes for the eye to respond." Learning that when colors very close in value are

> placed side by side it takes time for the eye to distinguish one from the other, he gained in his own painting "a softer, more poetic feeling."[66]

During his studies in Europe, Mayhew was drawn into the work of a wide range of artists. "I was trying to get a sense of artists who were interpreting their lifestyles at the time, their environments — Rembrandt and van Gogh, how they were painting in their time periods and were influenced by their cultural existences. Later on, this was very good for me, because as a teacher I utilized the idea of the artist as reflective of the social development of the time."[67] The Impressionists, too, had a significant impact on Mayhew, particularly in their attention to atmospheric perspective and the natural phenomenon of light and reflective light. "The density of the atmosphere in Europe is heavier than in the United States [according to Mayhew], [so] that when bright sunlight hits objects in the landscape, it changes them to purple and to blue-green and creates multicolor hazes in the sky."[68]

Mayhew held "five solo exhibitions between 1962 and 1965 at the Robert Isaacson and Durlacher Brothers galleries in New York, and the Sutherland Gallery in Boston."[69] A large portion of his energy, however, was devoted to his career as a jazz singer. To know Mayhew is to realize his astonishing life energy. He describes his youthful experience as a barrel walker, a biker ("That was a joy of mine. I'd ride miles and miles and miles every day"), a first sergeant in the United States Marines (for which he was head of an artillery outfit in the South Pacific, where he painted pictures of women on the soldiers' tanks), and a jazz singer. Mayhew sang professionally for four years in clubs in New York, freelancing at the Five Spot in Greenwich Village and other clubs in Greenwich and Harlem. He expresses great joy in recounting some of his escapades: "I was singing at one of those rattrap places, and a guy pulled out a gun and was shooting up the place. We ran in the bathroom to get out that way. The drummer was trying to get his drums out of the bathroom window. I said, no, forget it, get out yourself! (laughs).... But really, those ragtag places."[70]

Another of Mayhew's experiences was driving across the country, beginning in 1964. He often recounts the tremendous impact this had on him: "It was subconscious that I got more dedicated to [Indian American and African American sensitivity to the earth] and challenged by it, driving across the United States six times. Three over and three back. Each time I drove, I felt it wasn't enough. I really didn't understand until the next time I went over ... observing the feeling of nature, and the neglect of the dedication of people who are involved. It's no longer their land, because it's owned by others. This was a dedication [on the part of American Indians] that haunted me. I wanted to master it in some way. My paintings became very abstract, in some way ... part of the nature involved with a very free feeling. I found that it was depicting sometimes the mystique of what was going on."[71]

Spiral and Diasporic Engagement

When Mayhew returned in 1962 from Europe, the Civil Rights Movement drew him into an intellectual engagement with the contexts and implications of artistic production. As Schmidt-Campbell has argued, the movement from a "Southern, nonviolent movement protesting ... disenfranchisement and social apartheid was rapidly moving north as an often violent expression of the fundamental ironies of racial difference," yet this movement was not reflected in an art world focused upon the satirical ironies and commercial commentary represented by Pop art.[72]

In 1963, Romare Bearden and Norman Lewis held a meeting to form an "artists' contingent" to participate in the March on Washington.[73] After the march, its members (Hale Woodruff, Charles Alston, James Yeargans, Felrath Hines, Alvin Hollingsworth, Merton Simpson, Ernest Crichlow, Norman Lewis, Romare Bearden, Emma Amos, Reginald Gammon, and Richard Mayhew, as well as Calvin Douglas, Earl Miller, William Pritchard, Perry Ferguson, and William Majors) continued to meet in order to consider—according to a 1966 interview with group members—"what should be their attitudes and commitments as Negro artists in the present struggle for Civil Rights."[74] Although the group never reached a definitive conclusion on this issue, Mayhew maintains that "we weren't supposed to; that was part of the spiral ... [our] multicultural background," including African and European influences as well as "many other elements absorbed from American society ... [constituted] a unique sensibility which, like jazz, is indigenous only to this continent."[75] The name of the group, Spiral, was intended to capture the progressive nature of its thinking: "A racially neutral term suggested by painter Hale Woodruff ... the name reflected the Archimedean symbol of constant expansion upwards and outwards and described the mood rather than the aesthetic of the group."[76]

The notion of Mayhew constituting a bridge between the communal African American sensibility of WPA-era representation and Abstract Expressionism, advanced by Bearden, can be envisioned as part of the larger bridging structure of Spiral. According to Schmidt-Campbell,

> Before World War II, the Black artist was able to work with his artist colleagues in the WPA supported communities and the informal groups that clustered around the more formal ones. In New York, for example, the Harlem Artist's Center, the Harlem Artist's Guild, 306 W. 141st Street, and the 135th Street YMCA provided artists with spaces either to work, exhibit, or generally congregate as a group sharing a common endeavor. The sense of camaraderie and shared experience dissipated after the war, with the demise of the WPA.... Responding to their separate aesthetic imperatives[,] many Black writers and painters went abroad to work[,] including Romare Bearden, Beauford Delaney, James Baldwin, Albert Murray and Samuel Allen.[77]

The structure of Spiral supported the coming together of artists associated with the Harlem Renaissance, such as Bearden, with a younger generation, including Mayhew, Hollingsworth, and Gammon, as well as Faith Ringgold, Emma Amos, and Vivian Brown. Established artists, such as Bearden and Norman Lewis, worked with younger artists who had not achieved commercial success. Spiral also drew together artists responding variously to the exclusion of African American artists — in Doss's terms, the "institutional apartheid" and racism[78] — of the art market, allying a communal spirit with the more individualistic and introspective impulse of the Abstract Expressionists.

The Spiral movement stands in distinct contrast to "the masses of ... people, who were often puzzled by and reacted adversely to art that did not present a mirror image of the fictive 'black experience,'"[79] and "the more militantly race-conscious, cultural nationalis[m] ... espoused by proponents of the Black Arts Movement during the late 1960s and 1970s." Romare Bearden states in the conclusion of "Why Spiral"—"the 1966 Art News article that introduced the by-then defunct Spiral group to the art world"—that "[t]he Negro artist is unknown in America,"[80] and both Spiral and the Black Arts Movement challenged majority (i.e., white critical) expectations of an illustrative, sentimental or jazz-age art.

From 1963–1965, Spiral met once a week in the artists' studios or at 147 Christopher Street, in Greenwich Village, to discuss "artistic processes, existences and purposes; they challenged and stimulated one another's thinking."[81] The challenging nature of the conversations of Spiral was intended to reconcile individual creative endeavors with the objective of Civil Rights. Spiral members suggested different resolutions of this objective: Norman Lewis, an Abstract Expressionist, maintained that "black artists should be allowed to paint anything—and in whatever style—they chose,"[82] while Bearden reevaluated his aesthetic and became increasingly drawn to representing the figure.[83] Schmidt-Campbell argues that Spiral constituted for Mayhew "a means of confirming what he had already done: personally and individually acknowledge his African American past in his paintings without a breach of his aesthetics."[84] Certainly the group reinforced the support for community that characterized Mayhew's efforts throughout his career: as he stated, it "had an effect on every black artist in the country. The group provided a support mechanism for creative survival."[85]

An often-related anecdote in the history of Spiral is Romare Bearden's effort to engage the Spiral members in creating collage. Schmidt-Campbell maintains that this effort was inspired by reproductions of Mayhew's work in a magazine, and created at a meeting of Spiral; Mayhew states that he participated in the collage effort after exhortation by Bearden, while other Spiral members did not.[86] Ultimately, artwork was not created collectively by Spiral members, although the artists did achieve a common theme in their inaugural "Black and White" exhibition of 1965, restricting the colors used by the artists participating to black and white. Significantly, the original theme for that exhibition was "Mississippi, 1964"; Spiral characteristically moved away from the overt protest signified by such a theme, preferring an emphasis on aesthetic concerns which nonetheless signaled an awareness of social and political ideology.[87]

Spiral drew attention to the systemic exclusion of African Americans from gallery shows and museum exhibitions. Mayhew describes picketing museums in New York City; in 1971, for example, he was among a group of 15 artists who withdrew from the Whitney Museum's "Contemporary Black Artists in America" show because it was not organized by an African American curator along with the Whitney's Robert Doty. Mayhew describes this failure as "part of all the manipulation and control" characteristic of major museums: "Any time there was a black show, it was controlled by white curators who dictated which black artists should be seen. So you couldn't win."[88] Mayhew later showed his withdrawn work in a "Rebuttal to the Whitney" exhibition held at the Acts of Art Gallery in Greenwich Village. In a review of the two shows indicative of the critical reception of Spiral's ideology at the time, and perhaps a misunderstanding of Mayhew's intentions, John Canady wrote in the *New York Times* that he could not "be called a Black artist except by race ... Mr. Mayhew's peaceful landscapes have nothing to do with whiteness or blackness or anything except art, and this at an admirable level."[89]

Mayhew's commitment to the cultural expression and realization of his African American heritage is discernable on many levels. His concern with the political symbolism of landscape, his involvement with Spiral, and his continued support for artistic community all reflect an ideological commitment, an engagement with the world focused upon a conscious alignment with social and political concerns. But as the complexity of his engagement with the figure suggests, Mayhew's commitment was never manifested in the overt depiction of struggle, which he disparagingly terms "illustrational interpretation" or "storytelling."[90] As he stated in an interview in 2003,

> Most of the group in Spiral were completely abstract. Romare Bearden, Norman Lewis, Hale Woodruff, Charles Alston — most of these master painters were abstract ... involved in painting their personal sensibility.... What is African American art? Is it an image, of just painting black subjects? That's not true. It's the gut and feeling of the sensitivity of this person which is African American... the artist has the right to paint any way he wants to, not to the dictates of the art market, which is involved [with determining] this is black art and this is not black art.[91]

When questioned directly about whether he has been misrepresented or misunderstood as a consequence of not creating overtly illustrational or militant art, Mayhew states,

> Well, I guess for years they didn't know I was an African American artist because I wasn't involved with those kinds of subject matter, right? And the landscapes were accepted on the basis of that, so I had problems with the fact of, well, he's not painting disruptive subject matter which is a pain to our society, so there was that. I had problems with that for a while, but many of my peers respected what I was doing, so I just continued to do it. It has to do with the sensitivity of my culture, my dedication. My dedication now is really helping other artists and that was part of the whole group.[92]

Diaspora and Africa

The focus Mayhew places on his role in the community is characteristic of art of the diaspora. In Richard Powell's *Black Art and Culture*, diasporic history is defined in a manner that "rather than being intellectually bound to the perceived race or nationality of a creator, looks instead to the art object itself, its multiple worlds of meaning, and its place in the social production of black identities."[93] Richard Mayhew does not conform in his art to the narrative or illustrational style broadly identified as "African American," but it is clearly diasporic in its manifestation of Robert Farris Thompson's notion of "the flash of the Spirit"[94] — the retention, material or spiritual, and the reconstruction and conscious assimilation of Africa through communal sensitivity and engagement.

As Powell has argued, the art of the African diaspora is not reducible to a set of stylistic traits or characteristics, but emerges in shared historical consciousness and socioeconomic struggle. True diasporic expression is found not only in African stylistic traits, but also in what the Prices have described as "deeper organizing principles."[95] The communal production and performance associated with the African American community is one such principle. Indeed, one of the primary characteristics of African art is performance. As Suzanne Blier has argued, "It may well be that for African peoples, performance, which always implies music and dance, is the primary art form."[96] Although not normally associated with performativity, Mayhew's art, both in the context of its production and reception, resonates with the communal idioms that define African and African American art.

The name "Spiral" itself has rich connotations, both of African belief systems and communal sensibilities. In Kongolese belief systems, the spiral constitutes a cosmogram.

> The N'Kongo [i.e., an inhabitant of the capital of Kongo] thought of the earth as a mountain over a body of water [that] is the land of the dead, called *Mpemba*. In *Mpemba* the sun rises and sets just as it does in the land of the living ... the water is both a passage and a great barrier. The world, in Kongo thought, is like two mountains opposed at their bases and separated by the ocean.[97]

At the rising and setting of the sun, the living and the dead exchange day and night. "The setting of the sun signifies man's death and its rising, his rebirth, or the continuity of his life. Bakongo believe and hold it true that man's life has no end, that it constitutes a cycle, and death is merely a transition in the process of change."[98] As Robert Farris Thompson argues, the spiral permeates every aspect of Kongo spiritual symbolism: "The Bakongo symbolized the daily journey of the sun around the mirrored worlds of the living and the dead by means of the spiral shape of the *kodya* shell. They also expressed the same idea, architecturally, with the concentric spaces of the royal enclosure (*luumbu*)."[99]

The semantic associations of Spiral evoke the African notion of spiritual continuity, of connection between the living and the ancestors. Mayhew's art similarly served to connect past and present, to bridge the

Richard Mayhew and artist Emma Amos at a gallery exhibition in New York, ca. 2000.

legacy of the Harlem Renaissance with a generation responding to the Civil Rights Movement and the rise of Abstract Expressionism.[100] His art and associations suggest a number of extensions between worlds: the representational and the abstract, the political and the aesthetic, Africa and America. The element structuring all of these negotiations is the communal orientation of his work.

Diaspora and Community

"To me, the artist is not supposed to be a star. He's supposed to be part of a community — a necessary part."[101] Although Mayhew's aesthetic focus was not explicitly narrative and militant, and though his training has been described by some critics as "individualistic" in the manner of many post–WPA artists,[102] his work turns "19th century introspection" to a broad social context and objective. As Schmidt-Campbell argues, "Mayhew has linked the 19th century love of nature with a thoroughly 20th century introspection. His introspection, though personal, is not entirely private as is the case with Abstract Expressionism: rather, it is linked to an ethnic group association. His close ties to the Blues and Jazz also emphatically mark the paintings as 20th century products."[103]

Mayhew's art is not consciously intended to convey a social consciousness, but is instead aligned with an inner, ineffable message. "I don't impose reason on a painting. I don't get locked into controlling it.

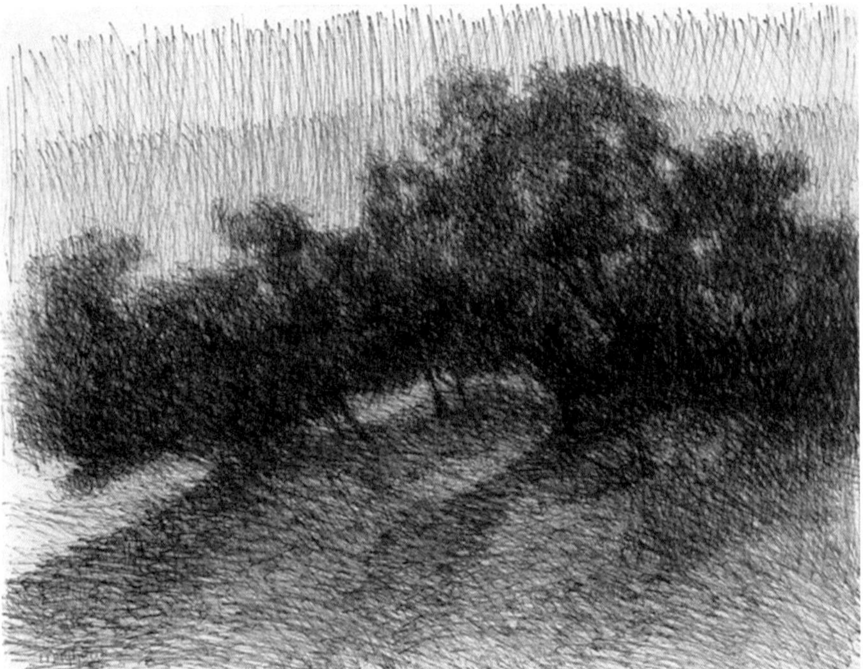

Graphite drawing of trees, ca. 1960.

Once you control it, you start losing the sensitivity of it ... There is a spiritual message in my paintings, but I don't know the message, even when the painting is finished. It's an elusive message."[104] Yet Spiral was always engaged with a social consciousness and purpose:

> Spiral members often examined the relationship of the artist to the black community and to the community as a whole in America. They were much stimulated by new studies of African culture that delineated the specific community role of the African artisan-artist in creating works with a symbolic religious meaning, a role that had continued into the nineteenth century.[105]

When Mayhew joined Spiral in 1963, the prevalent tone of art in the United States was one of reflection on the surface, of employing "popular American images to make fun of aspects of American commercialism and bourgeois life[.]"[106] Artists associated with Spiral — including Hale Woodruff, Charles Alston, Norman Lewis, Romare Bearden, Emma Amos, Reginald Gammon, and Mayhew, among others — challenged this aesthetic on an intellectual and an aesthetic level. As Mayhew concisely attests, "My dedication now is really helping other artists and that was part of the whole group."[107]

Richard Mayhew has been engaged in community activism throughout his career. Members of Spiral participated in the 1963 March, and in the Rebuttal Exhibition held in Greenwich Village in 1971[108]; Mayhew later became involved in establishing a community art center in Hillburn, in the Ramapo Mountains of Appalachia, attempting to relieve a community that was divided by poverty and racial prejudice. As he stated in 1973,

> What does the artist do? What is he here for? If I don't paint the kind of subject matter that relates to the community, maybe if I become involved with the community through an art center — maybe that is the role of the artist. How can community people relate to the artist? They do not always get a chance to go to museums and galleries. How can they respond and understand what art is all about unless there is a close rapport with the artist? Why can't we set up a community-art relationship by bringing in poetry, the theater, the visual arts and exhibitions, dance and music workshops where everyone can participate instead of being passive spectators? I felt this is what the role of the artist should

> be — being actively involved in his community where people can then appreciate what he is doing as a painter, because they then have a chance to see it and to know him.[109]

This sentiment is extended in Mayhew's involvement in the community 40 years later. Although Spiral ceased to function as a formal group when it lost its lease on the Christopher Street Gallery in 1965, its influence extends in the work and teaching of Mayhew and others, and in their willingness to draw upon multiple identities and cultures to exemplify the ideal of "be[ing] true to yourself in a creative form."[110] Mayhew continues to reach out, particularly to marginalized communities and struggling artists; he supports American Indian artists, visiting reservations and speaking to students about art and Indian traditions, and lectures frequently both about Spiral and creative survival strategies. Mayhew's advocacy of American art, and African American art in particular, reveals — as Powell suggested — that the diasporic character of Mayhew's work, its "African Americanness," is not "bound to [his] ... perceived race or nationality,"[111] nor to the formal aspects of his work, but is located in his continuous and ongoing commitment to his peers, his friends, his fellow artists, and the community around him.

Improvisation, Individualism and Creative Joy

For all of his prestigious affiliations and seriousness of purpose, and amidst a life characterized by continued engagement and artistic discipline, Richard Mayhew constantly demonstrates that the act of artistic creation is for him one of improvisation, surrender, and intuition. Mayhew worked in New York City as a singer, and the fluidity and experimentation in his work demonstrate his commitment to the improvisational aspects of jazz — what he describes as "improvisational internalized creative experience."[112] Mayhew listens to music as he paints, and his works have in certain periods alluded to musical phrasing and technique. His movement from watercolor to pastel and the scratching away and erasure of certain images and passages suggest a willingness to experiment and a pleasure in spontaneity and the act of painting. Mayhew's appreciation of Stuart Davis, Miles Davis, Cecil Taylor, Wassily Kandinsky and Romare Bearden also attests to the presence of music as a formative element in his work.[113]

Although preceded, and undoubtedly influenced, by rigorous academic training and professional experience with illustration and portraiture, Mayhew's method is surprisingly spontaneous. "When I walk to the canvas I don't plan what I'll do. I just smear paint on the canvas and I let it happen. I start with an abstract pattern and it develops into a representation of feeling.... I don't impose reason on a painting. I don't get locked into controlling it. Once you control it, you start losing the sensitivity of it."[114] Although Mayhew is aware that his paintings carry powerful meanings, he does not shape them deliberately, nor is he entirely conscious of or exclusive in understanding these meanings: "There is a spiritual message in my paintings, but I don't *know* the message, even when the painting is finished. It's an elusive message."[115]

Mayhew's commitment to improvisation and experimentation is evident in his rich experience as an educator. In 1970, at the Henry Street Settlement in New York, a center for visual and performing arts, Mayhew discovered that his presentations were greatly enriched by a multidisciplinary approach. Noticing that portions of the audience fell asleep during his slide lectures, the artist overcame "the intrinsically lulling effect of a darkened room and a single voice" by incorporating dancers and musicians — Larry Ridley, Harold Mayburn, Freddy Waite, Keno Duke — into his lectures, and later traveled with improvisational musicians, dancers, and artists

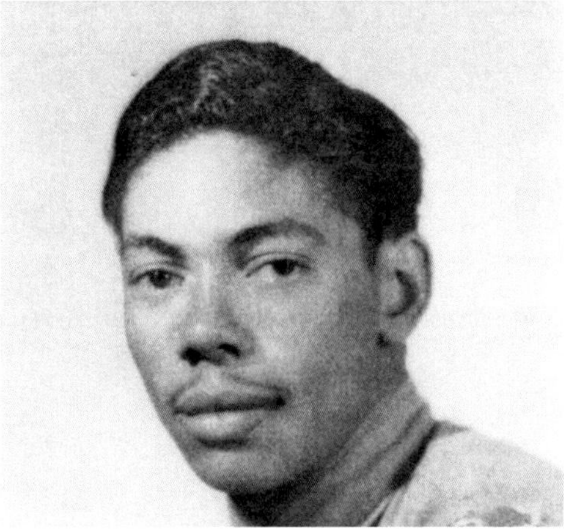

Richard Mayhew, 1950s.

to Mount Holyoke University, the University of Connecticut, and Smith College, among other schools.[116] His interdisciplinary method was realized in architectural form in 1972, through an arts program for a community of Native American, African American and Dutch ancestry in Hillburn, New York: "In a geodesic dome built especially as an arts center for the community, Mayhew established a full arts program which focused on the arts as a means towards stimulating social interaction. In this tiny hamlet of 1,500 people in the hills of Appalachia, Mayhew found that the instruction and activity of art was a means of establishing communal bonds by providing meaningful group activity, something modern communities seem to be losing."[117]

Mayhew's later career as an educator at the Pratt Institute, in Brooklyn, in 1963, the Art Students League in New York in 1965, Smith and Hunter College, and Pennsylvania, Cal State Hayward, San Jose and Sonoma State University, extended and expanded his interdisciplinary inclination. In the description for his arts course at Hunter College, Mayhew explained that "the Combined Arts Course is designed to develop an innovative creative community within the College by interdepartmental disciplinary interactions of the arts."[118] The artist's goal was to "break down the polarizing tendencies artificially erected by specialization," and to prepare students for the interrelationships of the arts, and their real-life complexity: "The real test of his academic course work ... [is] real life."[119] Mayhew describes many educators as "locked into the mold of redundancy and

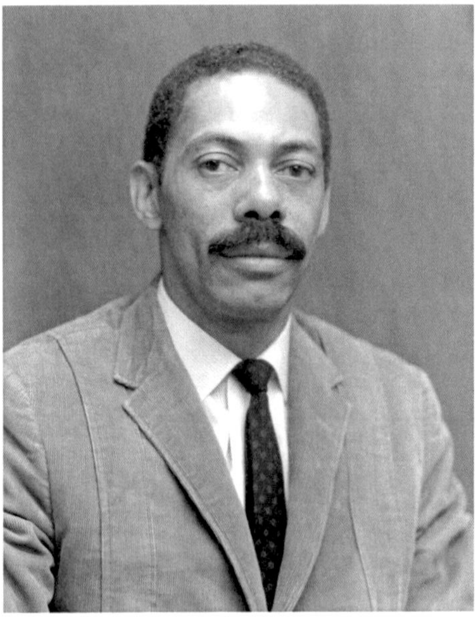

Richard Mayhew, 1970s.

repetition... But the innovators are the ones who make a difference. They refuse to conform to the limitations. I'm an interdisciplinarian, and that's a dirty word."[120] With evident delight, he relates his experience at Sonoma State University, and the performative, interdisciplinary structure he created as "a giant inflated balloon in which dancers and musicians performed ... [they] made a geodesic dome out of cardboard. Students made instruments out of anything they could imagine."[121]

After retiring from teaching, Mayhew returned to the Santa Cruz, California, area, where he had spent time on a sabbatical from Pennsylvania State University. The beauty and atmosphere of Santa Cruz and Soquel inspire his work: "California and the Southwest — big oranges and bright yellows and different changes of patterns. Here in California it's phenomenal, the color constantly changing. And green becomes a bright green and then it changes to an orange and gold ... and the sky out here."[122] Until very recently, Mayhew continued to travel across the country to gallery openings, lectures, and to visit New York, to see family and friends; his work continues to be exhibited in New York galleries as well as major museums, including the Art Institute of Chicago, the Smithsonian Institution, Carnagie Institute in Pittsburgh, the Pennsylvania Academy of Fine Arts, the Brooklyn Museum, and the De Young Museum in San Francisco. Mayhew is also an academician in the National Academy of Design, and has taught at the Brooklyn Museum Art School, Smith College, California State University at Hayward, Hunter College in New York, San Jose State College, Sonoma State University, and Penn State.[123]

For all of his improvisational spirit, Mayhew has remained faithful to his fondness for portraiture, expressed not only in early commissions, but also in paintings like the series of historic African American judges and lawyers undertaken for Edward Littlejohn, or his self-portrait of 1878 painted for submission to the National Academy of Design on his induction as an academician. Although not as well known as his landscape images, the portraits represent for Mayhew a continued commitment to making art that is important to him, regardless of his established "genre" or reputation. He continues to speak out passionately, even fiercely, about the denial and omission of African and Native American art, and the frustrations of working within a dominant culture's paradigms; although "the life of the poet is solitary," Mayhew ceaselessly celebrates the painting process, as, for him involving "that moment of creative joy."[124] Painting for Mayhew "is an obsession. I find I have to do it. It's the creative process.... It's like a religious commitment." According to Mayhew,

> When one is born they are born with a creative spirit to survive, and that instinct becomes retarded in fitting into a societal structure. My deity is internalized in the beginning. Everyone has it; they just deny it because of the environment they are in. Mine has been that internalized existence. I interpret truth, whatever that is. What came out of Spiral was, be true to yourself in a creative form.[125]

Mayhew describes the commitment to portraying the truth about his historical experience as "a dedication that haunted me. I wanted to master it in some way.... [I] was depicting, sometimes, mystique ... it has to do with the shadows in the foliage and a mystique in what happened there. I'm sure those bushes I looked at recently on [a Southern] plantation didn't exist in the early years. But the identity and the feeling about the oppression of slaves that lived on that plantation ... one has the history of knowing how destructive it was to a mass of human beings."[126] Yet despite the destruction and oppression that has characterized the history of African Americans, and the necessity of working within imposed art historical paradigms, Mayhew appreciates the luxury of producing images that acknowledge the beauty of his culture and of his meditative vision. He continues to demonstrate in his art and life the possibility of creative freedom. As he stated empathically to me in 2008:

> You're involved in the dominant cultuare. To the point, you're not you. You're them. You have to be them in order to survive ... but you have the potential of breaking out of the mold and setting up a unique interpretation [of the ... world].[127]

Chapter Two

"Shadows in the Trees": Art Movements and Critical Reception

For many critics and art historians, the intense identification with landscape and the African and Native American communities represented in Richard Mayhew's work situates him in the shadow of a series of dominant artistic movements, including WPA-era Realism, American "visionary" painters, and Abstract Expressionism. Although Mayhew worked in the era of the Black Arts Movement, his desire to convey the richness of both culture and land, and his immersion in the milieu of Social Realism, has established him in the socially oriented tradition of WPA-era art and the American landscape tradition. His stunning, lush and evocative landscapes have led historians and critics to align his work with "atmospheric" American art: the art historian Christopher Volpe, for example, argues that in his abstracted fields of color and landscape, Richard Mayhew advances a tradition begun by American artists in the 19th century.[1]

> [Hans] Hofmann theorized in essays such as "Search for the Real" that the painter intuits a "spiritual synthesis" between the "essence of things" and "the natural qualities of the art medium" resulting in a "higher third of a purely spiritual nature." Intuitively grasping these principles, Mayhew renders a version of what Hofmann called a "personal experience of life and nature" alternately in muted and in "pulsating, luminous, and open surfaces that emanate a mystic light."[2]

This luminous and mystic synthesis, for Volpe, locates Mayhew's work in a trajectory not solely of European modernism, but also within American "visionary" history, allowing us to understand his work as "neither traditional landscapes nor abstract geographies but improvisations and variations on the theme of an American vision of art and nature."[3]

Yet the Abstract Expressionist movement — with which Mayhew is associated as a consequence of his relationship with Hans Hoffman, Max Beckmann, and Robert Motherwell, among others, and the "fields" of color characteristic of his work — has engulfed and shadowed much of the artist's history. His de-emphasis upon individual ego, heroicism, and masculinity sets him apart from the champions of abstract painting characteristic of the era. In choosing allusion to landscape against "pure" abstraction, and in embracing abstraction as opposed to the representational template within which many African and Native American artists have been forced, Mayhew establishes a unique vision, contributing to the critical neglect of his work. Mayhew's refusal to embrace the emphatic nationalism of the Black Arts movement, despite his activism, has further cast his work into the critical shadows. This chapter addresses the trajectory of specific styles and modes of expression in Mayhew's work, the relationship of his work and worldview to established artistic movements, and the emergence in individual works of a uniquely meditative and spiritual art.

Beginnings

Richard Mayhew's art did not begin either as landscape or as color field/expressive abstraction. Early in his career, Mayhew painted commissioned portraits, *trompe l'oeil* and still lifes. Although Mayhew agrees with Bearden and Henderson's assessment that he experienced "visual homesickness" when he moved from Long Island to Manhattan,[4] he vehemently resists the suggestion that this accounts for his painting of landscape: "I was a still life painter! A portrait painter!"[5] A singer and artist in the Catskills, Mayhew painted portraits on commission, and became involved with painting careful renderings in still life: as he states, he painted "all the things around that particular time, the things my grandmother used to have on her dresser ... like a wire hanger.... I had rags and cloths hanging from the wire hanger, and I painted a hammer and chisel hanging from the wall."[6]

Mayhew's first solo exhibition of still-life images was held in February 1957 at the Morris Gallery in Greenwich Village.[7] Reviews noted that his work "convey[ed] his interpretations of isolate moments and places within a purity of representational element."[8] In the same year, Mayhew placed a work in City Center Gallery group show, which was described by John Canaday, staff writer for the *New York Times*, as having "unusual merit" among the exhibited works.[9] Mayhew's painting in the following several years, exhibited at the Atchinson and Midtown galleries,[10] was exemplified in the Thicket series, which Cooks describes as "characterized by deep ochres and somber tones ... depict[ing] a moody environment of dark, dense woods."[11] As Mayhew relates, early critics had difficulty placing his work within a specific genre. "Mayhew's *Morning Bush* (1960) in the 1961 Annual Exhibition of Contemporary American Painting at the Whitney Museum of American Art inspired one reviewer to claim that the notable newcomer's landscape "seems to come straight from the heart of the 19th century" and that "it took the right kind of nerve to include him" in the exhibition.[12]

One of the primary challenges for early critics was the confusion or overlap of styles they perceived in Mayhew's work. "They [didn't] know what category to put me in ... whether I'm an Impressionist ... [or] involved with the Barbizon school."[13] Critics compared his work to that of Monet, Gustave Courbet (associated with the French Realist movement), Albert Pinkham Ryder (an American artist influenced by the French Barbizon school, which followed French Realism), and the American painter George Inness. In a review appearing in the December 1959 edition of *Arts* magazine, Sidney Tillum invoked Inness for assistance "in locating the elegiac remoteness of Mayhew's landscapes."[14] Mayhew also studied directly with James Peale and performed and painted portraits in the Catskills, linking his work for many critics to the Hudson River School. John Canaday of the *New York Times* credited Mayhew with the courage to follow this wide range of artistic movements in an era of abstraction: his paintings were described as "especially gratifying because he works in the neglected field of landscape — and was doing so as long as 10 years ago, when there were so few young painters willing to go against the current of abstract expressionism, then all but universally triumphant."[15]

Perhaps the greatest influences on Mayhew's work, rarely credited in critical discussions, were his teachers, Edwin Dickinson and Reuben Tam. Dickinson, like Mayhew, painted portraits and quickly executed landscapes ("premier coups") with a lush, rich brushwork and deep tone; his portraits were sometimes obscured and often combined a representational focus with surrounding components of abstraction. "According to Dickinson commentator Mary Ellen Abell, Dickinson's landscapes leaned toward the ethereal from an intuition, like Inness's before him, that art can serve as a powerful visual analogue of experience" attuned to the natural world.[16] In this emphasis upon internal responses to, or correlates with, nature, as in his refusal to align his work definitively with representation or abstraction, Dickinson established an example of an elusive narrative, a liminal space between representation and abstraction, and a painterly, evocative saturation of tone also characteristic of Mayhew's work. Dickinson was a sympathetic teacher, committed to a sympathetic community of artists, like Mayhew: "A fantastic man. Unbelievable artist. Very humble, very sensitive, very supportive of me — he made me his assistant, which is very encouraging. Edwin Dickinson — it has to do with integrity. Creative thinking. And also technique.... He said it's not just the [method of application] ... [fine painting is] innate in your feeling."[17]

Reuben Tam, even less well known than Edwin Dickinson today, was a powerful influence on Mayhew's later development of abstract landscape, or "Abstract Impressionism," as Mayhew sometimes describes it. His extraordinary landscapes formed from broad and evident brush strokes, fields of color, and occasional emphatic lines of color reminiscent of de Kooning, have a meditative quality and optic transition between representation and abstraction that is more subtle and serene in effect than Dickinson's. Tam spent most of his summers on Monhegan Island, Maine, away from his home state of Hawaii, and his work suggests an intense observation of the ocean and the juxtaposition between the coast's stormy agitation and serenity. "One of the greatest abstract landscape painters," according to Mayhew; "very mystical, very simplistic, and very powerful."[18] Despite the similarities, Mayhew insists the influence of Dickinson and Tam was technical only: "They didn't encourage me in terms of direction; they encouraged me in terms of the creative internal consciousness, design, and composition, application, technique. I never imitated them."[19]

Many critical sources and reviews state that Mayhew studied with Max Beckmann and Hans Hoffman at the Brooklyn Museum of Art. Mayhew reveals that while he sat in on Hoffman's classes, he did not study directly with him, nor did he become a disciple: "One could see how [others] could be easily influenced by his direction and technique ... [although] I learned from him [about] the opaque and transparent application of paint."[20] Hoffman's dazzling employment of color, intense saturation of restricted regions of space, and his exhilarating juxtaposition of both color and atmospheric and geometric form were an inspiring vision for Mayhew, but the rigid didacticism of Hoffman's method did not appeal to him. Max Beckmann, with whom Mayhew audited classes, similarly provided an example of painterly rigor, fine draftsmanship and a fidelity to social origins that may have reinforced directions Mayhew followed, particularly in his forays into portraiture, but Dickinson and Tam remained his abiding influences. One can observe, for example, in Hoffman's *Indian Summer* the brilliant vibrancy and unexpected shock of color — as well as the allusion to landscape suggested by Hoffman's title — evidenced in Mayhew's *Love Bush*; Beckmann's portraits have the solemnity and simplicity evidenced in Mayhew's early portraiture — *Woman in a Red Dress*, for example — but the resonance in Mayhew's work is one of intense focus and conscious philosophical commitment.

A profound influence on Mayhew's philosophy of community aesthetic concerns, if not his abstraction or attention to the spiritual aspect of landscape, was the founding member of Spiral, Romare Bearden. Bearden, one of the most widely exhibited and critically acclaimed African American artists, if not American artists more generally, of the era, fought for the aesthetic freedom demonstrated in the widely divergent styles of Spiral, maintaining that it was "not necessary that the Negro artist mirror the misery of his people" because the "artist's greatest service consists in making his individual creations as he can."[21] Even as he embraced the aesthetic freedom of abstraction, however, he believed in the narrative content of his work, crowding "scenes of black urban and rural communities" using a great assortment of media, and dramatizing the "lives of black conjure women, farmers, nudes, jazz and blues musicians, artists, families and factory workers."[22] Bearden believed that "the Negro was becoming too much of an abstraction, rather than the reality art can give a subject.... What I've attempted to do is establish a world through art in which the validity of my Negro experience could live and make its own logic."[23]

Despite their profoundly different styles, Bearden and Mayhew both believed in artistic freedom and the expression of individuality, as well as the authentic depiction of personal experience. Bearden also provided the example of support and community orientation so important to Mayhew in his developing career. As Mayhew states, Bearden was "like a big teddy bear. Very warm, very giving, like a security blanket, he was always there for assistance and help — when we were a part of Spiral, he was the one who kept the group together, united the group, even though there were diverged ideas and feelings and so forth. So he was always involved with that sensitivity. And he was always very giving, on the basis of helping others."[24] Mayhew shares in detail the story of how Bearden began the collage work for which he is now famous.

> [Bearden] wanted all of us to work together in doing the collage; this is where it started. Because he was a fantastic Abstract Expressionist. I said, what can we [do to] unify ourselves, and he was thinking in terms of the Impressionists, how many of them came together and did similar work. He said, "Why don't we be involved with a collage together?" And so we started cutting out paper, and putting things together, and color forms, and images. He said, "why can't we get a big mural together?" That was part of the idea. And no one got into it. I started; I was cutting out papers with him and so forth. And they [other artists] said, "Mmm, Romi, this is not my thing!" Reggie Gammon, who was involved with collage before Romare Bearden, was the graphic designer, because he was used to doing pasteup. He was showing Romare Bear-

> den how to do pasteup, and did a Xerox copy of pasteup, which was all in black and white. That was his first one, and then he got involved with cutting that up. And cutting up more pieces and putting them together in terms of design. Because he did a book ... on design. He was involved with the whole design fact, based on the old masters, and the concept of design. And [Bearden] tried to apply that to his collage. Since no one wanted to do it, he said, "Oh, I'll show you!" (Laughs) It was like a challenge. He became so incensed by this and fascinated by it, he just took off in that direction.[25]

The relationship between Bearden's community orientation and this original, assemblage-style technique, between narration and abstraction, is a complex one. According to Celeste-Marie Bernier, "His photographic and painterly surfaces rely on fragmentation, juxtaposition and distortion to creative emotive, visceral and animated works which dramatize a 'new symbolic sense of reality.'"[26] For many Abstract Expressionists, this fragmentation, distortion and emotive quality was in itself sufficient within the work of art; emphasis was placed on the medium surface and the release of the individual artist from political or moral implications, rather than narrative content. Rather than employing "primitive" elements to signify an unexamined and unparticular unconscious, as Pollock did, Bearden placed together "unreadable mask-like faces and fragmented body parts [to] thwart audience tendencies towards voyeurism in consumption of black female and male bodies as spectacle."[27] Thus Bearden's style, while within the ambit of Abstract Expressionism, had an entirely different and specific purpose. As Ralph Ellison stated, his art replicated the "sharp breaks, leaps in consciousness, distortions, paradoxes, reversals, telescoping of time and surreal blending of styles, values, hopes and dreams which characterize much of Negro American history."[28]

The WPA Era, the Black Arts Movement and Abstract Expressionism

Throughout the period preceding the Second World War, the WPA supported African American artists such as Archibald Motley, Palmer

Hayden, Hale Woodruff, and Jacob Lawrence. African American artists' organizations flourished, including the Harlem Artist's Center, the Harlem Artist's Guild, the WPA Artists' Group at 306 W. 141st Street, and the 135th Street YMCA. Although the WPA had initially excluded African American artists, the defunding of WPA art projects — initiated by the House Un-American Activities Committee — was a blow to the organizational network that promoted their art.[29]

In discussing his association with artists of the Abstract Expressionist era that succeeded the WPA, Mayhew delights in emphasizing his association at the East Side Educational Alliance with the Soyer brothers, whose work was allied with Social Realism. Both the Regionalist and Social Realist art movements of the WPA era highlighted the moral ideals of American people, the value of community, and the indelible influence of landscape on social cohesion. As historians of the period noted, the Realist movement expressed "the aesthetic affirmations of a democratic society wrestling with profound social disturbances, yet dreaming dreams of a greater dignity for man."[30] Perhaps best known of painters from the era was Thomas Hart Benton, whose large-scale, WPA-funded murals depicted muscular workers and idyllic scenes of rural and regional life. Benton's most famous student, Jackson Pollock, was, ironically, the champion of individualism and the avant-garde, while, according to Mayhew, Betsy Benton, Benton's wife, dismissed Pollock as "a horrible student."[31] Pollock, in keeping with the abandonment of a "narrative, anecdotal" style accessible to the masses, and the emphasis upon "personal expression and social alienation" characteristic of Abstract Expressionism, correspondingly maintained that "my work with Benton was very important as something against which to react very strongly."[32]

Within the divide of perspective and ideology characterized by these two movements, Mayhew continued to make art aligned with the philosophy of the WPA era, but enjoyed the freedom of expression associated with Abstract Expressionism. While his emphasis on community engagement and heritage aligned his work with the goals of Social Realism, the abstraction and loosely delineated color in his work is aligned with, if not inspired by, the work of Mark Rothko, Robert Motherwell, Helen

Frankenthaler, and other abstract painters of the period. Mayhew's work stands apart from the violent iconoclasm of Abstract Expressionism—its "disruptive, chaotic, [and] conceptual innovations, stressing the thrilling ingenuity and upheaval of tradition"[33]—but the spontaneity of the movement facilitated his freedom of expression. While deeply rooted in the tradition of the Hudson River School, and, more broadly, American "visionary" art, Abstract Expressionism facilitated his allusion to landscape. As Mayhew stated of the arc of his career, "Early on, I've been completely abstract ... almost [as in] Helen Frankenthaler's work. Very free subjects, but still you could see some remnants and suggestion of nature."[34]

The emphasis Greenberg placed on the material components of Abstract Expressionism—abstraction, flatness, and the reduction of the components of painting to pure form—belies the intensely personal vision, political perspective and psychological motivations of the Abstract Expressionists, as well as the immediate political context of the production and reception of art, a critical issue for African American artists in the Civil Rights era. The paradoxical nature of Abstract Expressionism—its assertion of individualism and personal expression as formal qualities, its claim to the evacuation of representational meaning in the face of overt cultural signifiers—is nowhere more evident than in the status afforded female artists.[35] De Kooning's classic "Woman" series is but one example of overt representation, and a personal, and perhaps misogynistic, artistic perspective. As Erika Doss states, "Standard postwar accounts of Abstract Expressionism cast it as an act of violence and virility, its practitioners as heroic men of action."[36] Women were often excluded from exhibitions and critical histories, a situation Mayhew sought to resist in interaction with Betty Blayton, Vivian Brown, and Emma Amos, and later students, including Gayle Fulton Ross and Ponsoon Park Sung. That Mayhew acknowledges and expresses this historical exclusion sets him apart from a movement that disregarded African American and female artists alike.

Both Romare Bearden and Norman Lewis represented an aspect of Abstract Expressionism that was not accommodated within its ostensibly universal character, a character that, for Greenberg, was "uninflated by illegitimate content — no religion or mysticism or political uncertainties."[37] Abstract Expressionism advanced an ideal of "rebellious, individualistic, unconventional, sensitive, [and] irritable" art which "arose from the feeling of being ill at ease in the universe,"[38] a sensibility relieved only by recourse to so-called unconscious and "primitive" Native American and non–Western art.[39] Yet the same adoption of allusion to meaningful figurative elements in the work of Bearden and Lewis was marginalized as narrative and/or "ethnic," either overtly political and therefore not embraced by the movement, or insufficiently narrative and therefore not "black."

The negotiation of this paradox was variously addressed within the African American community and Spiral itself. The first president of Spiral and an early ally of the Soyers, Norman Lewis was active in the Artists Union, the Harlem Artists Guild, and the Harlem Community Center, created by the WPA.[40] During the WPA era, Lewis aligned himself with the Soyer brothers and the Social Realist movement, depicting the oppressive conditions of African American life; by the 1950s, however, Lewis stated, "I used to paint Negros being dispossessed ... and slowly I became aware of the fact that this didn't move anybody.... Negros were employed and they had jobs and stuff like that but it still didn't make art any better."[41] Lewis's commentary on the gallery and exhibition world reflected this new cynicism about the effectiveness of art as social protest: to "paint Black people in their struggle for existence ... was a waste of time because the very people who you want to see this kind of thing don't see it.... Black people don't buy art and it's only just recently that you see them in museums."[42]

Unlike Bearden, Lewis did not see the value in depicting the African American experience, nor did he believe there was a "black experience" in art. This perspective set him apart from both his peers and from many mainstream Abstract Expressionist artists who did not share his belief that art should consider public views and understandings.[43] Lewis's colorful and complex abstractions, with their thickets of geometric, vertical forms overlaid on muted color fields, were not intended to sever the relationship between aesthetics and social and political concerns; his *Harlem Turns White* from 1955, for example, suggests both in its title and in its employment of gestural geometric forms that could be construed as a mass of individuals the concerns of African Americans. His fierce commitment to his art did not obliterate his social concerns, or a degree of rage against institutionalized domination: "White America is so goddamn aggressive that it destroys anything that gets in its way."[44] Despite his status with fellow Abstract Expressionists, Lewis struggled to make his way in the gallery and exhibition system: "I teach, I have driven a taxi, I have been an elevator operator, I have been a pants presser, I have washed floors, I have been a cook, I have been a seaman, I have sewed dresses, I have sustained myself in whatever ... has been necessary to just exist."[45]

The position adopted by Lewis stands in stark opposition to the achievement of political objectives through art advanced by the Black Arts Movement. "Why Spiral"—the 1966 *Art News* article that introduced Spiral group to the art world—concludes with Romare Bearden's emphatic statement, "The Negro artist is unknown in America,"[46] a view that was widely shared among African Americans. Responses to the exclusion of artists, however, varied widely. While the formation of Spiral was prompted by the Civil Rights Movement and, as their exhibition catalogue of 1965 stated, it "could not fail to be touched by the outrage of segregation, or fail to relate to the self-reliance, hope, and courage of those persons who were marching in the interests of man's dignity,"[47] Spiral's emphasis was predominantly aesthetic in nature. Lewis, Mayhew, and other members of Spiral concurred with Ralph Ellison's position that African American art stands as "an affirmation of the irrelevance of the notion of race as a limiting force in the arts."[48]

The differentiation by Spiral of aesthetic from social and political concerns markedly diverged from the nationalist perspective of artists in the Black Arts Movement (BAM), including such groups as AfriCOBRA, Weusi and "Where We At."[49] As Sallah Hassan notes, the Black Arts Movement, emerging out of the Harlem Renaissance, found inspiration in African aesthetics and the wave of African decolonization in the 1950s and 1960s, and regarded its mission as trans–African and transnational.[50] Each organization had distinct objectives and modes of action, but the unifying emphasis was "Black Art for Black People" (Weusi),[51] as well as an "Afrocentric aesthetic vision" (AfriCOBRA),[52] Amiri Baraka, the poet laureate of BAM, explains that "the most politically sensitive of us began to pull away from the bourgeois rubric that art and politics were separate and exclusive entities ... the standard bourgeois aesthetic of separation of arts and politics was stupid and becoming more and more politically bankrupt."[53] Baraka's poetic energy and bluntness illustrates the more revolutionary tone of the movement: "The Black Liberation Movement and even the civil rights movements are held up each day to public ridicule as backward and passé, or else the most valid ideas of our struggle are replaced with the ideas of the sickest of the sickest and the most backward of our contemporaries, by Hanging Judges from the Caucasian Chalk Circle ... we have a new generation of the backward, the little neo-negro greedballs bloated with the arrogant ignorance of abject submission to imperialism. The various Fly Boys in the Butter Milk and Affirmative Action Babies, Colored People whose mission like the Spikes and Skips, just like the Tom Ass Clarences and Colin Powells, is to attack and give the lie to the idea and movement for Black Self-Determination."[54]

Among the more prominent artists in the Black Arts Movement, a member who adhered to Baraka's more strident vision of black energy and imagery, was Faith Ringgold. While Spiral was formed as a visual and philosophical response to the March on Washington, Ringgold's early series, *America Black*, was intended as an aesthetic embodiment of the Black Power movement.[55] Ringgold's posters on paper, designed for free distribution — such as "Committee to Defend the Panthers," "Power to the People," "Woman Free Yourself," and "United States of Attica"— and her powerful statement paintings, such as *Flag for the Moon: Die Nigger*, illustrate her political focus.[56] The commentary made by Ringgold in *Flag for the Moon*, acknowledging a lack of economic or ideological support for the racially disenfranchised, was embedded within the palettes and technique of the work itself.

> In 1967 I had begun to explore the idea of a new palette, a way of expressing on canvas the new "black is beautiful" sense of ourselves. In the painting of *Die*, I had depended upon the blood-spattered white clothing of the figures to create the contrast needed to express the movement and energy of the riot.... But I was now committed to "black light" and subtle color nuances and compositions based on my interest in African rhythm, pattern, and repetition.... In years to come my colors have lightened, but I feel more comfortable with "black light" even now.[57]

The position of the Black Arts Movement, in its various language and objectives, differed in tone from the philosophy and objectives of Mayhew and Spiral. Mayhew shared Lewis's view that the "artist has the right to paint any way he wants to, not to the dictates of the art market, which is involved [with the issue of] this is black art and this is not black art. They are talking about black art being ... symbols and painting of black subject matter. And that was completely contrary to the reality of what African American artists are."[58] Mayhew's activism and community-building efforts were accompanied by an insistence upon artistic freedom in expressing individual, cultural and social experiences, a position that marginalized him within the dominant paradigm of African American art, even as the position of Spiral continues to occupy an awkward position in critical and art historical accounts between the Harlem Renaissance and contemporary African American art.

The position African American artists (and particularly members of Spiral), occupied in the community and in the history of art is illustrated by the critical and art historical presentation of Hale Woodruff. Although Woodruff was primarily dedicated to large murals in the Social Realist style, the painting for which Woodruff is best known is in the style of Cezanne's *Card Players*.[59] As Mayhew comments, "That's what the media shows, right? They don't show you murals, which are in Atlanta, on all the walls down there, and out here in California, and in the Midwest, Indiana, and also Los Angeles—"Card Players" is really primitive symbolism, and he never painted that way. That was only one image. And this is what they dig up to show, 'Oh, this is Hale Woodruff?' The media again controls."[60]

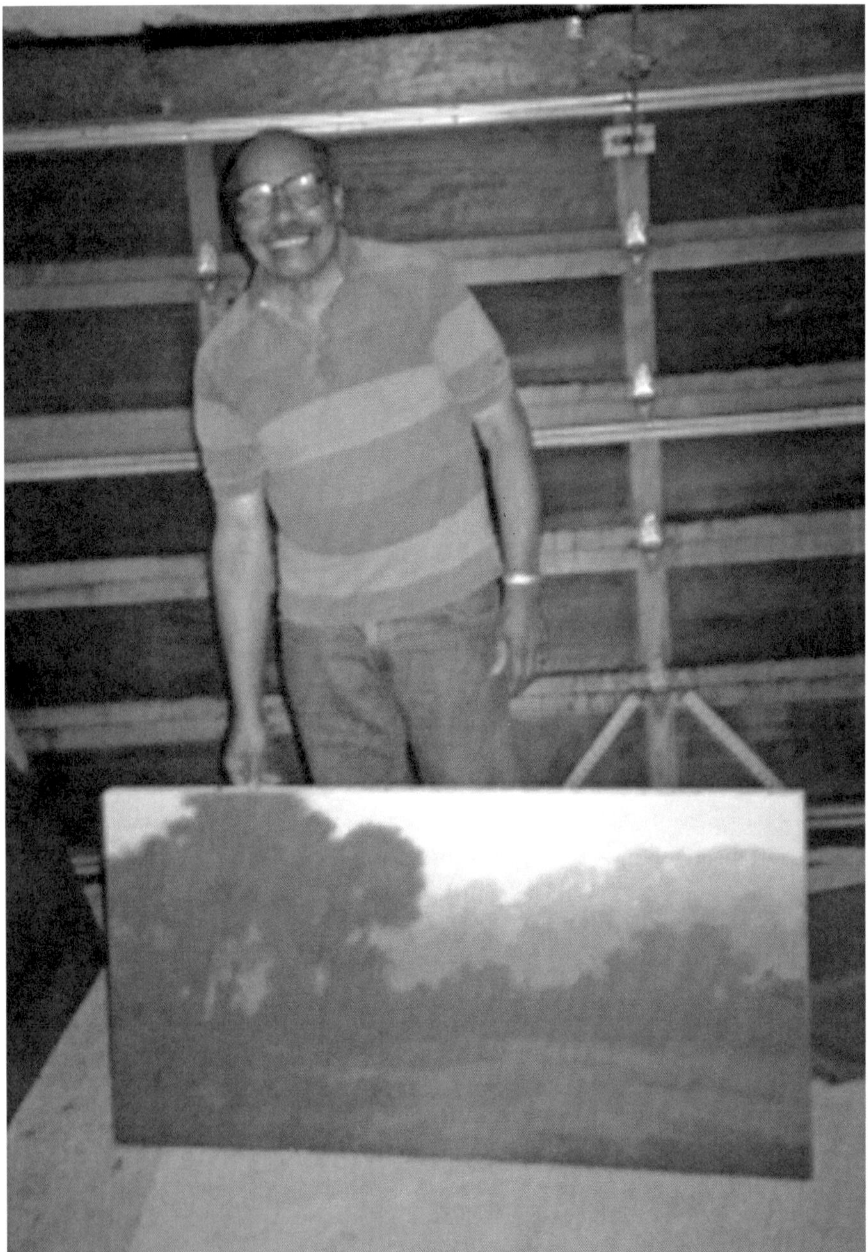

Richard Mayhew in his Soquel garage studio, 2012.

The marginalization of African American artists within the Abstract Expressionist era was primarily due to critical and institutional rejection, but it also occurred within the art movements themselves. The philosophical and representational connection on the part of African American artists to community sensibility and concern over the inclusion of the viewer was not embraced by the critical champions of Abstract Expressionism, despite the fact that Jackson Pollock, Wilhelm de Kooning, and many "second generation" Abstract Expressionists participated in a politics of dominance and, according to some historians, political propaganda.[61] The women of "Where We At" and artists like Emma Amos and Faith Ringgold suggest a degree of marginalization within Spiral itself: as Amos shared in an interview in 2012:

> The question is, why did they [Spiral] invite me? ... As a feminist, I knew then that this was a setup. Why would you invite a 22-year-old

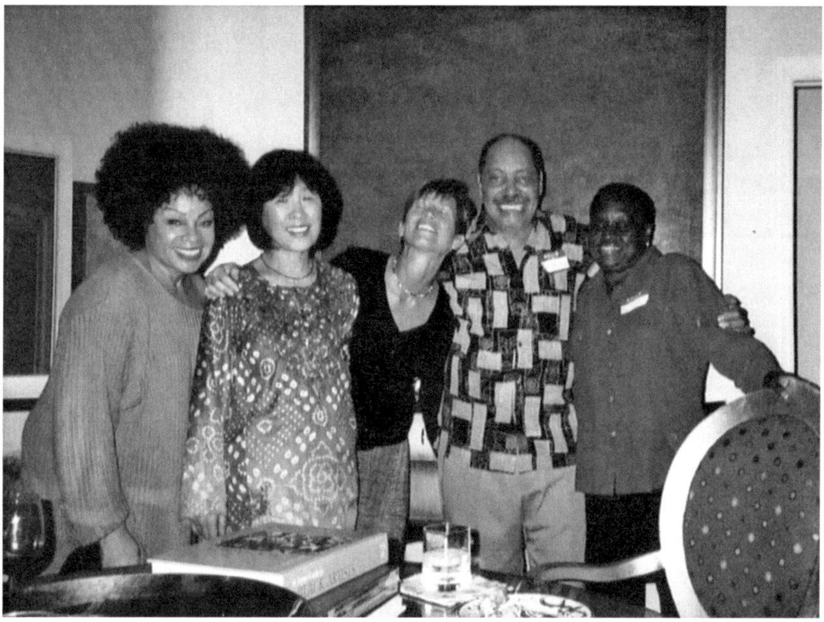

[Left to Right] Gayle Fulton Ross, Posoon Park Suro, Sue Byron, Richard Mayhew, and Ella Williams at home of Edward Littlejohn, ca. 2005

> girl to join a group like that? I was not threatening to them, or so they thought. (Laughs) They were wrong....Why didn't they invite [Camille Billops, Augusta Savage, Vivian Browne]? ... Why didn't they invite Faith Ringgold? They were scared to death of Faith. (Laughs) She threatened them beyond belief. There was no way in the world they were going to invite Faith Ringgold.... So I just want to introduce the fact these guys were wonderful, but they were just like what's going on now. Women are one thing and guys are another.... [The members of Spiral] were not comfortable with women as colleagues. They were not.[62]

Faith Ringgold similarly relates the feeling that she was not accepted by either Spiral or the art world of Abstract Expressionism: "In New York I found it difficult to exhibit my work because of my figurative style, the political content, the lack of social connections in the art world, and, also, because being black and a woman was not as fashionable as the Civil Rights Movement and the Women's Liberation Movement might suggest."[63] According to art historian Kay Brown, Ringgold helped found "Where We At" in response to her exclusion from Spiral.[64]

Mayhew's perspective on the exclusion of women from art exhibitions and organizations suggests both an active effort at inclusion and a resistance to feminist activism. He disputes the notion that Ringgold and Vivian Brown were not invited to join Spiral, but also maintains, "The women at the time, like Faith Ringgold, were very aggressive about women's rights. And that got in the way of them as a creative person, because they were constantly challenging it on the basis of male-female situation, rather than being involved in creative exchange with the other artists."[65] The exclusion of women from art exhibitions, organizations, galleries, and histories is now well documented. Yet Amos expresses her gratitude for being a part of Spiral: "It was a great honor to be a member.... It was life-changing to know them. I mean, how many of you can recall being members of a group of people who were 30 to 50 years your senior? And if somebody asked me now to do such a thing, I would pay them! (Laughs).... It's an amazing honor to have that happen to a kid."[66]

The survival of male and female African American artists in this atmosphere of exclusion, denial, and conflict is noteworthy. Despite his personal and artistic exclusion, Mayhew flourished in producing, exhibiting, and discussing aesthetic objectives with many of his peers, receiving affirming reviews and continuing the activism that defined his early career. During the late 1960s and 1970s, Mayhew continued to exhibit his work in "solo shows at galleries in New York, often the Midtown galleries (who represented him for more than 20 years), landscape-themed group exhibitions, and group exhibitions" focused on African American art.[67] Hilton Kramer, of the *New York Times*, called "for more of Mayhew's work in the 1976 exhibition Two Centuries of Black American Art,"[68] and other critics celebrated the expansiveness and masterful color of his work, even as he continued to champion the work of younger artists and students.

Later Years

In his foreword to the 1984 exhibition brochure "Richard Mayhew: Recent Paintings and Drawings," Jack Bolen describes the transition within Mayhew's work which occurred from the late 1970s to the 1980s: "Gradually the recognizable landscape elements diffused, and eventually disappeared altogether."[69] Throughout the sixties his work consisted chiefly of loosely brushed, somber-color fields or landscapes, painted in the dark tones and banded layers reminiscent of Rothko's final works. Images such as *A Thicket*, *Intermission* and *Interlude* seem to waver between a light color field fading across dark and variegated brown or green, and images of groves or isolated trees hazily emerging, out of focus, from the horizon. By the 1970s color erupts into Mayhew's work, the bands of color begin to soften into overall tones and/or landscape; in certain works, as in *Essence*, suggestions of landscape disappear almost entirely. Of a painting entitled *Indigenous Spring*, Mayhew states, "It's not so much a path here, as it is a feeling of time. And space. And the mood of early spring ... nature is constantly evolving, changing, changing. Constantly reinventing itself."[70] Of his painting *Sacred Path*, Mayhew states, "You see a lot of worn areas where people travel on these spaces.

And they leave their mark by doing the path, but not knowing where it really goes. So there's a mystery about the future. It has to do with shapes.... It's that worn spot where people walk — but then where does it go? Nothing is planned when I paint; I put color on the canvas ... it completely changed. The mood evolves [without planning].... So that path dictates a feeling of what's happening with those tree forms."

When asked if he sees in *Indigenous Spring* the ending of a path below, and a more transcendent space above, Mayhew states, "No, but [looking at the work is] your experience. Or your identity with what you see." Mayhew came to believe that overt representation was unduly restrictive: "Later on, I felt there is a certain mystique and more of a suggestion that nature was there. So I got involved with being more suggestive about it. I even had figures in there at one time. And the figures determined how big, how far and what location it was. So I took them out. Until tree forms became a certain identity with space."

At the same time that he moved into almost total abstraction, Mayhew insisted that attempting to paint mood alone, with no external influence, was restrictive: "It's a feeling of, if you love, how do you paint love? The Abstract Expressionists were discussing this. What does love look like? What does hate look like? Someone ... [said, I'm] going to paint hate, and got so involved with the joy of painting, it changed the feeling. Or he was painting love, and he got so frustrated, he painted hate! So there [must be] a particular feeling of time, space, and mood." Critical here is Mayhew's inclusion of the words "time" and "space." His "recognizable landscape elements" may have disappeared, but his focus upon the land at particular moments in particular locations was never lost.

As Mayhew's work moved into the 1990s and 2000s, it seems to extend the transition described by Bolen in its distillation of the essence of landscape beyond identifiable forms — except, occasionally, a tree or bush — and in its brilliance of color. The tremendous sense of balance, clarity, and emotional evocativeness make his paintings in reproduction seem vast in scale, although they are often two to three feet in size, and arrest the viewer with their vibrant emotion captured in landscapes or abstractions that appear absolutely still. Mayhew expands his color repertoire into color contrasts of brilliant pink and purple, orange and yellow, green and brown. Perhaps the most brilliantly evocative images by Mayhew in his recent period are bushes rendered in lush, intense, and saturated red. Of *Scarlet Noon*, Mayhew states that the image is "like — the middle of everything. The middle of the day. It's like — the middle of life. The strength and power of that experience." Mayhew also suggests that the brilliant, rich reds, such as those in *Love Bush*, have a passionate and even erotic connotation or intention.

Mayhew has discussed the extraordinary effects produced by such paintings, and what they suggest. Of *Forty Acres and a Mule*, shown in an exhibit at the Stella Jones Gallery in 2003, Mayhew states that "after I painted it, I felt that this is part of the land, the treaty rights which were never honored, and the 'forty acres and a mule' that African Americans never received after Reconstruction ... [the intense purple] has to do with the shadows as part of the mystery, that subtle area of sensitivity which is never really revealed, and of hidden feelings of thought, like the shadows in the trees over there." The painting is dominated by a brilliant, even firey orange that softens into a circular clearing of brown and green, surmounted by an exquisite horizon of pink, purple, and blue; one gets a sense of great intensity balanced by an archway of sky, with a small clearing, of human scale, in the center. Of his painting *Serenity*, Mayhew states that the viewer "responds to it as an abstract shape and space. [I was thinking of] mood. Feeling. Space. Shape. A feeling of time." And, indeed, these are the pivotal concerns in paintings devoid of human figures or specific geographical references.

Mayhew returns to landscape irresistibly, despite what is popular, current, or critically established. He enjoys working back and forth between watercolor and oil — "It stimulates the different effects and techniques ... [and] you don't get bored" — and between the brush and palette knife, skills he attributes to crow quill pen techniques from decades ago. Mayhew's technique in portraiture is something of which he remains proud: "I can draw a figure upside down backwards right now. I can close my eyes and do a figure ... [due to my study] of anatomy." He delights in signing some of his paintings twice, on opposite edges, so that there is no "proper" way to display them. This fluid sense of the painting's subject highlights the extent to which Mayhew's work involves the viewer in its apprehension. The resulting visual event engages the imaginative, or image-making, capacity of the viewer.

As part of the effect of his work, Mayhew prefers a very simple frame and a certain distance for the viewer, an effect different from the surrounding effect encouraged by Color Field painters: "If you get very close to it, you miss some of the mystery. You back away, you start to see it ... most paintings, that's [the] way to really view the painting, not too close. It has to do with hard edge as opposed to soft edge. And the soft edge is not so much the edges of form, but all the subtleties of color contrast ... I prefer just a small molding. Sometimes I put these elaborate frames on there and I found that they change the frame anyway, so I stopped bothering doing that, and then I felt that the subtlety of the molding is fine. The frame gets involved with, I guess, a decorating situation for one's décor."

Mayhew continues to turn aside the notion, advanced by Bearden and Henderson, that he retains a sense of place in his landscapes because viewers prefer it. "No, that's wrong. I never painted for anyone. I painted for myself ... [such an act would be] involved with the dictation and compromise of who you are." Mayhew's refusal to compromise who he is, how his art appears, and how he presents and interprets his own work, is a moral commitment on his part — a "spiritual commitment," as he would describe it.

In holding fast to his spiritual commitment to his African and Native American heritage, Mayhew shares the concerns, but not the aesthetic sensibilities, of postmodern art. Mayhew's relationship with contemporary African American artists, including Emma Amos and Faith Ringgold, is respectful, but like many of his peers, he has not embraced the "challenge of modes of cultural representation"[71] represented in the work of artists such as Kara Walker and Lorna Simpson. Walker's work — what Shaw has described as "nostalgic postmodernism" — employs panoramic installations, using silhouettes, to examine "racial" myths and stereotypes. In freezing the "motions of ... wildly gesticulating bodies [typically, African American female slaves] in erotic, satiric, and violent poses" that are "both attractive and repulsive," Walker challenges the viewer to examine whether she or he is seeing a racist or erotic image, or whether the image is generated by the viewer's own embedded views.[72] Lorna Simpson similarly emphasizes oppression and denial in representing bodies of African American women: in *Necklines*, for example, she employs photographs of a woman's mouth and neck area with the words "ring, surround, lasso, noose, eye, areola, halo, cuffs, collar, loops," in a suggestion of sexual abuse, confinement, and terror.

For Mayhew, the leap into postmodernism, particularly its sensational or ironic imagery, is one he is unwilling to make. His objective is to convey a spiritual, rather than transgressive, mood and message; he does not wish to provoke or question strategies of social responsibility[73] in the confrontational fashion characteristic of Walker and Simpson's work. Mayhew has rejected what Shaw describes as "the caustic bite of political satire and the scopophilic draw of pornography."[74] Such confrontation does not engage him, because the works provoke or reveal what he wishes to overcome. For Mayhew, the natural instinct is to be "spiritually sensitive, and loving, and supportive," in work communicating "peace and a feeling of tranquility,"[75] while addressing the shadows. Works like *Sonorous*, with its agitated, almost volcanic field of black and red, are evocative of clouds or a negative imagery of shadowed foliage, and surmounted by a small horizon of purple foliage against a pink sky—and *Transformation*, whose dark, almost black horizon line of dense black trees and pink field is dominated by a brighter backdrop of saturated purple trees and translucent white sky, the bright shadow to the foliage's darkness—allude to the oppressive histories Walker and Simpson describe, but these histories are buried in the shadows.

Chapter Three

"He Just Came Off the Reservation": Native and African American Art and the Civil Rights Movement

We have one of the artists. He just came off the reservation.
— Romare Bearden [introducing Mayhew][1]

Henry Louis Gates, Jr., has described incidents of racism as "moments of recognition"— those times when the individual must "realize that he or she is different, and that the white world sees black people as different, no matter how blacks feel inside."[2] Mayhew relates such moments with equanimity, but they have clearly had an impact on his perception of the world: "The dominant culture invades one's sensibility of thinking and functioning. African Americans championed the causes of sitting in the back of the bus, or sitting in a [theater] balcony — now people want to be in the balcony. I remember going to the movies. I had to sit in the balcony. And then the uniform, when I was in service [as a first sergeant in the United States Marines], I had to sit in the back of the bus."[3] Mayhew relates the experiences of his father, which had a profound impact on him: "He couldn't get [painting] contracts [because he was Native American] ... so he had to get a white person to get the contracts for him.... He was a very sensitive man, and very vulnerable, because of the conditions. And I didn't want to — in watching him, I didn't want to fall into that pitfall, which was a product of that kind of heritage. How easily one could not excel, because of being psychologically oppressed."[4]

One of the strategies Richard Mayhew has employed for dealing with oppression is situating himself in his own sense of place, an orientation he equates with transcending external and internal harm. He describes the senselessness of anger at a "racist" experience: "[An angry person] can think of themselves [instead] as a creative, constructive person. You're not caught in that pitfall of self-denial and destruction. Otherwise you find yourself involved with anger … psychologically, you're always involved with denial."[5] Mayhew's sense of equanimity is both geographic and internal, defined by a perspective toward landscapes and his defiance of expected creative output, critical categories and worldviews.

The history of African and Native American art is replete with responses to physical and psychological oppression. David Hammond, Robert Colescott, Melvin Edwards, Carrie Mae Weems, Michael Ray Charles, and Pat Ward Williams (to name but a few) have generated powerful cultural commentary and a push back against the expectation that African American artists create stereotypes of the black experience—"jazz, old people of the church sitting on the porch, sweet mothers holding up their babies," in the words of Gayle Fulton Ross.[6] Similarly, American Indian artists—Rick Glazer-Danay, Rick Hill, T.C. Cannon, Jimmie Durham, Jaune Quick-to-See Smith, and James Luna, among others—have called into question the expectation that certain "races" produce a particular kind of art. Yet as Gwendolyn DuBois Shaw indicates, not all responses to oppression are received in the same way by African and Native Americans. Artists like Kara Walker and Lorna Simpson are criticized by Mayhew's collectors and students, and by Mayhew himself, for presenting negative imagery, or for simply not producing fine art. Betye Saar, for example, questions "the validity of a black person's attempt to reclaim and reverse racist imagery through irony."[7] Fulton Ross, Mayhew's former student, states, "They may get the joke, but 90 percent of the world doesn't get the joke. We live in a racist world. And there is nothing funny about that anymore."[8]

Among Mayhew's close friends, opinions about the appropriate role of art and artists in response to oppression diverge widely. Romare Bearden believed that "there is an aesthetic that informs the work of black peoples," and sought to depict the narrative reality of African Americans, employing collages and photomontages to depict panoramic visions in which "the Negro experience could live and make its own logic."[9] Norman Lewis, maintaining, "I just see art. I don't see any black experience," argued that it was the quality of the art, rather than its political relevance, which offered "the most effective blow against stereotype and the most irrefutable proof of the artificiality of stereotype in general."[10]

Mayhew's positioning within this range of perspectives is complex, as the discussion of his participation in Spiral and his reflection on what constitutes African American art makes clear. Although Mayhew's activism, his community engagement, and his statements about artistic sensitivity demonstrate that Mayhew resists institutional exclusion and proscribed categories based upon "race," his experiences with oppression shaped his artistic objectives in subtle but significant ways. This chapter will examine Richard Mayhew's response to institutionalized oppression, specifically his personal and artistic response to the denial and suppression of the African and Native American experience, and his meditative and spiritual/internal response to oppression.

African American Experience

From the time of his early years as an artist in New York, Mayhew was aware of both institutional exclusion on the basis of "race," and the elitism that prevented much of the public from viewing art. In 1959, Mayhew and his friend and colleague Ernest Crichlow, in response to discussions about the reception of African American artists in the community and gallery system, expressed a desire to "communicate with the community," and decided to exhibit their paintings on a fence at a busy intersection in Brooklyn.[11] As Mayhew recalls, "Early on I got involved with the community with Ernie Crichlow and that's why we started showing things on the fence. He said, 'We're not involved with the community. The community never sees the work. They don't go to museums.

They never go to galleries.' We had a discussion about being artists and said that no one sees us. The community never sees the paintings. Ernie said, 'Let's put them on the fence in Bed-Stuyvesant.' On the weekend, people would come up and they were curious and they'd spread the word to other people and they came. There was no way to advertise the paintings. We put them out there where everybody goes by. They all came and were looking and asking questions."[12]

The struggle against elitism reflected in this "exhibition" echoes the position of Spiral, against the vision of Abstract Expressionists of individualism and heroicism, that art is not the exclusive domain of a rarified community:

> In examining ourselves, we soon realized we were also examining the present health of a wounded American society, as well as much of Western culture.... If possible, in these times, we hoped with our art to justify life. In time, we came to depend upon one another, and perceived that talent and aptitude were not the only means needed for creativity, since creativity is an aspect of human behavior, comprehensible only in terms of a dynamic social relationship.[13]

In addition to his early activism with Crichlow, and his participation in the "Black and White" exhibition with Spiral — with which Mayhew was not entirely happy, as he believed it should be installed in a museum and comprised solely of more established artists (e.g., Alston, Bearden, Hines, Lewis, and Simpson)[14] — Mayhew worked to advance his ideal of inclusion. Bridget Cooks documents his effort to rebut institutional exclusion through community activism and special exhibition:

> Mayhew exhibited work in the 1967 exhibition The Evolution of Afro-American Artists: 1800–1950, organized by Romare Bearden at City College of New York. He also ... picket[ed] the exclusion [of African American artists] from the Harlem on My Mind: Cultural Capital of Black America 1900–1968 exhibition at the Metropolitan Museum of Art in 1969, protesting as a member of the interracial activist organization called the Black Emergency Cultural Coalition (BECC) led by artist Benny Andrews. In March 1971, he organized the panel "The Black Artist" for the Art Students League, one of a series of eight. Joining him on the panel were curator Barry Gaither, artists Benny Andrews, Vivian Brown, Lewis, Faith Ringgold, and others. In the fol-

> lowing month, Mayhew was included in the show Rebuttal to the Whitney Museum Exhibition at Nigel Jackson's Acts of Art Galleries in New York. The exhibition opened concurrently with[,] and in response to[,] the Whitney Museum exhibition Contemporary Black Artists in America, which it developed as a result of pressure from the BECC to mount a show focused on Black artists. Although the Whitney organized the exhibition, it did not comply with all the BECC's demands, particularly the hiring of Black curators to oversee exhibitions of Black art. Mayhew was one of fifteen Black artists who were selected to be in the Whitney's exhibition but he withdrew in protest. Mayhew did participate in David Driskell's 1976 Two Centuries of Black American Art exhibition, which originated at the Los Angeles County Museum of Art and traveled around the country; it was the first comprehensive survey of work by Black American artists at mainstream American art museums. In 1977, he received a major exhibition of his paintings at the Studio Museum in Harlem.[15]

The resistance to institutionalized oppression represented in these exhibitions, protests and other forms of activism sprang in some measure from Randolph's call for participation in the March on Washington and Spiral's formation on the 100th anniversary of the Emancipation Proclamation.[16] But for Mayhew, as for so many African American artists, the impetus for action was personal as well as political, and emerged from his experiences with racism, as well as those of his family and his fellow artists. Mayhew clearly takes great pride in his family. His grandmother "was a powerful woman in the community. When people needed information and so forth, they used to come to her. And when they were sick she would go and help them.... So there was an inherited state that I found myself in."[17] Mayhew's parents also offered an example of strength: "[My father] was a very statuesque man, very tall, very handsome, and involved with a survival kind of instinct, even though he was in the middle of this oppressive situation. Very proud man, even though he was living a mediocre kind of existence.... I had great respect for him.... [Both of my parents had] this kind of stature. No matter how oppressive things were, they were survivors.... It was implanted in me as a youngster: not to submit to the oppression and destruction of your heritage or yourself."

The overt racism which his family experienced had a powerful impact on Mayhew. "I once witnessed a very disturbing thing, just a very disturbing situation," he recalls. "I went in a shoe store ... [and my father] was getting a pair of shoes ... they were too tight, and [he] set them [down to try to give them back].... And [the store owner] said, 'You bought 'em.'" Mayhew's father cut the ends off of the shoes and wore them. Such examples of daily humiliation led Mayhew to leave Amityville: "I left that town, I still had the pitfalls of one who had lived in that existence. And I needed to get out of it. I needed to leave. I didn't want to be involved with the limitations — where my father really never left that town. And the mediocre existence because of oppression. The oppression is unbelievable."

Mayhew recounts what happened to him when, in the New York years, police accused him of breaking into his own art studio: "I had a little school on Sixth Avenue, right near Twenty-second Street. There's a church now, still there, and the studio was next door to that church. One time I went in there late at night. I forgot to close the door downstairs, and the police go around at night checking all the buildings, and the door was open. They came upstairs and I was there, and they said, 'What are you doing here?' A black man in that area ... I said, 'Well, I'm an artist, this is my studio, and I teach' and they said, 'Well, the door is open downstairs, and you broke in.' So, one of the officers, while I was talking to him, I was sketching. He came over and he says, 'Oh, wow!'"

While the officer was taking the report, Mayhew sketched a picture of him to demonstrate that he was a skilled artist, and that he was indeed in his own studio. Mayhew's action was at once a creative and defiant response to discrimination, and a response to an offensive and unnecessary intrusion. Such a display of discrimination is hardly atypcial. Mayhew notes the story of a friend, a prominent businessman and collector in Detroit, who owned "land and properties and hotels and [yet said], 'When I walk in the store, I still keep my hands in my pockets so they won't think I'm stealing something.' He's a millionaire, right? It's still affecting [his] head. The insecurity was implanted." As Mayhew states,

"This prejudice — it's there. It's always there. The genocide, psychologically, is there."

Mayhew's response to discrimination reflects both an awareness of the internalization of racism, and his own more restrained and creative orientation: "You can internalize anger, and get involved with alcoholism, drug addiction, and anger ... you lash out about something and end up in prison, which happens to many, and ends itself that way." Mayhew describes the anger of good friends such as Reginald Gammon, Marlon Ross, and Norman Lewis, among others: "Marlon Ross was very strange. He would have the most foul language you can imagine, right? But he'll cut you off and hug you.... Norman Lewis was great, very bright, very brilliant. But he was very angry. He would vent his anger in communicating with people. Someone would come to the door and right away he'd say, "What the hell are you doing here?" Slam the door, then open it. That was the reaction of defense, and the opening up.... [Some of the younger participants in Spiral secretly sought to record conversations, but older members] didn't want any kind of recording, because of the constant furor over the exchange of ideas. And Norman Lewis, trying to make a point, slammed his hand on the table, and the tape falls to the floor (laughing). He didn't want a tape, he took it and threw it against the wall."

The anger over discrimination, denial, omission, and outright violence toward African Americans, Mayhew avers, harmed the artists psychologically: "Anger doesn't help, you know. If you become angry, it's self-destruction.... You poison yourself. This is part of creative survival, and it's part of, don't get caught up in self-destructive denial. I've been around a lot of African American artists who've become angry about being denied. Norman Lewis is a perfect example of it. He was just very bitter, very hostile, because he completely ignored what he was doing. Great artist. Completely ignored. They wouldn't buy his work, you know? Publicize his work? He ended up driving a cab, in New York. Brilliant teacher. But there was this constant denial of who he was."

Some of the artists with whom Mayhew was close, such as Charles White and Ernie Crichlow, channeled their outrage in gentler ways, depicting, as Crichlow did, beautiful, figurative forms: "You find there was this other area, the anger was involved with creating beauty. To show that there was something here besides ... my doing [it] is in terms of landscape." Mayhew's approach has been a determination to rise above obstacles, and sustain a kind of spiritual sensitivity: "Other [African American artists] were denied ... it came [for me] because I've been aggressive and ambitious about it! And challenging the system."

In addition to this resistance, Mayhew consistently displays — in art as in life — a private and somewhat elusive spiritual outlook that seemingly sustains him: "The inner self is not visible. Even you, when you look in the mirror, you don't see yourself. Who are you? Who am I? That's the inner self, which no one can ever touch but you! You're the only one who ever knows! ... So there is that uniqueness which is the beauty of human existence. It's the intellectual internal creative existence."

Native American Art

The most emphatic and entrenched resistance Mayhew describes is the lack of recognition by, and segregation within, academics of American Indian artists. Native American art has long been subject to the perception that art must be made by individuals raised in "traditional" households, and adhere to the requirements of Indian apprenticeship, traditional belief, and registration with the United States or Canadian government. As Janet Berlo and Ruth Phillips attest, "The application of a 1990 U.S. law that legislates such a definition has resulted in such absurdities as the exclusion of celebrated Cherokee artist Jimmie Durham [who refused to register] from recent exhibitions."[18] Moreover, the history of Native American art is overlaid with colonial romanticizing:

> The modern trade in Native art turns on this aspect of doubleness. On the one hand, the market for Indian art grew in tandem with the entrenchment of assimilationism and the dogma of the Vanishing Indian. Yet, on the other hand, the commodity most desired by buyers

> ... was "Indianness" itself.... As many Native critics point out, non–Native patronage has been a mixed blessing. Individual patronage ... has all too often stimulated to production of repetitious and stereotypical images of the Indian as noble savage, tragic warrior, or new-age mystic — a phenomenon whose continuing vitality is evident at powwow booths and commercial art galleries from Ontario to Sante Fe. Institutional patronage, on the other hand, has imposed arbitrary hierarchies and systems of classification that disrupt Native unities of thought about objects and about the visual art as an integral part of culture. Until the 1970s few art galleries — and vitually no large urban museums — collected or displayed twentieth-century Native Art.[19]

Oscar Howe, a graduate of the Studio School in Sante Fe — an institution that encouraged "an 'authentically Indian' way to paint" — was one of the first artists to break away from the stereotypical and romanticized image of modern Indian art.[20] After one of his abstracted images was rejected by the important Philbrook Annual Exhibition in 1958, Howe stated, "Who ever said that my paintings are not in traditional Indian style has poor knowledge of Indian art indeed. There is much more to Indian art than pretty, stylized pictures.... Are we to be held back forever with one phase of Indian painting, with no right for individualism, dictated to as the Indian has always been, put on reservations and treated like a child, and only the White Man knows what is best for him? Now, even in Art, 'You, little child, do what we think is best for you, nothing different.' Well, I am not going to stand for it."[21]

As recently as 1986, when Mohawk artist Rick Glazer-Danay had work removed by the director of the Roberson Center for the Arts and Sciences in Binghamton, New York, from the traveling "Art of the Seventh Generation" show on the basis that it was "soft-core porn" and not appropriate Indian art, Glazer-Danay stated, "My work is always appropriate Indian art. My work is how I define myself in the 20th century."[22] Another contemporary Native American artist, Rick Hill, reiterates: "We had to legitimize ourselves, correct stereotypes, present our view of history, before anyone would ever *see* the art ... for too long we've let other people tell us what our art is, what it means, and who are the best artists. But we have to lay claim to that.... I look at my job in the overall Indian political scenario as a way of claiming our art and declaring self-determination. We are going to tell the world what that means."[23]

Perhaps the most striking, and politically resonant, example of exclusion is that of Jimmie Durham. Durham, a Cherokee American artist, creates "assemblages and installations that find their principal source in his Native culture, which he uses to deconstruct the stereotypes and prejudices of Western culture and installations" [24]:

> Jimmie Durham's artistic work and intellectual engagements have systematically focused on questioning the global hegemony of modern Western system of knowledge, or the "authentic" order of things. The melange of these scraps subverts the essential order of the hegemonic power of modern culture embodied by the museum itself.[25]

Yet, despite Durham's sophistication and prominence in the art world, he has consistently been denied access to major exhibitions because he refuses to conform to the U.S. federal policy of registration.

James Luna, a Pooyukitchum/Luiseño artist, and one of the leading figures in contemporary Native American art, is also largely excluded from surveys of modern artists. Luna's performances and installations address issues affecting Indian communities, and their exploitation by contemporary American ideology and corporate culture. In *Artifact Piece* (1987), for example, Luna was installed inside a clear museum case with personal objects, including family pictures, diplomas, and divorce papers, around him.[26] In a performance piece entitled *Take A Picture With a Real Indian* (1993) the artist invited observers to be photographed with him; at different junctures he wore a loincloth, a bone breast plate with a feather in his hair, and business attire.[27] That the audience did not take photographs when he was wearing the latter "costume" suggests that Native Americans have been romanticized, idealized as vanquished, or wholly commodified:

***Interview — Luna**: You've been called "one of the most dangerous Indians alive." What are you trying to say?*

Mayhew: Well, at times the message can be potent. One of my subjects is with ethnic identity—how people perceive us and how we perceive ourselves. Not everybody can talk about that, so I guess that makes me a dangerous character.

Why do you make yourself the subject of your art?

Mayhew: Because I know myself better than I know anything else. How do you talk about things like intercultural identity. Do you talk about it in the third person? If you sacrifice yourself, so to speak, then it becomes much more dynamic. I like to think that in my work I'm talking about something I know because I've lived it, as opposed to something that I read about.... When you're asked to take a picture with a real Indian, what does that mean? ... There was an Indian in a breechcloth with everybody going, "Oh!" There was a big ooh and aah when I stepped up on that pedestal with my war dance outfit. They forgot about all the rest and really lined up to have their picture taken. This is the memento that they really wanted."[28]

Both Durham and Luna are categorized within the history of art as Native American, rather than contemporary, artists — as *Artifact Piece* suggests — by virtue of the romantic essentializing of their identities. Yet the body of their work is largely excluded from such institutions as the American Indian Museum in the Smithsonian. This exclusion suggests the liminal position Native American art occupies, and Mayhew's response to this exclusion constitutes his most fervent response to injustice. "Native Americans are completely denied today, so there's a pain there of seeking acceptance and respect for the Natives of this country! I have a great pain in the suffering of that area ... if you say you're a Native American artist, there's no acceptance at all."[29]

Mayhew's outrage extends to a wider societal denial of the existence of Native Americans, and the particular problem of alcoholism and addiction: "Genocide. It's genocide! It's hard to escape it. It's everywhere! ... Complete omission. So you don't exist. And you know what the reason for that is. Land control. Land rights. Property rights. And identity rights. Unless you can prove you're Native American, you're not accepted by the government as being Native American. Now, come on! Every other group can say who they are, and [be] accepted, but Native Americans have to be certified by the government, [because] they can make claims on the land.... It's big business, right? The addiction is part of that ... on the weekends, in order to have some enjoyment, they get their pay, they go get a bottle. To get happy. To drown the oppression and disappointment.... Try that, get happy! And then all the movies, you never see the real culture of Native Americans.... What do they show? They show the drug thing, the oppression ... so you don't have any real images of who they are — all the movies ever done, there's no real image of who they are. Native Americans, the only time you see them on television is [in] Westerns. And then they have whites playing Indians! Now there's more and more, like *Dancing With Wolves.* But who's the hero?"

Mayhew credits his identification as an African American artist to his early lack of attention to his Native American heritage. "I've always lived as an African American. I'm Native American. I'm two-thirds Native American, and only one-third black. So I've always denied my heritage." This denial, which began with his family, extends broadly to national denial: "It has to do with my mother completely denying her heritage as Native American. She didn't want to know.... The fact that the oppression, and omission, and denial, and how Native Americans were treated and thought about — today.... [It is said] there are 250,000 Native Americans. There are 30 million descendants of Native Americans in this country! And they're completely ignored."

Mayhew has taken an active stance in promoting, encouraging, and teaching Native American artists. In 1985, on sabbatical from his position at Penn State, he taught at a school in Sante Fe, and felt a great identification with the Native American students: "The completely comfortable feeling I had there, I don't know if I'd had it before, although I was searching for my identity. The eagerness of them to learn to create was fabulous, it was almost natural; they wanted to do it. You can't believe what they did. In the middle of nowhere, out in the country in the desert, they built a beautiful school of Native American art, an art school, which is involved with theater, and filmmaking ... the technology of creative thinking. That was really a pleasure. With Native Americans there's a very spiritual connection. I went there, and I found it." Mayhew also went on to establish the Creative Center for the Arts and Sciences in Marin County, California, which supported Native American artists.

One of the striking experiences in writing about Mayhew's art is that this fundamental connection is initially submerged.

Hess: *Part of my struggle in writing a book about you has been that people say you're going to have a difficult time putting him in the context of other Modernist painters because your subject matter isn't angry, political...*

Mayhew: I'm painting *Forty Acres and a Mule.* That's the political connection. I'm painting the treaty land that was never honored for Native Americans. Which is still going on. Civil Rights, that was working very well for African Americans and other ethnic groups, but never Native Americans. No other group has been denied their heritage on the basis of the United States giving them the right to their heritage, or who they are. So that's part of the paintings that I'm involved with, the whole spiritual sensitivity and concern, which becomes landscape.[30]

Academic Restrictions

A significant aspect of institutional resistance faced by Richard Mayhew, as with other African and Native American artists, is the inflexibility and constricted nature of art history categories. Both in galleries and oral accounts, African American and Native American artists are often categorized and segregated from the breadth of American art. As Mayhew states, "If you say you're a Native American artist, there's no acceptance at all. African American artists have been accepted, but in a separate category ... my painting had fallen into a category which they can't define. They can't fit it in this category, can't fit it in that category, they write about it as a metamorphic form ... [it] really matters. It matters in terms of the contributions society will accept as inspiration and stimulation and functional creative consciousness.... All the books in academia ... it's always leaning to the area of the dominant culture, [the one] in control. And so, as a result, the sensibility of so-called minorities or the so-called subcultures never reached a level of equal development."

The influence and emphasis within academics of dominant culture may be attributed to its unmarked character. Richard Dyer suggests in *White*,

> The invisibility of whiteness as a racial position in white (which is to say dominant) discourse is of a piece with its ubiquity.... Research ... shows that in Western representation whites are overwhelmingly and disproportionately predominant, have the central and elaborated roles, and above all are placed as the norm, the ordinary, the standard[, a human norm] ... white people are systematically privileged in Western society, enjoy "unearned advantage and dominance" ... [and] set standards of humanity by which they are bound to succeed and others bound to fail.[31]

These standards construe perspectives, representations, and cultures that do not conform to the unspoken "norm" as troublesome, extraneous, and/or threatening. As Mayhew stated of his work at Sonoma State University, "I was a threat there. Academic politics has to do with the dominant culture's contribution. In academia, I was a thorn in their side always ... teaching interdisciplinary study of the arts and sciences — they were not ready for that! They didn't even understand what the hell I was doing. 'That's not a regular design class!' [they said] I said, yes, it is." Mayhew's methods of instruction were constantly questioned and misunderstood: "I took my class to the museum and got my hands slapped for doing that."

Mayhew describes the repeated and persistent experience of attempting to overturn the omission of minority artists in the history of art, and the repeated rejection he faced. He describes himself as a rebel, aligned with the Impressionists in their rejection of what was prescribed in the Academy, in all of the institutions at which he taught — Penn State, the University of California Santa Cruz, San Jose, Sonoma State, and elsewhere — everywhere except the Native American school at which he taught. "In academia I was constantly involved with the challenge of acceptance and rejection of minority artists ... the dominant culture is involved with maintaining the status quo, and if they start accepting the power of the subculture as being equal to their culture, then they start to lose foothold control." Mayhew describes the effort to teach African and African American art, and how he ultimately was able to "get into the curriculum or get into the books in the libraries ... [yet] I was on one of the committees to read over some of the books in terms of inclusions.... I looked and they just changed the paragraphs around."

The recent establishment of the Museum of Contemporary Native Arts in Santa Fe, and the discussion of current Native American lives in the American Indian Museum of the Smithsonian, mark an advancement in the exclusion of Native American culture from public discourse. It is in academic contexts, however, that omission is most evident. In text surveys of art histories, and particularly in college art courses, mention of contemporary artists is virtually nonexistent. The fact that Mayhew is known as an African American artist, although his heritage is primarily Native American, is telling; the mixture of the two seems to confound analysis. Is there a role contemporary artists can play in the presentation of art history? What underlying premises are challenged by their inclusion? Perhaps, as Dyer suggests, the unmarked category of white art,[32] the universal assumption that underlies such surveys, are revealed, and a floodgate of the contemporary arts of other cultures is opened, a disorienting and perhaps threatening prospect.

In discussing the omission of Native and African American art from historical accounts, Mayhew also weighs in on the neglect of contemporary female artists: "European heritage came to deny ... African Americans and Native Americans.... They've always been involved with beautiful craftmaking and developing. And for years African art being [considered] craft instead of fine art, that was part of the dictation of the media again, and the dictation of a controlling culture that says what is important and what is not." Mayhew speaks eloquently about the acceptance of African American women as primarily "folk" artists in the gallery system: "Who selects whom? There's Betty Blayton. You have no idea who she is. See that? She's fantastic. She was involved in the early '60s, long before Faith Ringgold reached any recognition. She was involved with the Children's Caravan in New York, showing primarily minority students the arts. As a result she neglected her input into the art market. She was a fantastic printmaker and painter. And then there's Vivian Brown! They weren't in favor in the court."

Omission from academic discussions is also his concern: "In our society, and in academics, the woman gets less money than the male, in the same subject. How come? How is that controlled? How is the art controlled? It's the same thing. Who controls this?" Mayhew demonstrates a nuanced understanding of the challenges faced by female academics:

Hess: *How do you survive in a dominant culture that doesn't "know" you? How do you come to terms with that paradox?*

Mayhew: How do you come to terms with being a woman in a male-dominated society?

Most men don't see that.

Mayhew: It's a male-dominated society.

When asked what aspects of the Native and African American experience might be compromised in the teaching of white art historians, Mayhew reveals the same concern with academic omission and denial: "You're coming out of the dominant culture, which dictates [what is appropriate].... And how much you're able to bridge that gap. It's hard, because I know a lot of white historians and white artists who have crossed over. They know, but they can't influence the larger picture. So when they look at you, they see you as the dominant culture. How much you can convince them is hard.... You know the bridge. You might be able to walk across the bridge; you end up in the center of the bridge. To be able to cross over, then you're the rebel. Right? Once you cross over you're the rebel. But if you're in the middle of the bridge, you come bouncing both sides, placating both sides."

When I informed Mayhew, with a laugh, that I thought I was in the middle of such a bridge, he said, "You have to be! In academia, this is what my problem was, right?" Mayhew has completely crossed the bridge. As a consequence, to some degree, he has left the greater fame he might have achieved behind him.

One of the most emphatic themes in every interaction with Mayhew is an awareness of the elite context of artistic experience, and a desire to break free of the dominant culture: "Unless you go to the museum and gallery, it's not your world at all." Dismissing the importance of his retrospective in 2009 (held at the Santa Clara and Santa Cruz museums and the Museum of the African Diaspora in San Francisco), the artist states, "It happened a long time ago. It doesn't matter.... What *does* matter is my contribution. But my work can be enjoyed only by the elite." This elitism is linked for him to the very foundations of thought: "Intellectualism is based on the philosophy of Europe ... [it is] based on ... educational structure and ideology." He seeks continuously to subvert and dismiss this elitism, despite his acknowledgment of the satisfaction of the positive response of others.

The perspective adopted by Mayhew is, hence, a relatively radical one. Mayhew seeks to maintain his technical and spiritual gifts in painting, yet open the canon to creative and alternative ideas about instruction, and what constitutes art. The contradictions in this perspective seem not to trouble him. He accepts the views and efforts of almost any creative endeavor, while he himself adheres to the more traditional and academic painting mode. The sense of place Mayhew has created — straddling traditional and quite radical perspectives on the art process — seems comfortable and natural to him. The calm and sense of order captured in such works as *Blue Breeze*— with its brilliant purple foliage against an orange sky, like a photonegative of a still forest — contrast with *Contemplation*, which presents what appears to be a path leading to the horizon of a lake, until the path dissipates, and the bright pink and purple sky threaten to overtake the greenish black of the trees. The contrast between these visions, arresting and lovely, illustrate Mayhew's complexity — his integration of the spontaneous and the technical, the abstract and the representational, the awareness of oppression and the celebration characteristic of culture — that has defined the course of his life and career.

Chapter Four

"Forty, Forty, Forty": Creative Consciousness, Landscape and the Sense of "Place"

> "Forty Acres and a Mule" ... slaves were supposed to get forty acres and a mule ... they never got that ... all the treaties which were supposed to be given them, never honored.... That's part of the paintings I'm involved with, the whole spiritual sensitivity and concern, which becomes landscape. How much I'm doing the landscape is based on this whole sensitivity and concern for the land, which is the spiritual reflection of self.— Richard Mayhew[1]

The Kiowa author N. Scott Momaday writes extensively about the relationship to land in *The Man Made of Words*. "There is great good in returning to a landscape that has had extraordinary meaning in one's life. It happens that we return to such places in our minds irresistibly. There are certain villages and towns, mountains and plains that, having seen them, walked in them, lived in them, even for a day, we keep forever in the mind's eye. They become indispensable to our well-being: they define us, and we say, I am who I am because I have been there, or there. There is good, too, in actual, physical return.... I, too, happen to take place, each day of my life, in my environment. I exist in a landscape, and my existence is indivisible with the land."[2]

The turn to landscape — indeed, the fierce refusal to abandon allusion to the land, despite critical consequences — has long defined Mayhew's art, and his spiritual connectedness to his heritage. The dense, lush foliage of the East Coast, with its closely growing trees, deep shadows, and roar of cicadas in the heat, contrasts dramatically with the open landscapes of the West Coast, washed with sunlight, cool rolling hills, and the glimmering calm of the ocean. One can see with the passage of time Mayhew's dedication to these specific landscapes, as well as the desert spaces of Arizona, and the gradual transition in his work from densely wooded forests to the yellows and oranges, the brightness, of his home in California. Mayhew's activism, too, focuses around the places which have been denied to Native and African American artists — the "forty thousand treaties" made to keep Native American land, the forty acres denied African Americans during Reconstruction, his forty years of fighting for access, inclusion, and recognition.

The sense of place Momaday suggests, however, can also be seen in terms of Mayhew's orientation in the world, a sense of groundedness and appropriate presence. This inner confidence is constantly evident in Mayhew, and he clearly sees the consequences of an absence of centeredness and place in his peers. Many of the Abstract Expressionist artists at the Cedar Bar, Mayhew suggests, dealt with pressure by becoming arrogant, although they were tremendously talented and bright — Jackson Pollock, Wilhelm de Kooning, and Andy Warhol, among others. Mayhew is quite articulate about the explanation for this attitude, and the underpinnings of humility: "It has to do with insecurity. These people became so confident, some of the great writers were there, they were so humble about it. That was beautiful. You don't have to talk about it."[3]

Richard Mayhew had many teachers who handled their gifts, fame, and the oppressive circumstances of their existence with grace and clarity. His grandmother Sarah Mayhue, the Hudson River School painters in Amityville, the supportive members of the MacDowell Colony, the artists at the Penzioni Bartolini, his instructors Edwin Dickinson and Reuben Tam — all of the colleagues and mentors he encountered in New York City — provided him with examples of inner confidence and the ability to handle challenging circumstances (including racism on the part of art institutions) with strength and grace. Romare Bearden, Norman Lewis and Hale Woodruff, among others, held fast to the mode of creative expression to which they were committed, regardless of what was popular or critically acclaimed. But Mayhew's adherence to a sense of place in landscape and in his inner "sensitivity" (as he describes it) cannot be easily attributed to these influences alone.

Mayhew approaches fame and his gifts and challenges with humor:

Mayhew: Someone says, "You're a famous artist!" Why are you so humble? I said, if you create … it's very humbling. You don't know from one moment to the next … if it's successful. Not to anyone else, but to you!

Hess: *I've never seen you say to someone, "I'm Richard Mayhew."*

Mayhew: No, no. They'd say, "I don't know who you are anyway!" (Both laugh) [Robert Motherwell was a] very brilliant man. He was brilliant. Very sharp. Very intelligent person. And he said that the creative process is very humbling. You don't really know who you are. The outside world sees you one way, you see yourself completely differently. You don't see that person when you look in the mirror, that they are talking about. And it's true! I look in the mirror and I say, "Oh, yeah." In fact, I see a thirty-year-old when I look. (Laughs)

Mayhew humorously refers to his limitations, but his extraordinary life energy and positive outlook invariably emerge in such accounts:

Mayhew: Someone told me, "You shouldn't be traveling by yourself—what are you doing traveling by yourself at your age?" I said, "I think I'm forty years old—what the hell are you talking about?" (Laughs) It's a state of mind. I was with a guy, he says, "Hey, Mayhew, Mayhew, Mayhew!" I was running at the airport. (Laughs) I was too late for the plane. I said, "Get out of my way, I'm catching a plane." He called me, he said, "Man, I see you running through the damn airport!" (Laughs)

So what is your secret?

Mayhew: It's a state of mind. If you think you're forty, you're forty. (Laughs)

> Mayhew believes that being famous as an artist can be restrictive. "It's hard to deal with that reality. Fame has its pitfalls in terms of your family and friends. They see you differently. They treat you differently. And I don't like that. All of a sudden you're different. I'm like the same

> scrubby youngster making drawings. (Laughs) I get a lot of respect.... But then, it's hard to live with that. You look in the mirror and say, Who the hell are you? You know, that kind of ego-ness I don't have. Others — maybe I would like to have that, what they have, they're really involved in this ego trip, how happy they are within themselves. But sometimes I wonder, are they really? (Laughs) Because I don't have that, I don't see that kind of egomania, or the fact that all of a sudden I became famous. What contribution have I made at being an artist? My indulged, joyful existence, my whole life — what contribution was that? That's hard to deal with. That's why I got involved in different activities in the community. It's very meditative, because when I'm painting, there's nothing else out there. I'm inside the painting. Someone says, You're really a star. And I say, No, no, no, I live a very humble kind of existence."

Not all of the artists in the Abstract Expressionist milieu had the egotism associated with prominence in the art world. Romare Bearden set an example of philosophical reflectiveness and community advocacy and support; Hale Woodruff, one of Mayhew's closest friends, advanced in his teaching and his work the social ideals he absorbed from Henry Ossawa Tanner, Alain Locke and his internship with Diego Rivera. Woodruff demonstrated a remarkable courage and independence of vision, and his social activism advanced the ideals of Spiral, which he himself named: Bearden and Henderson share, for example, the story of how Woodruff was determined to open all channels of art to his students and the African-American community at the High Museum in Atlanta.

> Woodruff insisted on seeing the director. Identifying his own background in art and his role as a teacher at Atlanta University, he gained permission to bring his student classes to the museum.... When he appeared ... for a lecture by Grant Wood, whose paintings *American Gothic* and *Daughters of Revolution* had provoked much controversy, Woodruff was denied admission. The next day Wood learned of this. In a rebuff to the museum officials, Wood called Woodruff and asked if he could visit him at Spelman.[4]

Benny Andrews, too, employed his position in the community to advance the causes both of his students and of African American artists as a whole:

> In 1969, Andrews and painter Cliff Joseph (b. 1922) formed the Black Emergency Cultural Coalition (BECC), protesting the exclusion of black art and artists from mainstream museums, and the lack of input from the black community in such exhibitions as the Metropolitan's Harlem on My Mind.[5]

Mayhew describes Andrews as an extraordinarily positive influence and an artist with an outer focus — in part, because of his children — that protected him from the isolation that afflicted other artists.

Mayhew fully embraces the feeling of meditative sensitivity as critical to his work, a sensibility inspired in part by Reuben Tam. Mayhew describes Tam as "a very brilliant man, one of the most intellectual persons I encountered other than Hale Woodruff ... there was a strange kind of intrigue of people like that. He had that kind of mystical, spiritual sensitivity." Again and again in gallery exhibitions, museum installations, and interviews, discussion turns to the issue of the spiritual as manifested in nature, although this spiritual aspect is ascribed to different sources.

Volpe attributes this sense of the spiritual in Mayhew's work to the influence of "visionary" artists, such as Inness:

> Inness began his career under the spell of the Hudson River School, but through the influence of transcendentalism and, more properly, of the writings of Swedish mystic Emanuel Swedenborg, Innes became, just as Mayhew would, a painter who wished to communicate interior states rather than duplicate what he saw.[6]

The art historian Halima Taha suggests that Mayhew's work encompasses aspects of the mystical, Gnostic belief, and Eastern religions, and a belief that consciousness and connectedness with others can only be fully realized through a deep grounding in nature.[7] The echoes of any number of spiritual traditions, or the affinity or alignment of his work with them, can thus be traced in Mayhew's views, but the community orientations of Spiral and the Social Realists is constant.

The perspective adopted by Woodruff, Tam and Andrews is one Mayhew constantly aspired to achieve — the ability to pursue creative interests fully, without neglecting or becoming separate from the community. Mayhew states, "Being an artist is a self-indulged existence. Very happy, joyful work, and I love to paint, and I love doing it! Like when I was doing singing, I loved to sing, I didn't want to be paid for singing, I just loved to do it.... [But I was concerned with] the fact that I wasn't making a contribution to the community. So I got involved with extracurricular activities. I got involved with all kind of special programs, in upstate New York, and I got involved when I came out to California, the Center for the Arts and Science, and special art programs. So I felt that was my contribution. My self-indulged existence as an artist ... was kind of selfish.... As a singer I also felt there was a role of self-enjoyment, the same thing as an entertainer. It was a pleasurable encounter. But how much is that contributing to the needs of our society? Someone said, "We feel that you are making a great contribution to us as an artist,' and I questioned that. What was the contribution? They said ... ['You provide] a very inspirational, and stimulating motivational existence.' It's hard to think of myself doing that for others. Because, there again, there's that ego trip that goes down ... it was hard for me to live in that state of mind, because doing a painting is constantly a frustrating, creative challenge."

Mayhew believes, then, that the life of an artist is a joyful but humbling one, a meditative experience that carries with it the responsibility for social action. When asked to describe himself, Mayhew discusses "the sensitivity of the mystique and meditative state of painting. It's a challenging dedication, and it's like a committed disease in some ways. And someone says, like a calling, like heads in a practice of religious, have a calling for the rest of their lives. So it is like a calling. It's difficult for one to understand unless they have that kind of commitment to the creative process. It's a joy in doing it, it's a fascinating existence. You get really lost in it."

Despite this description of joy and deep connectedness involved in making art, Mayhew describes the calling as one of deferred reward and, often, isolation. "The enjoyment of ... [being a musician] is different than being a painter. As an entertainer you get instant applause, applause in the moment. So it's encouraging, right there. As an artist, there's no instant applause. It comes much later. Or maybe it never comes.... [I saw] Edwin Dickinson in the lounge of the Whitney Museum, his retrospective was there, and I was asking him about the show, and he says, 'Oh, when you see yourself in retrospect, you'll find you haven't done a damn thing!' (Laughs) No matter how much it reaches the ultimate, you end up going to the next painting, because this painting is never finished! No painting is ever finished."

Mayhew describes the isolation inherent in the art making process: "I do get lonely.... It's such a solitary life. I feel very lonely and isolated. It's not here. No one to talk to. There's nobody here ... this is very disturbing to me, because I'm at this stage of being completely isolated. I get a lot of work done as a result of it. Because in New York there's always so much going on.... The human support relationship is very important. Peers are very important. It's part of the social functioning, which is really living life in community, that African American system of relationship. And if you don't have it, you're isolated, you're on an island."

While Mayhew's commitment to community engagement remains strong, his relationship with his peers is attenuated. Of his colleagues in Spiral, Mayhew states, "There's a certain credibility and intellectual development there that I miss. But people are not there anymore. All of these people died away! [Romare Bearden, Charles Alston, Calvin Douglas, Perry Ferguson, Reginald Gammon, Alvin Hollingsworth, Felrath Hines, Norman Lewis, William Majors, Earl Miller, Merton Simpson, Hale Woodruff, Benny Andrews, Tom Feelens, Al Loving, Ernie Crichlow, and others]. That's what sad about this. I miss them. It's shocking, because you have such a close identity with them; it's almost as though you're passing with them, really."

The pressures of working in isolation, Mayhew suggests, are particularly acute for artists without extended families. "Their work is their children ... sometimes they're under strain. Many of the prominent artists (I won't mention their names) had nervous breakdowns on the basis of this completely dedicated isolationism. The inside mindset that one is involved with ... contributes to some kind of breakdown.... My children are so enterprising and successful, which is very rare. Many children of successful artists suffer all kinds of maladies and problems, because of,

I guess, living in the shadow of the fame. Visual artists are vulnerable, and there's no fixed possibility of survival."

Maintaining an independence and freedom of perspective in the face of these challenges — or in the face of social pressures to conform generally — is quite difficult, as Mayhew acknowledges. "[Individuals] become oppressed along the way, and they start losing the natural instinct to function and survive.... They become submerged into a regimental kind of functioning, in terms of an ethical instinct of creative thinking and sensitivity.... Certain forms that one has to abide by deny that uniqueness, and one gets caught up in the formulas, and no longer involved with the creative sensitivity of self. [People] have to conform to a pattern of functioning that denies who they are, or what their potential is."

One of the purposes of Spiral, and certainly an abiding concern for Mayhew, was breaking through that regimental form of thinking imposed by society and by a dominant culture. The passionate investment Mayhew has in this objective is evident in almost every sphere of his life. In his breaking away from Amityville, his decision to become an artist, his travels, his singing, his activism, his choice of artistic forms, his widely varied friendships, his mode of teaching, his refusal of the isolation and egotism characteristic of the Abstract Expressionist, his openness to life — in so many ways Mayhew has led a life of clarity, the clarity of independent thought and dedication. "There is the creative survival instinct, finishing a painting, how much you can be defeated by the challenge, or writing a book — how much you are able to accomplish what you wanted, and being able to follow through on all the possibilities, and being accepted by a publisher. And how one becomes philosophical about it, is part of the whole creative instinct. That's what salvation is."

As Mayhew himself admits, defining this point of view, this combination of meditative absence of ego, creative clarity, independence of perspective, and dedication to a spiritual way of life — which involves, for him, dedication to the community as a whole — is difficult. The challenge has proved daunting for many critics, and even for the artist himself: "It's hard to identify that as some kind of intellectual, conscious

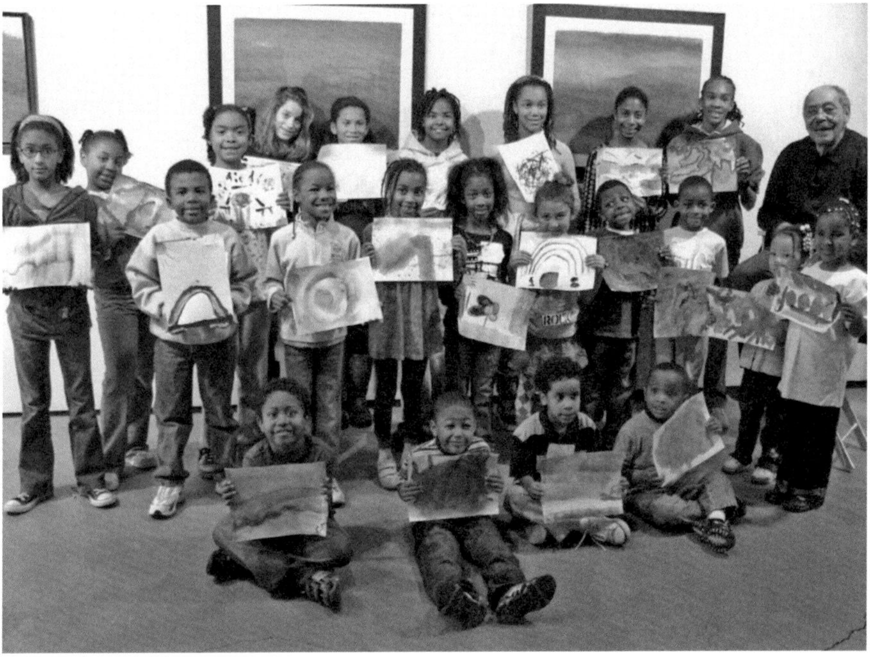

Richard Mayhew teaching young children to draw, New York, ca. 2000.

knowing, and to evaluate, that is sometimes difficult, because it is so abstract, and it has no basis of explanation and clarification. So I kind of live in that kind of space. And that's a religion." The degree of faith in a way of being and perceiving that can't be clearly articulated is striking, but as Mayhew admits, can't be consciously sustained: "It's hard for me to me to think that way, thinking, "meditative state." I can't think that way, I paint the way I feel." Efforts to highlight this unusual and striking quality in Mayhew invariably result for him in a good-natured laugh, as if to highlight the absurdity of using language to describe spiritual or visual experience in words, or to undermine any impression of self-importance.

Despite this playfulness, there is, nonetheless, the sense in Mayhew's work that the viewer is drawn in because it suggests something quite deep in themselves, although they may be unaware of what the depth is.

As Mayhew indicates, his work is increasingly used in rest homes and hospitals; one of his paintings is on the cover of *Dying Unafraid.* The sense of calmness, of a meditative kind of state, is both soothing and intoxicating, and Mayhew relates this sense to the continuity in landscape and life: "Nature is constantly involved with replacing itself. Just a puddle on the sidewalk, after a rain, is just another reflection of the forms in nature, right? And then the trees: [they go] through the cycle of the change of seasons; it's always involved with reinventing itself, each spring.... They go through a cycle of sleeping and waking. Because they sleep and they wake up, right? ... Even in sleeping they're still functioning sensitively. Right now, this is like part of winter, and I cut all my rose bushes back, but you can notice that they're regrowing already. In summer the cycle goes on, in regrowth. So from that, there's no end. Which has to do with religion, with everlasting life! Continuous."

Mayhew ties this regeneration and continuity to an inner creative sensibility that cannot be replicated or fully conveyed in words: "When one dies, it's the fact that one is going to keep on living! It has to do with how much is the mind that continues, or the spirit continues, according to many religions. And the fact that the body is destroyed, but that spiritual sensitivity is part of some of the philosophers in terms of energy and space. It recontinues in space. In anyone involved with germinating some continued form of sensitivity, it's part of the energy of space forever."

Yet for all of the depth, seriousness, focus and spiritual quality of Mayhew's approach to art making, he remains an expansive, humorous, outgoing friend, a lover of people, eager to celebrate and laugh. His sheer exuberance for life, his passionate energy, his powerfully affirming nature and his playful approach to challenges have the effect of encouraging and inspiring others. "I feel that anyone can paint, and anyone can draw. It's just a matter of how dedicated and committed they are."[8] There is room for everyone on the playground, he seems to suggest, as long as they want to play. Mayhew's easy demeanor, his resistance to restrictions and his sensitivity only underscore a life of play, despite extraordinary discouragement.

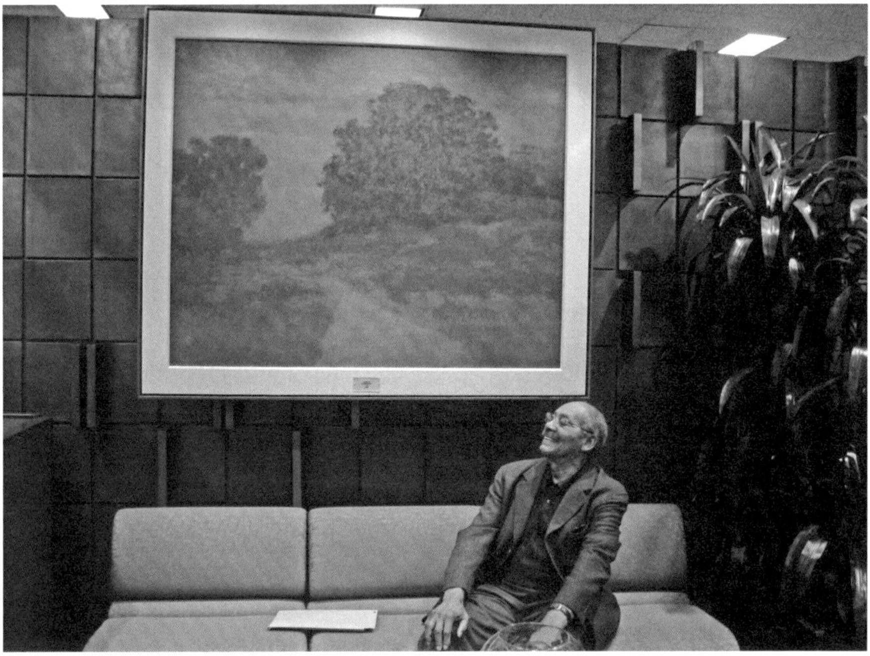

Richard Mayhew with one of his paintings, New York, ca. 2000.

Mayhew aligns the internal meditative state he seeks to achieve with the process of art production itself: "It changes in terms of application of paint, in terms of color, in terms of form, in terms of space, in terms of mood. I'm constantly involved and concerned about mood, which is part of that meditative state, which takes place in the course of working, really. I'm completely lost sometimes. I don't know what day it is or what time it is." This process is reflected in individual works that reveal an elusive and subtly shifting tone. Of *Mood Indigo*, Mayhew states, "It was painted while I was listening to Ellington. The work represents the involvement with the special sensitivity of moods and space that only the Duke had on the essence of feeling jazz that's hard to capture. It's so elusive, that mood in his music; this work summarizes it." Again, "In *Santa Cruz No. 8*, the rolling canyon and falling fog sets up a poetic space. Early in the morning the sky is green, and space is very subtle....

Santa Cruz No. 5 summarizes the moodiness of Santa Cruz … a special feeling of a lyrical, musical kind."

One of the most striking aspects of this meditative commitment and dedication to process is the modest environment in which Mayhew works. Mayhew's home, although lovely, is small; his studio is an attached one-car garage. As Gayle Fulton Ross states of her visit to his working space. "I'm listening to this artist I respect, I admire, I'm in awe of, knowing he's done all of this work, all of these years, and he's still … [not got] a studio."[9] The space Mayhew establishes in art production seems irrelevant to him, although he once expressed a desire to paint in New Mexico, where he had an overwhelmingly positive experience with the Native American school.

Mayhew's focus is spiritual, joyous and increasingly internal, although always inspired by nature and, by extension, his heritage. A student and friend, Nashormeh Lindo, states of her son's response to Mayhew's increasingly ethereal, lush, and majestic paintings, "There is no darkness in them."[10] This is not meant to minimize the profound seriousness of his work, which is motivated by a history of achievement as well as oppression. Mayhew himself describes his paintings inspired by a visit to the South as having to do "with the shadows in the foliage and it has to do with a mystique that happened in that area. I'm sure those bushes I looked at recently on the plantation didn't exist [then] … but the identity and feeling about the oppression of the slaves that lived on that plantation … one has the history of knowing how destructive that was to a mass of human beings." Mayhew desires only to present us with his experience, generated from many visions and experiences; both light and dark emerge, and he has no hand in determining the outcome.

***Above and Beyond*, 2009**
Oil on canvas
48 × 48 in. (121.9 × 121.9 cm)

C1

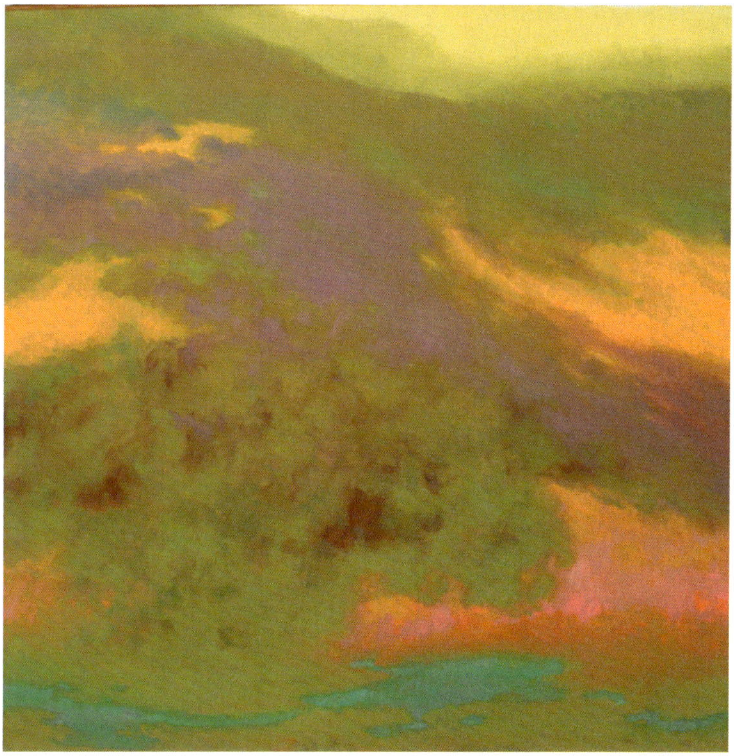

COURTESY ACA GALLERIES, NEW YORK

***Arroyo Secco*, 2009**
Oil on canvas
60 × 72 in. (152.4 × 182.9 cm)

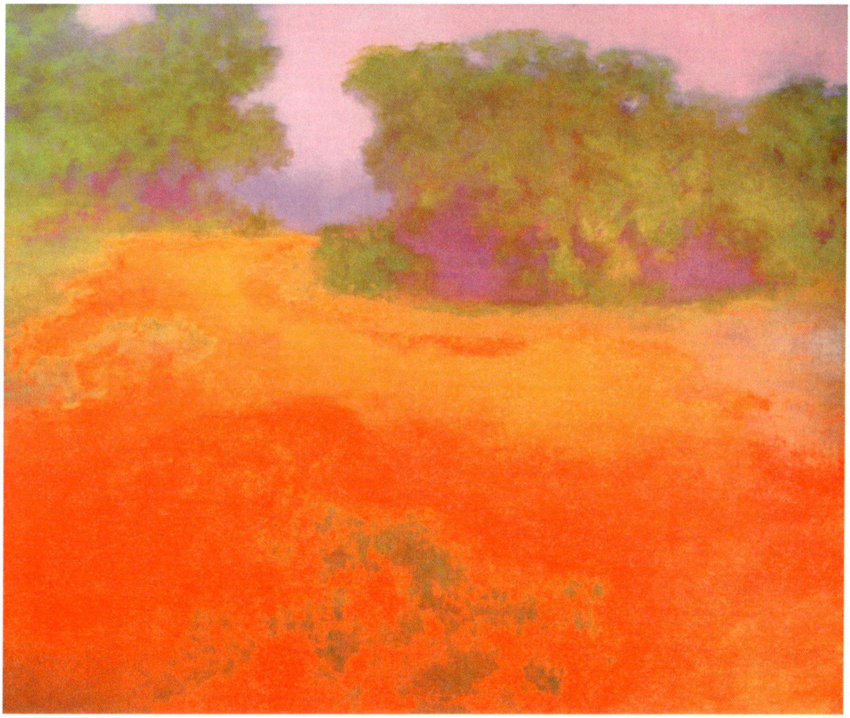

COURTESY ACA GALLERIES, NEW YORK

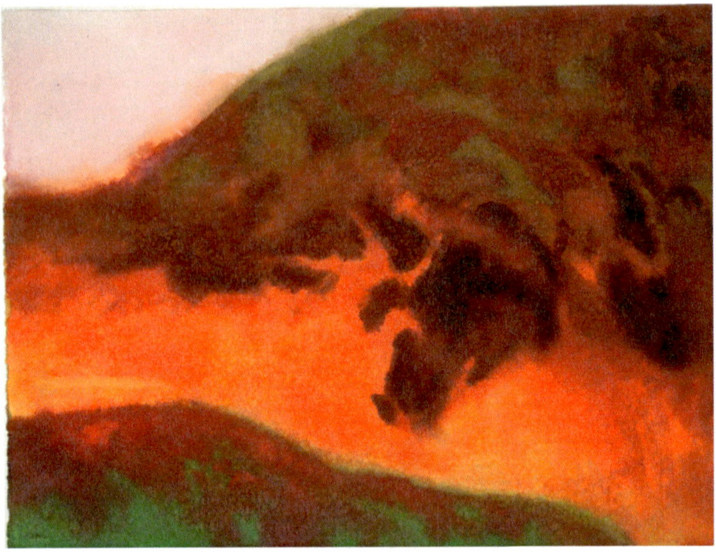

COURTESY ACA GALLERIES, NEW YORK

***Counterpoint*, 1997**
Watercolor
30 × 40 in.
(76.2 × 101.6 cm)

***Coyote Creek*, 2008**
Oil on canvas
33 × 52 in.
(83.8 × 132.1 cm)

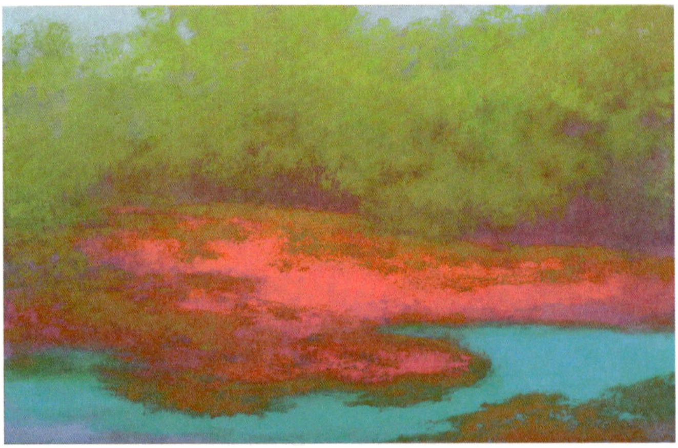

COURTESY ACA GALLERIES, NEW YORK

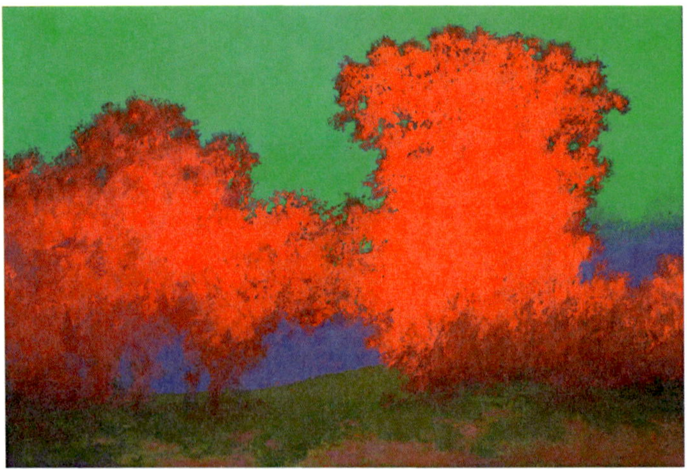

COURTESY ACA GALLERIES, NEW YORK

***Crescendo* (no date)**
Oil on canvas
24 × 36 in.
(60.9 × 91.4 cm)

***Diablo Pass*, 2008**
Oil on canvas 48 × 48 in. (121.9 × 121.9 cm)

Courtesy ACA Galleries, New York

***Summit*, 2004**
Oil on canvas 54 × 54 in. (137.16 × 137.16 cm)

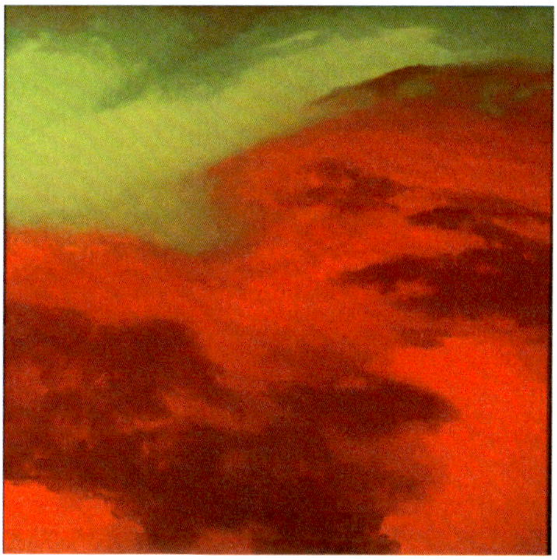

Courtesy ACA Galleries, New York

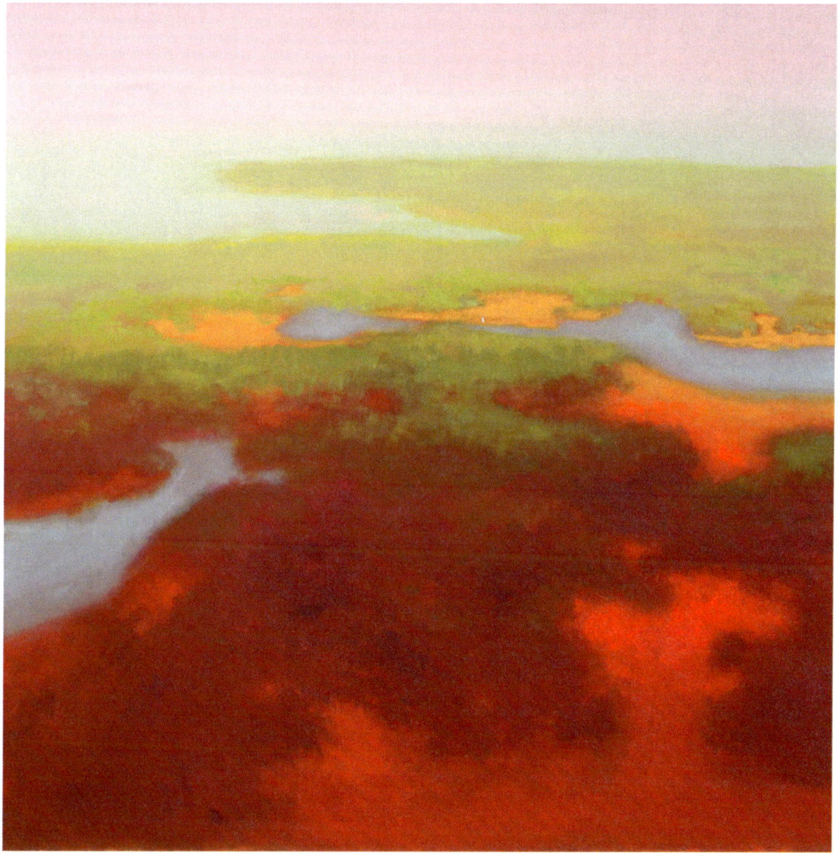

Courtesy ACA Galleries, New York

***Elkhorn Slough*, 2009.** Oil on canvas 36 × 36 in. (91.4 × 91.4 cm)

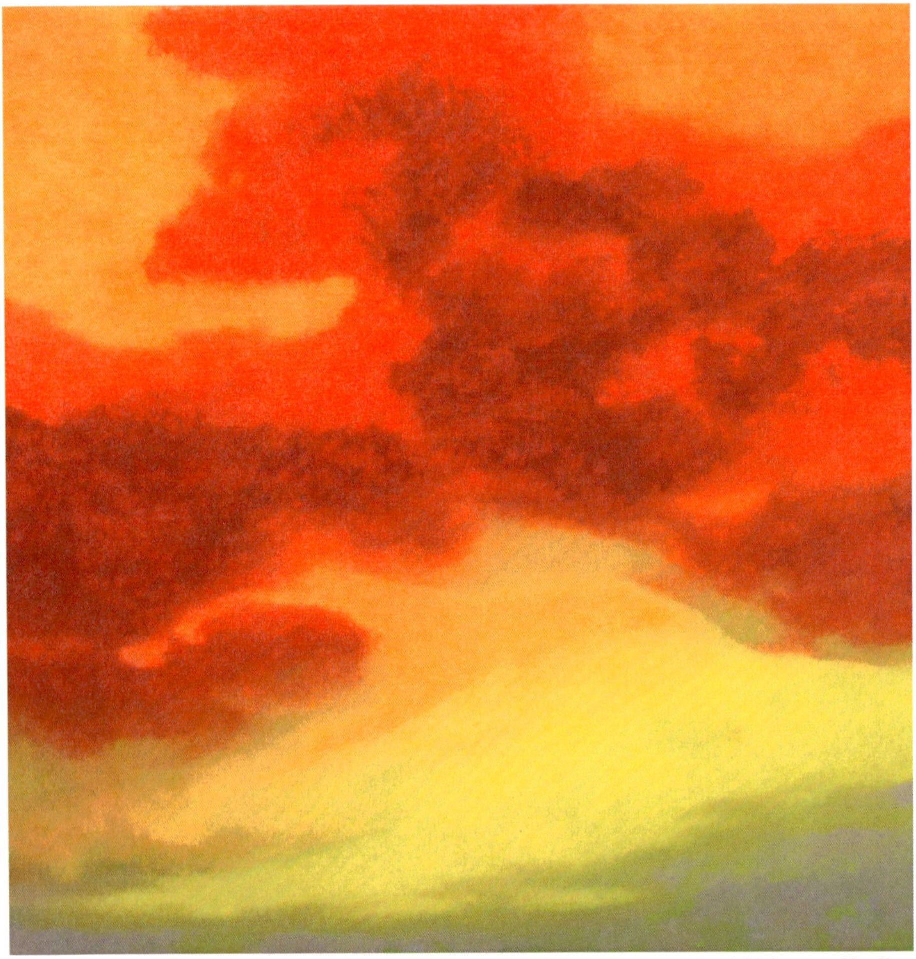

COURTESY ACA GALLERIES, NEW YORK

***Overture II*, 2010**
Oil on canvas
48 × 48 in.
(121.92 × 121.92 cm)

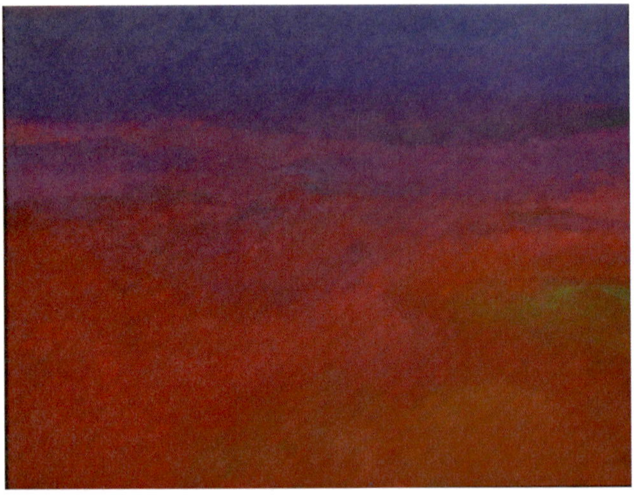

COURTESY ACA GALLERIES, NEW YORK

***Fog*, 2004**
Oil on canvas
36 × 48 in.
(91.44 × 121.92 CM)

***Jigsaw*, 2009**
Oil on canvas 36 × 36 in. (91.4 × 91.4 cm)

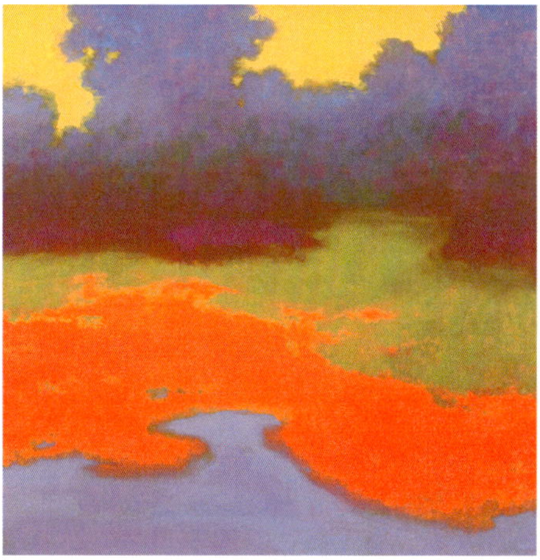

COURTESY ACA GALLERIES, NEW YORK

***Lumbee*, 2009**
Oil on canvas 30 × 30 in. (76.2 × 76.2 cm)

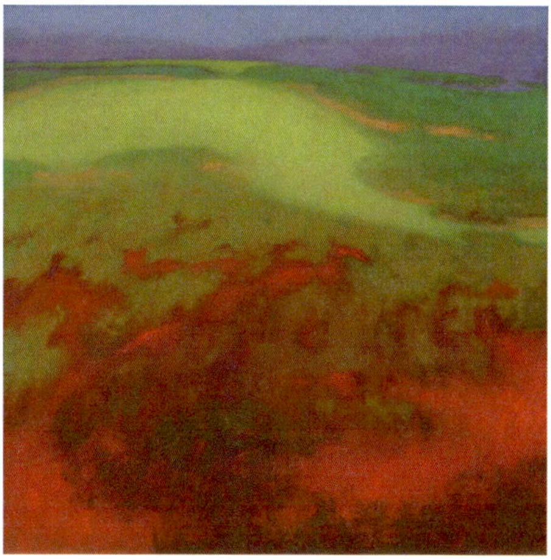

COURTESY ACA GALLERIES, NEW YORK

***Mellow Mood*, 2008**
Oil on canvas 18 × 24 in. (45.72 × 60.96 cm)

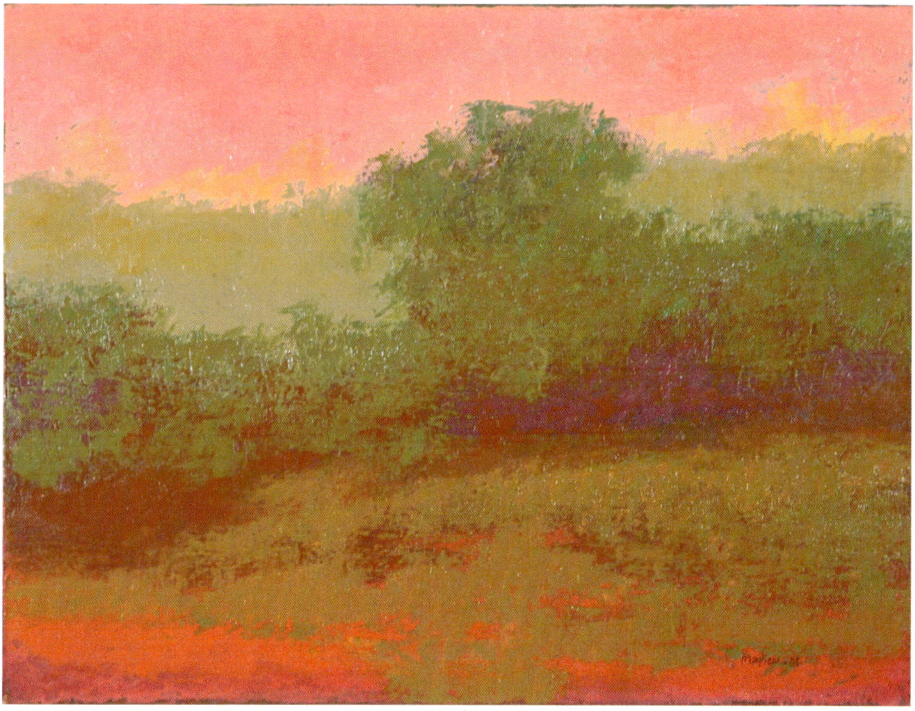

COURTESY ACA GALLERIES, NEW YORK

***Mist*, 2004**
Oil on canvas
30 × 36 in.
(76.2 × 91.44 cm)

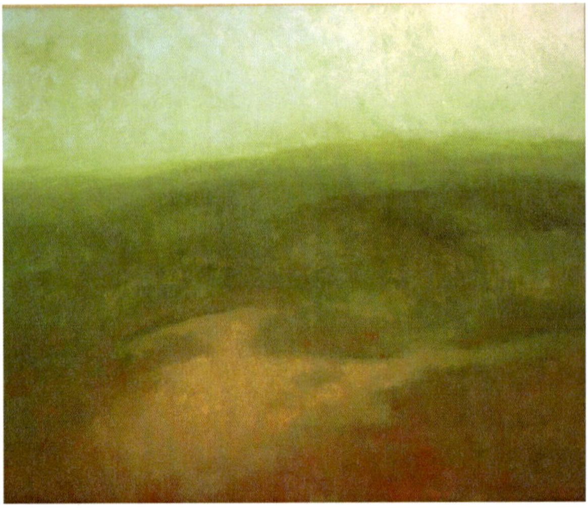

COURTESY ACA GALLERIES, NEW YORK

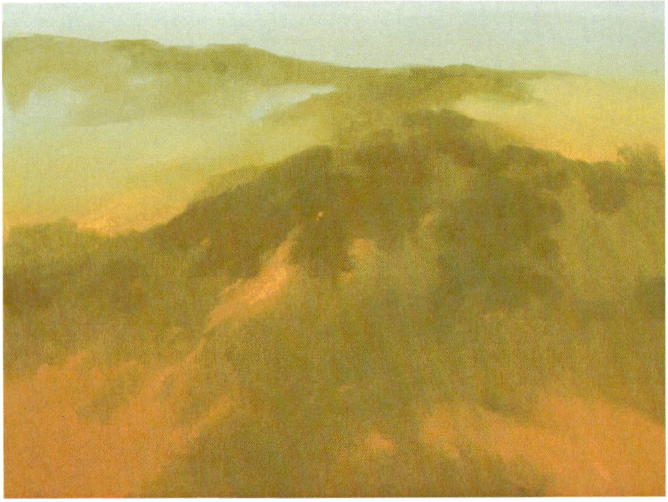

COURTESY ACA GALLERIES, NEW YORK

Misty Mystic
(no date)
Oil on canvas
40 × 30 in.
(101.6 × 76.2 cm)

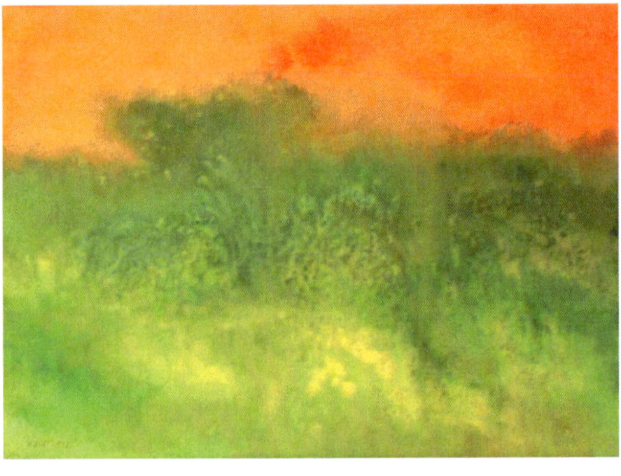

COURTESY ACA GALLERIES, NEW YORK

Monterey Series
***2002 #1*, 2002**
Watercolor
9 × 12 in.
(22.86 × 30.48 cm)

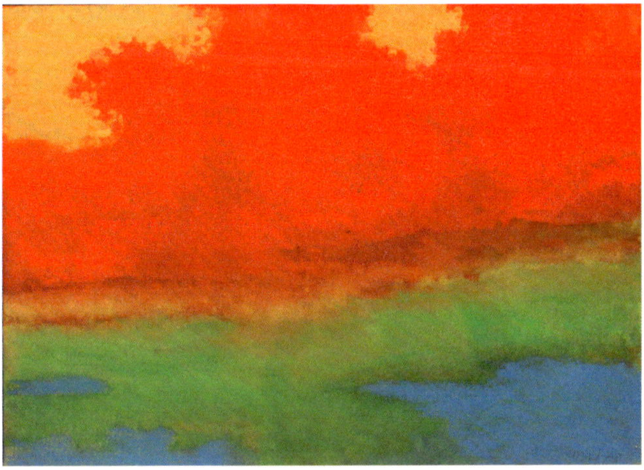

COURTESY ACA GALLERIES, NEW YORK

***Monterey Series 2002 #7*, 2002**
Watercolor
10 × 14½ in.
(25.4 × 36.83 cm)

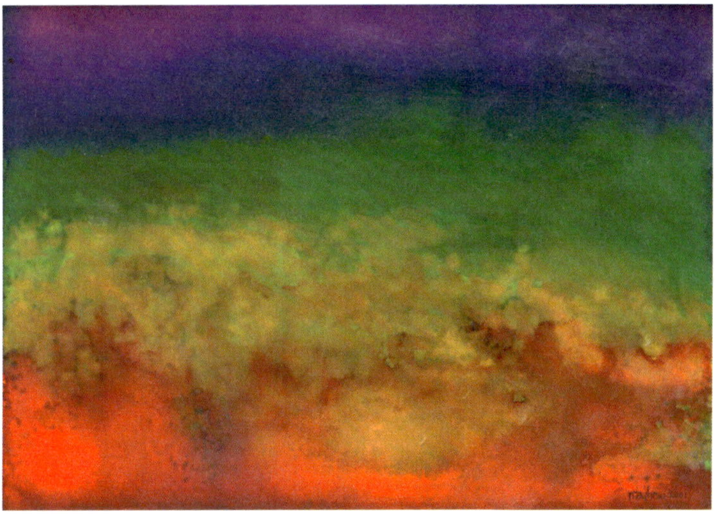

COURTESY ACA GALLERIES, NEW YORK

***Monterey Series #4*, 1996**
Watercolor on paper
13¾ × 16¾ in.
(34.9 × 42.5 cm)

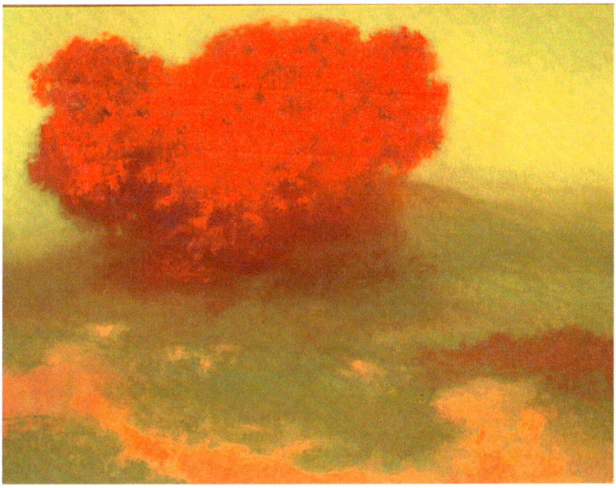

COURTESY ACA GALLERIES, NEW YORK

***Morning Glow*, 2009**
Oil on canvas
30 × 40 in.
(76.2 × 101.6 cm)

***Morning Mystique*, 2004**
Oil on canvas 30 × 40 in. (76.2 × 101.6 cm)

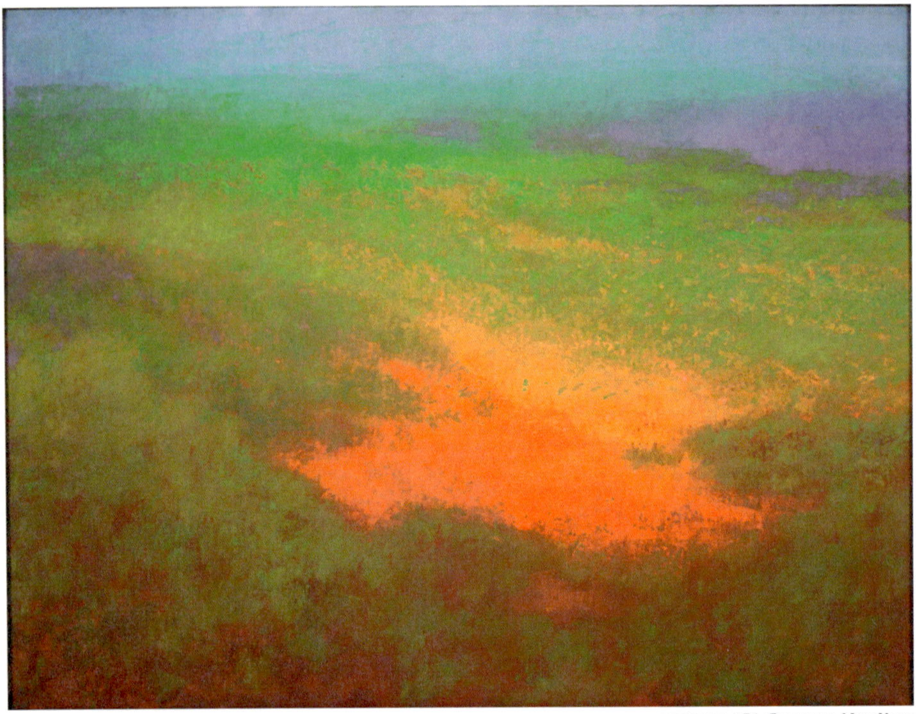

COURTESY ACA GALLERIES, NEW YORK

***Ollieberry Lane*, 2009**
Oil on canvas 30 × 30 in.
(76.2 × 76.2 cm)

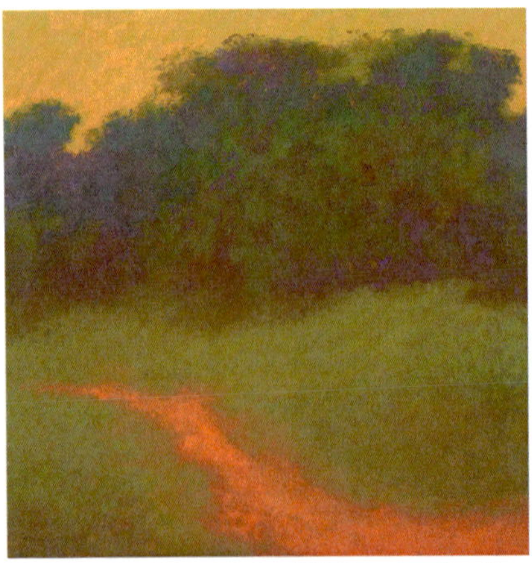

COURTESY ACA GALLERIES, NEW YORK

***Hill Top*, 1962**
Oil on canvas
39 × 45 in. (99.1 × 114.3 cm)

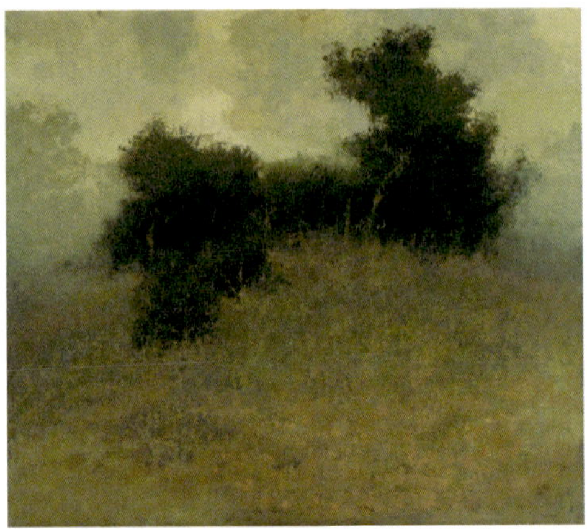

COURTESY ACA GALLERIES, NEW YORK

***Orchestration*, 2006**
Oil on canvas 52 × 60 in. (132.1 × 152.4 cm)

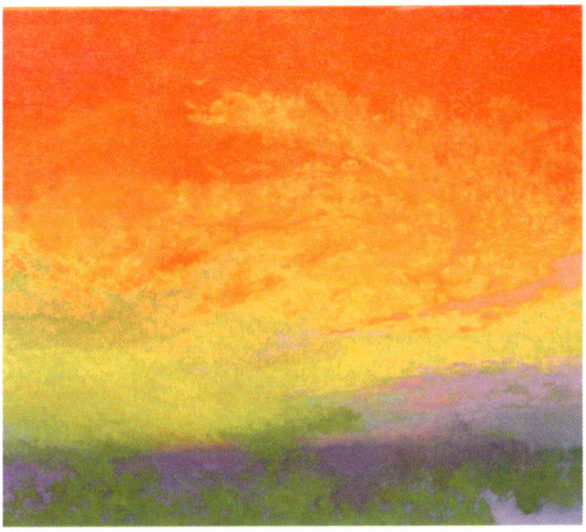

COURTESY ACA GALLERIES, NEW YORK

***Serenade*, 1990**
Oil on canvas 42 × 46 in. (106.7 × 116.8 cm)

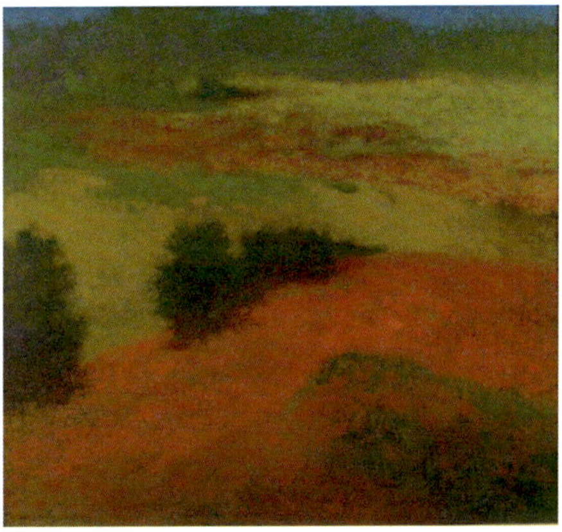

COURTESY ACA GALLERIES, NEW YORK

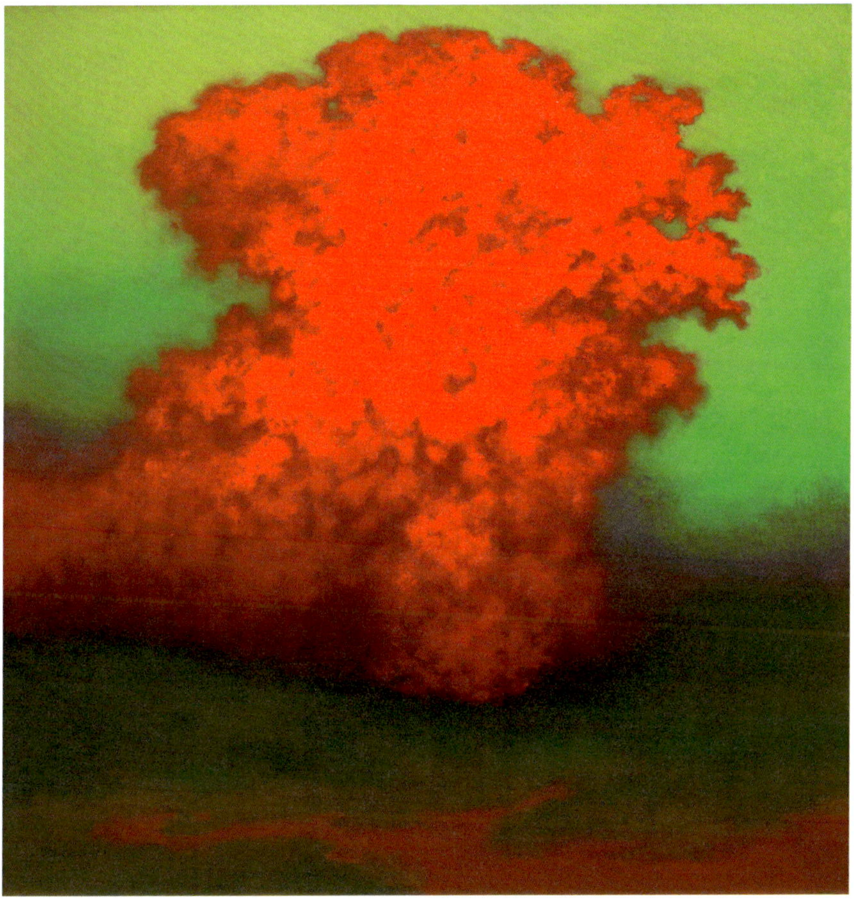

COURTESY ACA GALLERIES, NEW YORK

***Scarlet Solitude*, 2011.** Oil on canvas 48 × 48 in. (121.92 × 121.92 cm)

Serenade Series #4, 2004
Watercolor on paper
30 × 22 in.
(76.2 × 55.9 cm)

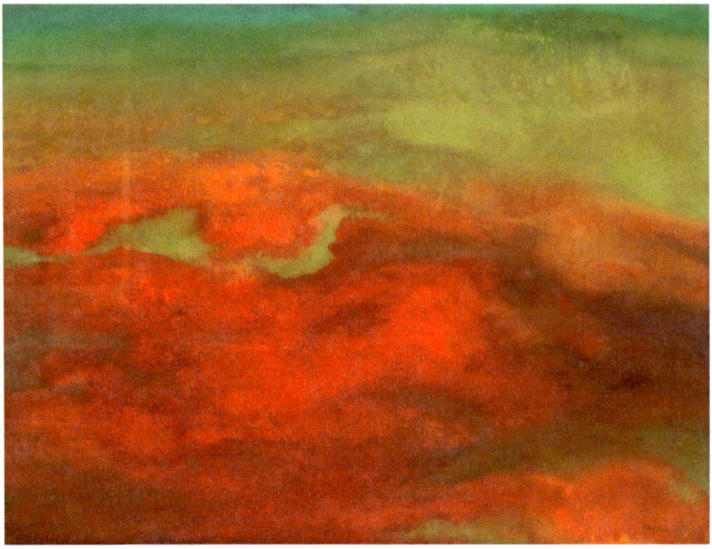

COURTESY ACA GALLERIES, NEW YORK

COURTESY ACA GALLERIES, NEW YORK

Soquel Serenade IV, 2008
Watercolor on paper
10 × 14 in.
(25.4 × 35.56 cm)

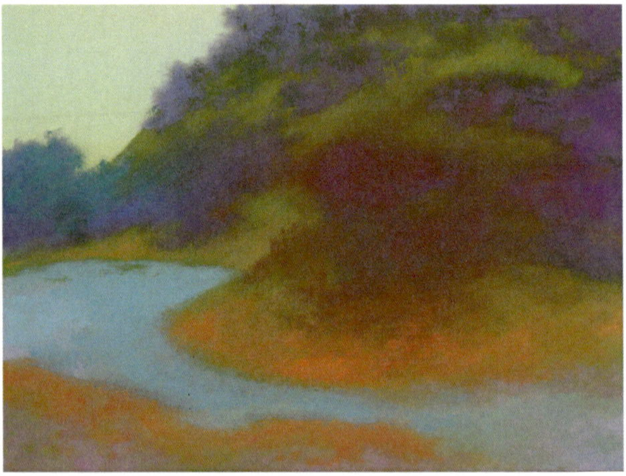

COURTESY ACA GALLERIES, NEW YORK

Soquel Valley, 2006
Oil on canvas
30 × 40 in.
76.2 × 101.6 cm)

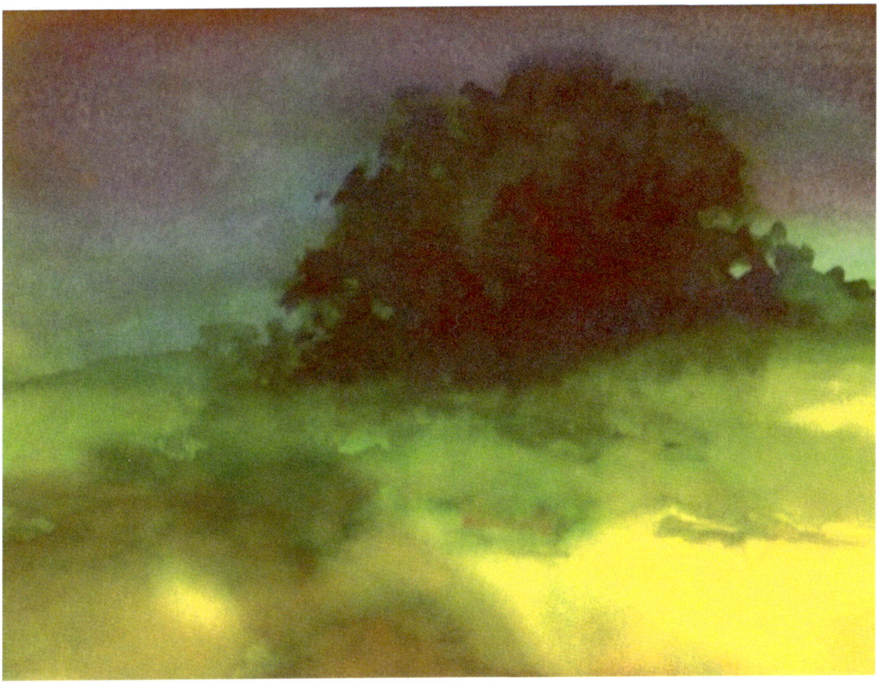

AUTHOR'S COLLECTION

Untitled, 2009. Watercolor 10 × 14 in. (25.4 × 35.56 cm)
Inscribed "for Janet" and signed by Mayhew on back.

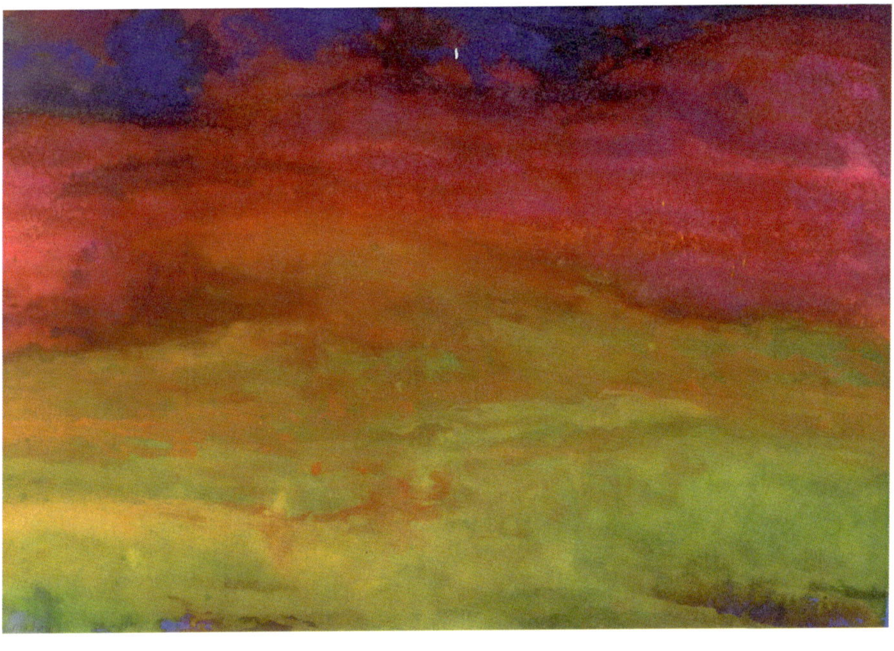

COURTESY ACA GALLERIES, NEW YORK

Toccata **(no date)**
Oil on canvas 48 × 36 in. (121.9 × 91.4 cm)

***Transgression*, 2008**
Oil on canvas 56 × 60 in. (142.2 × 152.4 cm)

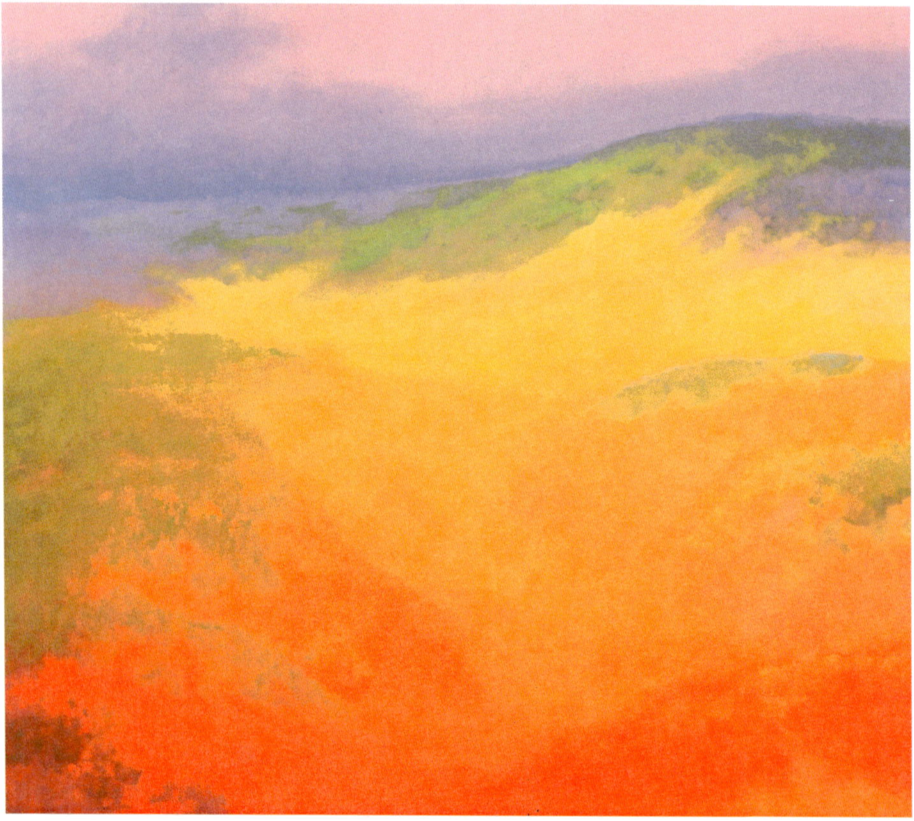

COURTESY ACA GALLERIES, NEW YORK

***Vista*, 2004**
Oil on canvas
36 × 48 in. (91.44 × 121.92 cm)

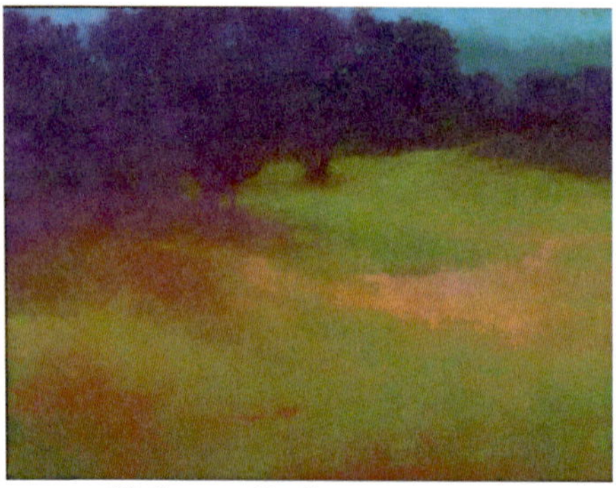

COURTESY ACA GALLERIES, NEW YORK

***West Bay*, 2004**
Oil on canvas
36 × 48 in. (91.44 × 121.92 cm)

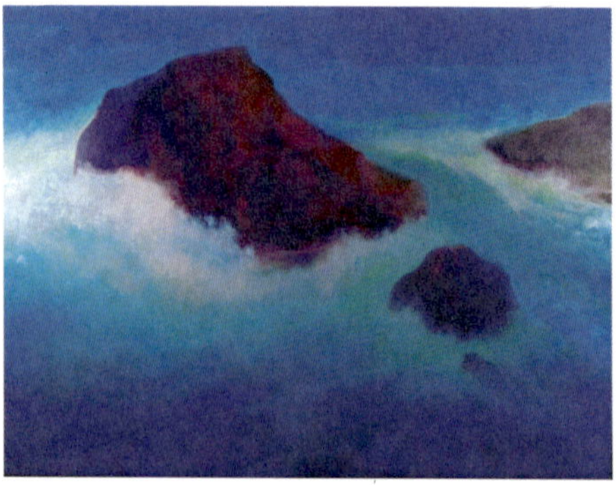

COURTESY ACA GALLERIES, NEW YORK

Chapter Five

Collectors and Students

In seeking to spread his vision of creative survival and integrity, Richard Mayhew approaches his mentorship of collectors and students with great commitment and gentle deference. Mayhew's modesty defines his pedagogical approach: "The student teaches you to teach him."[1] His modesty belies the enormous effect he has had on generations of students: as Nashormeh Lindo relates, "After [a symposium organized by Mayhew in conjunction with the exhibition "Since the Harlem Renaissance: 50 Years of Afro-American Art"], I had felt whole again. I knew that my outlook and my life would change and that I was finally on my way ... [college courses which did not address African American experience] owed me a debt; Richard Mayhew paid the bill.... Richard Mayhew is not only a fine artist, he is a friend and mentor. He is one of the elder statesmen of American art and a national cultural treasure. He has earned his place in the canon ... he has given and continues to give service to the artistic and educational community by encouraging and mentoring younger artists and writers and by his body of exemplary work. He is, in some measure, an unsung hero, and I am forever indebted to him ... he is an inspiration."[2]

Mayhew maintains that his artistic work always came first, citing Hale Woodruff's advice: "Be careful. Teaching is a creative process. Make sure you don't lose your creative sensibility as an artist, and become a creative teacher ... you've got to pull a curtain between the two."[3] Nonetheless, he takes great pride in the success of his students, regardless of the career path they ultimately choose. "Most of the students that I taught never became artists," he observes. "They became very inventive, creative people, whatever field they went into. They became very effective as a creative person in their lifestyle. And the ones who did go that route, did very well."[4]

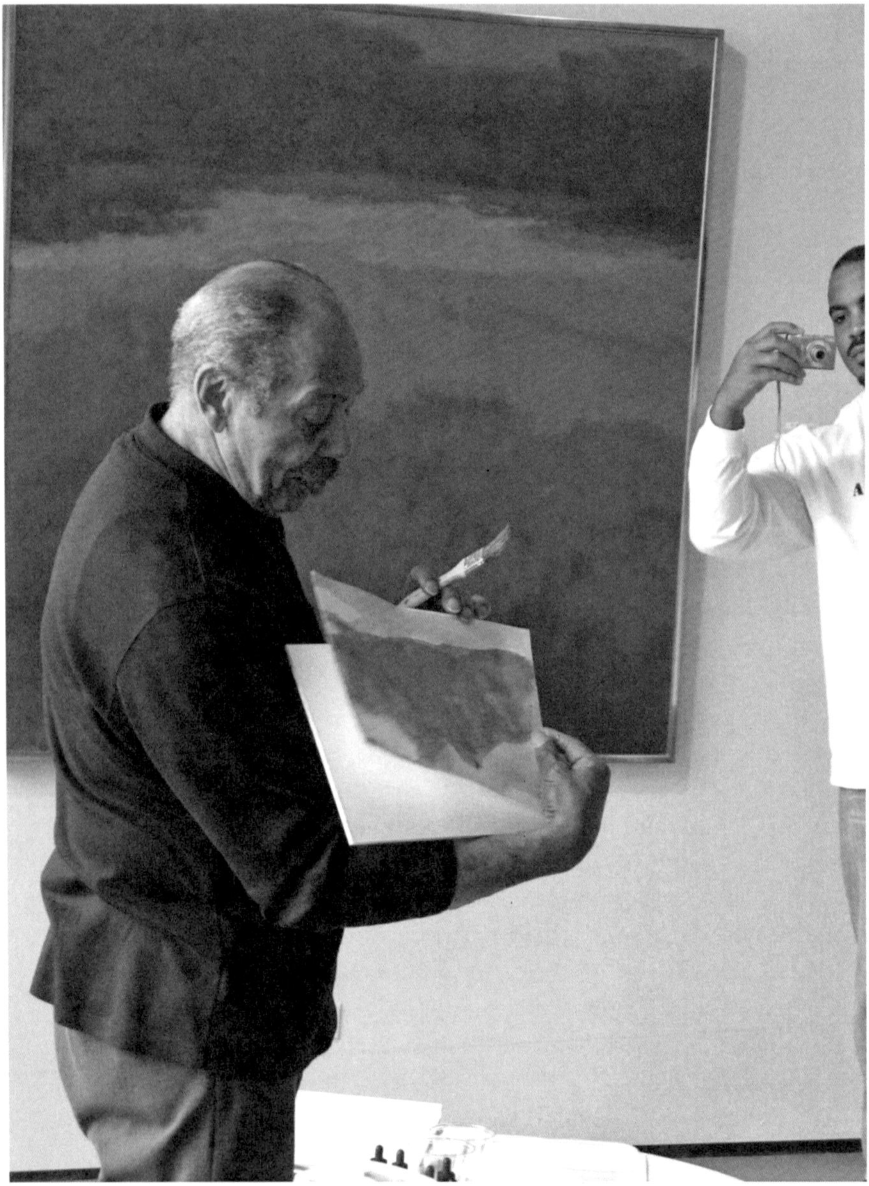

Richard Mayhew demonstrating artmaking, New York, ca. 1998.

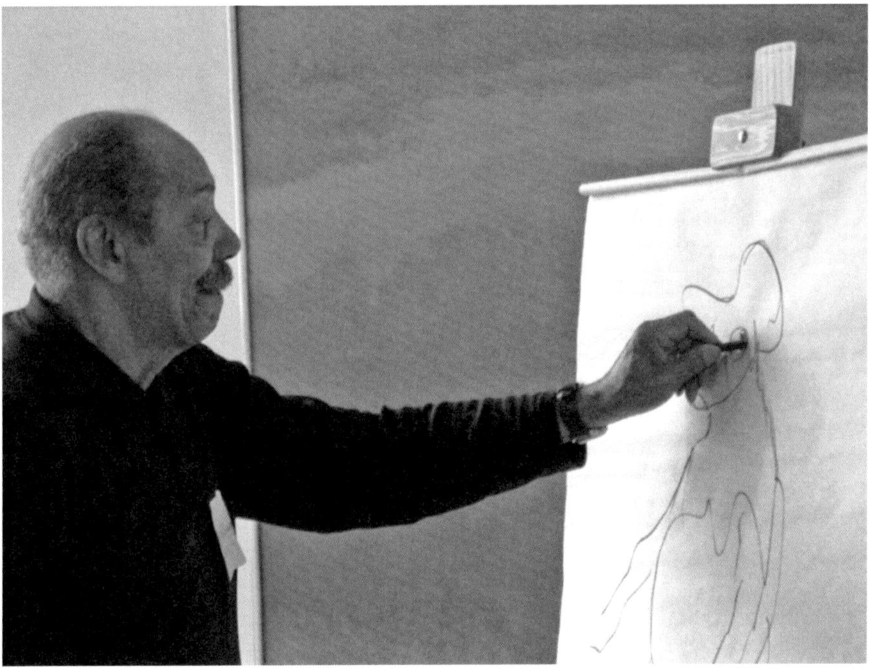

Richard Mayhew demonstrating his technique. New York, ca. 1998.

One of Richard Mayhew's primary collectors, Edward Littlejohn, and two of his students, Gayle Fulton Ross and Posoon Park Sung, exemplify the gifts Mayhew bestows in mentoring and befriending those he encounters, and the teaching methods he employs. The following interviews took place in December 2006, in Sarasota, Florida. The effortless continuity of these discussions underscore Mayhew's influence.

Ed Littlejohn

Hess: *My feeling is that Rick's art is more than just landscape—yet I'm trying to decide how much. How much can we read into someone's work and decide what their work is about if they're not explicitly telling us?*

Littlejohn: Personally, I think very little. I don't see it. Are we talking about racism, the African-American experience as an artist — is that revealed in your work? That's been a major debate among African-American artists for years, as to what *is* an African-American artist. Do you paint your culture and your people, or are you an artist who happens to be African American? And that was a big issue in Spiral, one of the issues that divided Spiral, although you had Norman Lewis and Richard Mayhew, who were not particularly — you know, they did abstraction. But the other side of that whole thing is what is the role of the African-American artist in the Civil Rights Movement? In the 1960s, that was a big issue. My view is that you have to have this discreet category of artists, African-American artists, but I don't think there's any such thing as African-American art. The reason why you have this discreet category of African-American art is because it's imposed upon historically, because of the larger culture of the art world — the museums, the dealers. Why should there be racism in the larger community still in existence today, and not in art? I've always thought artists were kinder, more gentle kind of people because of what they do — that's not true. Racism in the art world is as rampant as anywhere else. So if you're going to succeed as an artist you're going to have to as an artist who's an African American, I think you have to come together as a group. And that's what was happening back in the Harmon Foundation and others where you had exhibitions because you couldn't exhibit your work anywhere else! The thing that [I marvel at] in studying these artists, particularly major artists who committed themselves to art and in their struggle to become artists, was how they continued to do it! I don't know how many artists fell off because they say it's not worth it, we can't do this, there's no way you can make a living at this, there are too many roadblocks, the world is not going to let us do this. You know, I was talking about the vanguard artists — they talk about African-American artists [not being] good enough to be in museums, and you have Major Walker telling the directors of museums [to] be careful not to let this kind of art intrude — I don't know how these guys continue to do it! I have very great admiration for these artists who struggle to be artists and to produce major, masterful works in the kinds of conditions in which they had to work. I have a picture of Norman Lewis sitting around a table with all the white artists in the Castskills — with Pollock, and all — and in the article, the commentary is that one of the white artists is saying, "Norman Lewis is the best painter among us." But he never exhibited with them. And a lot of these guys died impoverished. You read about how they struggled to support a family, make art, and go overseas, and almost starve[d] to death. So it's quite amazing that they do this; it's necessary, it's still necessary that they have this group. When I was on the Arts Commission of Detroit and was involved with the Detroit Institute of Arts — actually had some black people involved in the museum — that subject came up all the time. Why do we have to have the center for African-American art? Why do we have to identify — weren't we all just artists? — well, the world is not working that way yet. When the world comes where you look at an artist and you accept that artist for his talent and his work without regard to his race or ethnicity, then you can change! Until then, you have to have the venues for these artists and identify these [individuals as] African-American artists. If not, they're going to get sucked up in the whole process!

You can come in the house and just sit there and look at the Mayhew painting, and a calm just comes over you. It's like this painting. Rick is renowned for this so-called spiritual aspect. Native-American/African-American spirit is somehow imbued in his work. Well, if it is, I get a feeling that somehow [it] comes out and greets me when I come home, and it calms the waters, and I look at it and say, "God, how fortunate I am to look at this, because it gives me so much pleasure." So, I like being surrounded by it. And, to me, it speaks. You know, it's Abstract Expressionism, so-called ... it speaks to me more than a lot of the figurative works that can be more [exciting]; it's just kind of quiet. And I've never been able to figure out how Richard is able to get up close to a painting, paint something that's totally abstract, and doesn't even know how it looks when you get twenty feet away from it! And it just bursts into a landscape! And I say, "How the hell did he know when he was going to paint?" He doesn't have a twenty-foot brush! You've got to get up close to it and paint it, so how did you know how it's going to look? And this whole spiritual thing with him, I think there's something in his work. There's no question in my mind that Richard Mayhew is the greatest living landscape artist that we have in this country. I look at landscapes in books and online and wherever you can, and I see nothing that compares to Richard's. Maybe it's this spiritual thing that we talk about. And, plus, if I'm not mistaken, he plays jazz while he paints. I think that's captured, somehow, it sings. This painting sings. I don't understand how he does it.

There's a lack of understanding in the critical literature of Rick's spiritual aspect. Would you say there's an easy equation between his landscapes and spirituality that is not rigorous?

Littlejohn: Yeah, I would think so. I don't think the average person, unless you've studied Rick and have read and looked at his work, is particularly aware of that. Now I've got to believe Rick is so committed to his heritage — he said he was two-thirds Native American — and the closeness to the earth, the elements and wind — I think it comes through, because Rick, of course, paints by memory; he doesn't paint looking at a bush or a photograph. He paints from memory, and I think that aspect of his care-giving culture comes through the paintbrush onto the canvas, and somehow, it's almost mystical. How are you going to define something that's a mystical thing? It's like [Supreme Court Justice] Potter Stewart [said] — "You know it when you see it, even though you can't define it." I can't define it. If you put a Richard Mayhew a mile and a half a mile away and had a stack of other paintings, I would know it. I would know the Richard Mayhew because it would be singing to me. It would be singing to me.

You've known a lot of artists personally. I've never heard anyone say a bad word about Richard Mayhew. He's just a very gentle spirit. Do you think that has something to do with this sensibility that one has in looking at it?

Littlejohn: I guess. I don't know. You mean because he's a good guy? He could be the worst bastard in the world and paint the same way. Yeah, I think so. Now maybe that's part of the spiritual thing that comes through, because he's a spiritual person himself, and he gives a part of himself that ultimately turns up in the paint. I don't know. But, you know, I find that there are some artists, particularly younger ones, who tend to be arrogant, way beyond the scope of their talent. But most of the major artists I've known have been very — like I think Benny Andrews is [a] wonderful, decent man, and he was committed to helping others. I had written a chapter in a book I was working on, these civil rights lawyers on Attica Prison. In the course of doing that, I turned over a big folio that Benny Andrews had done on Attica Prison, raising money — he got artists together — and he was out there at the same time Spiral was in existence. Spiral was just really a discussion — I think they had that one black-and-white exhibition. But, at the same time, Benny Andrews was picketing the Museum of Modern Art, that Emergency Coalition which Rick Mayhew says he was a member of. He was out there picketing, protesting the fact that these museums did not include the work of African American art[ists]. And then these guys somehow survived! Not being able to be shown, not being able to get galleries. Jacob Lawrence broke through in major white galleries in New York. He had the first exhibition there. Jacob Lawrence. Always Jacob Lawrence, Romare Bearden. You know, Jansen's history of art might mention those. I think David Driskell is a very gentle, kind person, very giving; I've taken him to dinner several times; he's been to my apartment many times. Rick's been down here, visiting me here. What he's contributed to the art world, art students and posterity, as an artist, and I think his spirituality, is evident in Mayhew and Mayhew's paintings.

What would you, as his friend, like to see in a book about Mayhew?

Littlejohn: I would like to see that the paintings somehow be linked to a very humane person — so you could say, "There was a good man. He was a good man, and his work reflects his goodness." I think, in the future, people will see a Mayhew painting and say, "That's Richard Mayhew." I think his exploitation of color is what dominates his painting. He is a masterful painter at bringing together color in a way that I have not seen in other landscape. Maybe that's because when you're painting from memory you have the ability to do that because they don't exist in nature. If you read his own personal history, he talks about how he was focused on color. In Europe, when he was looking at some of these master artists, not only from a technical point of view, but part of his two years in Europe was focused on coloration. When he puts red in a painting, I just think they explode. His use of color is masterful.

What do you make of Rick saying that he prefers a plain frame on his pictures?

Littlejohn: Well, I don't pay attention to it. Because I think artists become very accustomed to gallery frames, the temporary frames. And I think a part of why they want that afterward is not just that it's inexpensive in the gallery space, but they want something that doesn't interfere or detract from the art itself. You can frame pieces where your eye is focused on the frame, rather than the art. You're looking at a frame where the frame is dominating the scene, when you really want your eyes to focus in. Richard Mayhew's paintings [are the only ones] I've ever framed to match furniture. I hate people that say, "I've got to frame this because it's got to go with the couch." Framing is important. I think Richard is wrong. Artists say, "My work speaks, just let the work speak." Bullshit! Some artists have a lot of critics. Richard doesn't, that I know of. I don't know anyone who doesn't respect him. And it's amazing to me that [in] all these years there's been no book written on Richard. But do you know what I think it is? I think it's because he's a landscape artist. Landscape, and he doesn't command the prices that he should. I can't afford to get any more Mayhews, but he doesn't get the prices that his experience and his talent should get, and I think it's largely because it's landscape and not figurative. I was raised in the inner-city communities, and primarily Detroit. There was no culture or art or even books in our household. So I had no exposure to the culture. It was not in the schools either — I don't recall ever having any exposure to art, or seeing art, or being apprised of art, or told to look at art — had no exposure until I was an adult! I pretty much grew up [with the idea that] you buy a house, you start a family, you have to put something on the wall. So you go through that poster phase, buy a fifteen-dollar poster and put a two-hundred-dollar frame on it and hang it on the wall. I got pretty good at picking good posters. At some point I decided that my culture and history and community are important, and that I ought to focus on African-American art. Now, Mayhew had a lot to do with that, because the first serious piece of art that I bought — and we're talking, at that time, serious in the sense that it was an oil canvas by him — serious because it costs money. It was [sold to me by] Sherrie Washington; she was the exclusive dealer of Mayhew in Detroit. Detroit was the primary venue for Mayhew. She says, "Detroit is to African-American art what it once was to automobiles." And it, by far, was the best place for African-American artists in the United States. [The first time I went to her gallery] it was a Richard Mayhew exhibition. So I saw his work. And I saw him. And he gave a talk, and I got very interested in him, and I made a commitment to buy a piece. It was a major commitment for me at the time. As a product of having had that piece, I got interested in collecting. I was quite enamored with Richard, both the work, which as they say, speaks for itself, but [also of] Richard as a person. There's something — they say [a] spiritual quality [to] his work — well, there's something spiritual about Richard that you're proud not only to have his work in your collection, but proud it was done by a person like Richard. One thing I found out about artists visiting towns — it was particularly true about Benny Andrews. I was interested in Benny Andrews at the same time as Richard — it's surprising that these artists come to town, and they don't have anything to do. Most people don't know that. And the dealers find them a burden, because they have to feed 'em, they gotta take 'em to dinner, they've got to have this kind of thing for them — you've got to take them around, you've got to pamper them — so I learned early on, I hear Richard Mayhew's going to be in town, how about I take him to dinner? Or, something's going to go on, it eventually got to, "Richard Mayhew's going to be in town; I'll have a reception for him in my apartment." Richard and I became friendly because of me reaching out. And what you do is, these master artists love to talk. Not only about artists — and I'm interested in African-American art, I think right then I decided to concentrate, I got rid of everything else — I think you can build an important collection if it's focused on something. The purpose for me was not only to build a relationship, but to learn. So I'm indebted to Richard, in a sense. And he is a very encouraging person. There's nothing ostentatious about him. His ego — of course he has one, but he's not ego-driven in the sense that "I'm an important person." He takes time with you, he will talk to you, he will help you — so he was very helpful to get me started. And I still love his work.

When Rick lectures, he doesn't even show his own work.

Littlejohn: Not only will he do Spiral, at the end of that, he usually has a lecture where he talks to young artists about the business of being an artist, and [advises them not to] make the mistakes that other artists have made, and how you go about handling your work and dealers — you always get that end with the view of helping younger artists become successful artists. So he's very giving in that sense. Collecting African-American art became a passion for me, a magnificent obsession, that began with Richard Mayhew! And it's a good beginning! It's a wonderful start. Very few of us start at the top as opposed to the bottom.

Gayle Fulton Ross

Ross: Years ago, when I met Mr. Mayhew, I was in my early twenties, struggling to raise my son, struggling to do my work, and he had just those very necessary words that were optimistic. You have these artists that you're in awe of, and tell them your struggles, and they're continuing to have the same struggles, but they persevere through those challenges. I said to Mr. Mayhew, "I have this dilemma. I don't know whether to paint abstract or figurative, because I happen to like both. I love both." And he said, "Well, dear, you have to choose. You have to choose or find a way to put them together. Because until then, nobody knows how to sell you. So once you pick one, you can go to the other." I knew of his color work, color landscapes. Gorgeous. The man has an eye for color that is outstanding. He was getting ready to do a figurative show with Stella Jones in New Orleans. He said, "You see, I can do what I want now, but at least they know how to position me. When you go off and do something else, then it's 'revisiting' the figure, or 'discovering' the figure, okay?"

In his work, there is a quality that I admire. There are other artists who do similar work; however, they don't have that quality, and the brilliance of color. When you see Mr. Mayhew's work, it's very giving. You walk in the art and it's giving and it holds you. He is a very generous, charitable artist, in that he spends time talking, and the amazing thing is that in his conversations with other artists especially and I'm sure other people, his giving is educational; he's teaching. He's telling you what he knows. And if you're interested in learning — and I am, still, every day — here you have an artist older than I, who's making the same journey. I'd be a fool not to listen to him. The last time I talked to him, we discussed studios. I explained to him I no longer had my giant space, but I'd make it work. And when I went to see the portrait of Jacob Lawrence in the early '90s, he had less space than I did. He had a very modest home. You saw it, tiny. Did you ever see Jacob Lawrence's space? Jacob Lawrence's space was just like an alcove in the attic of his house. So I said that to Rick, and he said, "Mine is, too." He said, "My plan is, hopefully, to sell my house and get the studio I've been dreaming of." Well, I was amazed! I'm listening to an artist I respect, I admire, I'm in awe of, knowing he's done all of this work, all of these years, and he's still looking for a studio.

Mayhew keeps such a young attitude, as if this is what you do, until you just don't do it anymore. And you keep a spirit about you. You know, his fly collections, he still travels, he still paints. Artists don't get sick; they just die.

His color, when you really study what he does, blows you away. And his ability to mix and soften and transition and manipulate it and not use anything back in it, is amazing to me. It inspired me to incorporate color back into black and white. His shapes and his forms that are within painting — it all is sort of ethereal and luminous. And he is another artist that I just don't think received his due. I really don't. And he's not unhappy, because I know how he thinks, because I'm the same way, and maybe he helped me with this. I'm doing what I love to do. He's a gentle, kind, spirited, blessed man. Isn't that what anybody wants in life? His work demonstrates his heart. Many times I've heard, artists are what they do. Then, if that's the case, his painting describes a wonderful, wonderful human being whose journey through life metaphorically translates into these ethereal, luminous, colorful, positive paintings. We all have moods — that's why we paint. Everything in life is not beautiful. In every life there's trial and tribulation. Perhaps that's the moment he painted that particular painting. But, then, we go back to that level of who we really are, and you can come out of this darkness, and then you do what you do. You would never know [when something bad is happening] in his life. He wouldn't tell you. He's not going to share that. Painting brings him joy. I don't know if that joy is just as cathartic for him as some artists. I think the joy is doing it, as well as what he does. In my studio, the strongest information he gave me was that — I was telling him of my struggle to decide between the abstract and the literal representation of the world. And he said, "Well, if you'd like to know what I think," and I said, "I do," and he said, "Your figures are very strong." So I kept saying, "So you think I should stay figurative?" [And he said,] "I just told you that your figures are very strong." So, I know that I'm stronger there than I am in my abstract work. It was not a criticism; it was a suggestion. He didn't take away my choice. I received an invitation to Mayhew's last exhibit; it was so gorgeous, just the three images in color, that I changed — that's why the abstracts are as colorful as they are.

When you see his work, especially a body of it, you really appreciate it even more than when you see one. One, because you stand in the middle of it, and the colors take you on a journey that you're just not going to ever have. Then, certain angles or positions of a tree, or a bush, or a skyline, or a horizon, constantly change the mood of whatever it is you're seeing. Well, that's not formula work. Formula work is when an artist chooses to go for that one painting that made them money, and they keep kind of painting the same painting ... all you feel is one note. I've decided to position myself as an abstract artist, and surprise people with the figurative. And he said, "That's good! That's good."

Hess: *Why do you think Richard Mayhew is not better known? Because he is not self-promoting, because landscapes are not accepted, because people expect African-American art to be narrative or figural?*

Ross: That's exactly right. Mayhew's work is universal. His language is universal. He is an American artist who is black, like Sam Gilliam, Martin Puryear ... these are artists whose work has significance, in some sense historical significance and credibility, but no one should pigeonhole them because they are black, and their work transcends that anyway. Now you have other artists who paint only the black experience — jazz, old people of the church sitting on the porch, sweet mothers holding up their babies — we've all done it, but you can outgrow that. That's not to say that it's not beautiful work. John Singer Sergeant did portraits of wealthy white women — gorgeous, beautiful portraits. Nobody called that white art. So there is a place for portraits of black people, red people, brown people, yellow people, gay people, I don't care. The implication is what makes them lose the value, not the work. I like a universal language spoken by artists. That whatever the ethnicity means nothing. If I'm emotionally attracted to it, I don't care who you are. I'll always go back to the figure. If I do ten paintings, eight of them are going to be of black people. That's only because it's easier to paint what you know. And they're probably going to be black females. Again, it's only because I paint what I know. My journey as an artist is really just about me. It's about what I'm feeling and what I'm going through. What the world is throwing at me in the news, or any other area. And how I'm absorbing it and how I spit it back out. My studio is right here on the [Florida] Keys — I can walk to the beach, [but] I will never do a beach painting. I'm not going to do pink flamingos, and I'm not going to [paint] children playing on the beach. I don't have any problem with that, and when they're done wonderful, they're done wonderful. That's not what I feel. I'm really more political, and I'm really more involved in the activity not only of my art, but of other artists. Mr. Mayhew gives of himself in such a way — he not only paints his images, gets them to the marketplace, but along the way, he has nurtured a lot of other artists to be empowered by his ability to stay focused and keep his eyes on the prize, which is getting your work out. In that area, it keeps me strong. Without the Mayhews, the Benny Andrews, without the Beardens, without Catlett, even in my case I loved Augusta Savage — without them I could not persevere. That is my world. I could not persevere. I would make no sense. But you read their stories, you listen to them when you can, and you find that you're not alone, even in a solitary business. Solitude is important, but you're not alone. And their journey, each one helps me — they kind of knock down the bushes and the trees and make a path for you. And so, hopefully, I'm making a path behind me.

What do you think of contemporary artists, such as Kara Walker and Lorna Simpson?

Ross: I respect them. And yet … they may get the joke, but 90 percent of the world doesn't get the joke. We live in a racist world. And there is nothing funny about it anymore. It's only funny when everybody gets the joke. It would be nice to live in a world that it's not an issue, but it is. Race matters. I am a black artist, but I'm really an artist. I'm an artist; I'm an American; I'm a female. That's what I am. I don't like being defined. I don't want my work defined by my color. I do understand that description is necessary in the art world when you're trying to write about an individual. In this case, Mr. Mayhew, who is an artist, an American artist, who's black.

Posoon Park Sung

Posoon: We were very fortunate to have [Richard Mayhew] as a professor at that time. He was very good teacher — not only good, but a very good person. He really cares about students. So, immediately, students really love him and would follow him. And he's from New York.

He brought us to New York one semester, and arranged the place that we could stay. And then every day he took us to galleries, from the morning 'til they closed. Except for eating time, we were at the gallery. All day. And that was so great. We really learned a lot, and he knows everybody. He knows a lot of people. We bumped into people, he'd bump into people, and he'd say, "Oh, it's a writer, or a poet, or musician." He took us to top galleries, and he knows the director, and the director talked to us about how you become a professional, how you get into a gallery — things like that, in a more realistic way. So that was a really good part. I teach at a class now at the university and I talk about him — what he did for us.

Hess: *When you starting painting in graduate school, how did Rick approach your work in terms of color? Was that an emphasis with him?*

Posoon: Not really. He just kind of talked ... he didn't make students do a certain style or direction. So he just talked about problems that the students had, and from there, he would talk about what is good and what to think through a little bit more. I don't think he really directed in one direction. That's what I do, too, for my students. Everybody has their own idea.

I see a relationship between the figure and a field of color in both your work and Ross's. Do you see that as a legacy of Mayhew?

Posoon: I'm sure there is some legacy. But, eventually, you go your own way. I remember when Richard Mayhew was talking to me about my work — he always said there's mysticism in my work. So he lectured at my show four years ago. He came to Tampa for a big show, and he said that, I was very happy, he said that my work has a consistency from graduate school 'til now. He said, "The mysticism is there." He came to my show at the Jean Kelly Gallery this year, [and] he said the same thing. So I look at my painting, [and] I think I agree with him. The layer after layer of color [and the mysticism] — so that part, maybe. He used oil, I use acrylic. I represent in my work what we are, and what we will be — different time and space. My painting always has a certain darkness, and then always have a light. So I always have a balance of dark and light.

We always have to go through some darkness. And darkness is not necessarily the bad one. If we don't have a dark then we don't see the light. That's what I wrote in an art statement in my catalogue. But darkness — every day we have a light daytime, and nighttime. There's a balance So then after darkness, the light comes. After light, the darkness comes. So I experience certain things in my life, and I guess that's what I'm expressing in my work — more of like a yin and yang.

Would you ever paint an image that was all dark, with no bright light?

Posoon: I would not know yet. But my paintings, like *the birth*, are very dark, and some people say are a little scary, not peaceful, but to me I look at different things, and there is a light, with a different eye. I haven't made any paintings totally dark. The human being — we do have a body and soul. Some people connect very quickly; they become spiritually connected, they become much closer. But if they're not really connected, no matter how long we're acquainted, you don't ever get close. So I'm just really meditating [to] myself; I have to know myself first. Even when I was young I always was thinking. Thinking is a big part of my life. It doesn't take me that long for painting, but thinking takes a lot longer. (Laughs) So, when I'm ready for painting, I know pretty much what I'm going to do. Artists have different approaches; that's what I do. But some artists, they do not know what they are painting — they will just start, and then subconsciousness is coming. I tried that way, but the result wasn't always successful. Usually I know composition, colors, and mood, and all that — an idea that I have, when I start it, it appears quickly.

Mayhew was different than other faculty. He was much more involved with students, and the sharing of his experience, more than other professors. That's one of the activities he gave us — taking us to New York. And he wanted to share with us how he did it, and what kind of people he knows — that was a very generous thing to do. That part I always have appreciation towards him and I would like to do that for my students also. I often talk about him in class, with students — I probably talk about him most. When he came to lecture, he said to people,

"Posoon is more than [a] friend — she's like family." So we are more like family. His son and my son, they work[ed] together before, and they are friends now. So it's not like a friend, it's more like family. I feel very fortunate to have someone like him in my life. And people say that, "Oh, he's your mentor." And he was. He is.

You are going your own way. You're not painting "in the style of" Richard Mayhew. And yet it seems that in both his and your work, there's a holding back. It's not extremely explicit in message, it's not insisting, and that, it seems to me, is a common element. You don't insist in your work that I accept some message or view.

Posoon: I don't like to insist. People, when they ask me, "What is the meaning of your painting,?" then I always ask them back, "What do they see?" Rather than explain. Yeah, I'm sure that Richard Mayhew — his work has some certain degree about the mood, and the melancholy — also my work refers to that. I want people to look at my work in their own way. I don't really have a particular expectation. But there is always a response one way or other. My work is not direct.

Prints of Mayhew's work appear in convalescent homes. I don't see your work in spaces like that. Perhaps they're too dark, or — in other words, places where people are dying, Rick's work is hung, he's told me. I'm not sure I'd want to be gazing at [your] work of a man in a void as the last thing I saw. It seems more complex, more addressing some of the difficult moments in life. Is it hard to hear that?

Posoon: No! No, no, not at all. Art to me is — painting is, to me, everybody has their own interpretation. I would enjoy that many people have their own. It's not what I meant, but they see that. Usually people have a bit of a fear about the darkness. It doesn't matter whether they like my painting or not; they always say, "Oh, I love your painting of that, but I'm not sure whether I could put this in my living room." (Laughs)

It reminds me of that Buddhist meditation on mortality, and how confronting certain limits can be empowering.

Posoon: Right.

And your home is very cheerful, and even in your bedrooms you have these paintings that are very meditative and dark in tone. And that's an interesting combination.

Posoon: That's probably an American or modern attitude about life: I look at life as both sides. Death, for instance, directly speaking, people don't want to talk about death. But I like to talk about death. To me, death is not a scary thing. In this painting [*Passage*], there is a skull, and the person is insecure, or something, looking — and probably people look at it more negatively. But I don't look at it negatively. I like to give them a more — make them think about their life. People in America, this modern time, they don't want to think about reality. They always say, "Your work is a little bit sad." But, to me, it's not sad (laughs). Some people don't want to go through that process of thinking … and yet they know what it is. That's why, to me, it is a success (laughs). It's more liberation. It's just the whole process of life is — you evolve. You transcend to a different level. If you want to remain — as we all know, life is not just sugar; it's not all rosy. So we know, we confront it, we surrender. It's actually a very natural thing. I like to bring the subject, because it's in my mind. I'm in the process of life. That's what I want to talk about, and through different elements we can do it. Whether you like that or not, we have to view that. And life is not always something that you want, that you get what you want. You have to go through the whole process.

PART II

Interviews

Chapter Six

Conversations, 2003–2007

> To the extent that ... [a storyteller] re-creates his vision in words, he re-creates himself.... He declares in effect, "Behold, I give you my vision in these terms, and in the process I give you myself.'
> — N. Scott Momaday[1]

In the interviews I conducted with Richard Mayhew in the California cities of Santa Cruz, Capitola and Soquel from 2003 to 2007 and in 2012, the artist's commitment to spiritual expression and community involvement is evident. Mayhew discusses technical aspects of art, his connection to African-American and Native-American heritage — particularly the integral relationship of that heritage with the land — and his own commitment to survival in the face of enormous pressure on the part of the dominant culture in America. Empathy for the struggles of others, authenticity, and modes of negotiating life "as an artist or human being in a society that denies your existence" — these themes thread through the interviews, as well as a constant concern with the lived, embodied, and individual experience of art.

The challenge of relating Mayhew's experiences to some degree lies in his humility and deflection of attention in conversation away from his own experience and toward a representation of spirituality, the spirituality of American Indian culture that has been crushed by "oppression, denial, and omission." Mayhew takes an almost visceral joy in color, in painting, in landscape; the historical narrative that one might desire from an interview is subsumed within his discussion of this spirituality, and his stories about his family, fellow artists in Spiral, their achievements, and his philosophical stance toward oppression. Although he relates the story of how, as a young artist in New York, police would not believe that his studio was his own because of his "race," and how his father was forced to buy shoes that were too small because he had touched them, the overwhelming focus of his narrative in these interviews is meeting challenges with equanimity and following through with possibilities: "How one becomes philosophical about it [racism] is the whole creative instinct. That's what salvation is."

The oppressive quality Mayhew perceives in academic discourse has always been evident. Academic culture, for him, is inherently involved with dominant culture, and its formal expression he finds constrictive and cold; he discussed with me frequently his frustrations with the constraints imposed upon him at Sonoma State University. The following interviews were transcribed to reveal, in Mayhew's terms, his true self, his sparkling wit and expansive friendship, the sheer exuberance and joy of his artistic sensibility that defy the somber photographs reproduced in his gallery brochures and most articles about him. Mayhew's use of color and form was a personal and private joy, but his work is intended to offer a vision of the spirituality and beauty of cultures that have been oppressed and denied. Spiral was a group formed to conceptualize creativity expansively, as continuing without end, and in this sense the almost-preternatural energy revealed in these interviews aptly represents their objectives, and energy that would seem to defy both academic boundaries and physical death: "[Trees] go through a cycle of sleeping and waking. Because they sleep and they wake up, right? Even in sleeping they're still functioning sensitively. Right now, this is like part of winter, and I cut all my rose bushes back, but you can notice that they're regrowing already. In summer the cycle goes on, in regrowth. So from that, there's no end. Which has to do with religion, with everlasting life ... How much that part of nature, how much is that part of the human existence? When one dies, one is going to keep on living! It has to do with how much is the mind that continues, or the spirit continues, according to many religions. The body is destroyed, but that spiritual sensitivity is part of some of the philosophers in terms of energy and space. It recontinues in space. In anyone involved with germinating some continued form of sensitivity, it's part of the energy of space forever."

⁂

Hess: *I wanted to start by asking you about your technique a little bit, your watercolors. Because I know in the film [a documentary of Richard Mayhew] ... you were explaining how you did some of your watercolors.*

Mayhew: I use liquid watercolor, and mix it with paste in the cup. And I pour it on paper, and I spread it with the brush. It's kind of spontaneous what happens with it. Since I don't plan anything, it automatically starts to take up certain forms, which then I move around and develop and control to some degree, but I want a lot of it to happen on its own. Sometimes I use pastels with the watercolor. Once it is dry, I use some pastels in it. And I saw, when I was in Paris, traveling around, Degas's work, where he worked some pastels into the watercolor! (Laughs) No one talks about that, right?

No, they don't. You're in that tradition, anyway.

Mayhew: Oh, Lautrec did it, several others did it, pastels and watercolor, combination, so that was not me being original, but the way I use it has a certain different effect.

Do you use that same technique now that you've tried painting the figure for a while, too?

Mayhew: Well, I've been painting the figure all the time, just not exhibiting it.

It's always a challenge to one's craft. Working from watercolor back and forth to oil, is also so you don't get bored. Working back and forth from one media to the other, it stimulates the different effects and techniques that you use. The watercolor technique, and using some of the kinds of drawing brush effect on it also, came from actually drawing with a crow quill pen, on rough paper. So there's one media that stimulates the effect and technique you're going to use in the other. And also I started using a palette knife instead of using a brush—[this] came from the early technique of just using a crow quill pen on paper. Because then you are stimulating certain kinds of texture effects that you wouldn't get any other way.

Did you participate any in the dialogue on representation that was coming out in the fifties?

Mayhew: The dialogue with whom?

With the figure. Greenberg, saying, "No, we don't want in Pollock's work," when Pollock did his Blue Poles, that's no good. You see a lot of, this is a generalization, but African-American artists, at the same time, keeping the figure in the work.

Mayhew: The figure was important in the sense of, during the Civil Rights Movement, showing the figure which has been denied and omitted, and not doing the African-American image. Many of the Western painters were not involved with doing an image — and not showing African American images in a lot of European painting. So it's how much one wanted to see their own image, or were involved with their own kind of cultural identity. There was that, and also how much spiritual sensitivity was involved with it. I felt in the landscape I was doing this, instead of just painting. I didn't want to just paint the figure for political reasons; I wanted to paint for the uniqueness of multicultural sensitivity. And this is what Romare Bearden did, even though he was involved with mimicking and responding to the cultural activity of Harlem, and also from the South, where he came. But he was concerned about that, too. He didn't want to just make figures for making a comment about Civil Rights, he wanted to make some kind of documentary sensitivity in relationship to his cultural feelings and sensitivity. So I felt the landscape was a part of the "forty acres and a mule." There was the whole thing about African Americans not receiving the land they deserved, and also Native Americans, since that is a part of my culture; the land is the whole thing to them. The land, the sky and the water, that's it. That's the whole religious sensitivity there. The two cultures overlap in terms of the land being important to them. I started traveling back and forth across the United States. Three times, three over and three back, that's six trips! (Laughs) I don't think I could do that now.

That sounds pretty grueling.

Mayhew: Actually observing this country and the heritage of

African-American and Native-American area[s] and, actually, the land. That's it. That's the whole spiritual sensitivity of African-American and Native-American life. And they [are] close together in terms of bonding the heritage. I don't want to get away from things like the image or the figure, because ... it's not ignoring that, and every once in awhile, I do the figure, so how much in terms of political reasons ... the politics of doing any kind of art, there's a certain political effectiveness. I'm concerned today [about] the fact that art is the sensitivity of the continuation in terms of society. How much the figure is playing a certain part of that particular image, when you paint the figure, is how much you are painting a certain kind of effect which is projecting and dictating a certain thought, or a certain feeling, or a certain person, or a certain comment, so the picture attracts one into, this is what they see. This is what response is. And so the figure to be a landscape is more abstract to the point that [it is] also involved with a certain emotional identity with time and space, where the figure is locked into a particular space and time, or a particular image. So many of the artists that were involved in doing this, they look to Africa in terms of how much the image was painted there. Because most of the paintings in Africa are abstract, except for Benin, which is more representational and unique, but also in a certain symbolistic form, rather than just the mimicking and responding to a particular image. So there is this concern about the artists that were involved with doing the figure, and how much they got involved doing that. Many got trapped into a commercial interpretation of the image. Certainly Jacob Lawrence did not; he was involved with the historic imagery of the figure. But then again, his figures are very abstract. Many wanted a more realistic interpretation, many artists got involved with more illustrational interpretation of a figure. And there again, many were locked into a certain storytelling situation, and that became a problem for many of the artists ... whether they are more abstract, or representational. A perfect example is Reginald Gammon, who is part of Spiral. Master craftsman at doing the figure. But recently he got involved in primitive techniques of the figure.

Where would you put his Black and White, that's right in the middle of his career? He has a painting in Sharon Patton's text called Black and White, and that's the one image they show from Spiral's opening.

Mayhew: Reggie Gammon's painting? Oh, okay. Because he really worked extremely detailed representational, and the whole [unintelligible] is completely primitive in technique, you know. And going that way is rather like, William H. Johnson did this earlier, he was an expressionist, impressionist, right? In the later years he became involved with primitive, symbolic, hard-edged images, almost like cut-outs. A complete different change, a drastic change, really. I talked to Reginald Gammon recently to find out, "What are you doing?" Because we communicate a lot. I'm trying to arrange in New York for all of that group to come together. Because each one came away with their own impressions of what Spiral was. And their own influence of what happened during that time.

Do you feel that [Spiral] was solely a response to the Civil Rights Movement, or that it was about expressing the African-American artist's place in the community?

Mayhew: Well, there was a concern about minorities in our society, so, in terms of African Americans, it was their personal identity, but [all] minorities were affected. It's still a part of the problem in terms of omission and denial of the society. And, certainly, my views are not the only solution to that, until society becomes a multicultural government, rather than a singular government of one culture being dominant in its cultural and governing body.

In a lot of your work, and in your statements in art history texts, the focus is away from specific images for you, and onto the community as a whole.

Mayhew: Not necessarily with specific images. It's a matter of how the specific images are portrayed. So you're not locked into a certain comment that limits the image that one is painting. And, there again, it has to do with one's exposure to art, and when you paint a certain image, this is what they associate with, and they don't intellectually see beyond that point, in looking at the work. *Guernica* is completely abstract, based on African sculpture, right? That's not related to that at all. The heritage of Spain is certainly a part of the Moorish sculpture, right?

You mentioned earlier the covering over of Guernica.

Mayhew: That painting was done in protest to war, completely. The difference over war.... That painting was loaned to the Museum of Modern Art for four years in New York. When the Vietnam war broke out, the artists went there and said that, since that is an image that the United States is not honoring, they took it back to Paris. So there it is again, in looking at the *Guernica*, if one is not used to abstraction or symbolism, they wouldn't even know what is going on ... after a while it becomes a masterpiece; it loses the identity of what the original work was all about. And, right now, that's what it is. It's just a masterpiece, and not related to what is an island of protest against war. Mmm-hmm, right. It's strange about symbolism or images of figures; it's like Charles White's painting of figures, very realistic, but also based on certain symbolic issues of the time, and he painted ordinary people. He didn't paint any special people. Ordinary people and ordinary lives. He did a slave series that was based on slavery and images of how figures were treated in slavery. Beautiful interpretation.

You seem to have such an affinity for that work, and yet, when critics discuss your work, art historical accounts of you, are — emotional, evocative.

Mayhew: Because of limitations of the visual response to a certain subject. And how they respond to the figures. The figures I'm doing now — I wanted to see what the reaction was at the show I had recently in Detroit, and how much the people were responding to me. These were all about African-American women — actually, minority women — and how they look at them, and they said, "Oh yeah, there's that, it's a social comment." [But] it's not just a social comment; it's a painting of feeling. And the paintings are all based on strong color. So color plays a role in interpretation of the appeal or the mood of the subject, rather than just an image of the figure.

What does the color red mean for you? I'm thinking of Woman in a Red Dress.

Mayhew: The red dress has to do with the strong power of the image of the woman. One way of doing that is using color. And so one identifies and says, "Oh, yeah, red dress, a social something." They see identifying it with another person. But, really, the red is a part of the power of the expression of feeling of that woman And, also, her gesturing — there were comments in a review about that, and they were saying, "There's this strong woman which you can see in her face, there's pride and also — "

Pain.

Mayhew: The pain. Mmm-hmm. Right. Mmm-hmm.

Did you agree with that?

Mayhew: Mmm-hmm. Yeah. Oh yeah, that's part of it, yeah. The fact that, how much one's ambition was always denied, and so, as a result, there only half accomplishments, never arriving at the great accomplishments that one had desired. I know my father was like that. And then my brother and myself. He [my brother] saw himself in terms of the accomplishment that he never made, that we're making. And so he felt very proud and strong within his own feeling based on the fact that the heritage was carried on to the ambition that he had always wanted to achieve in society.

What would you say if, because of the color in your landscape, they're so evocative in abstraction and color, they [critics] put you more with Mark Rothko and color-field painters than African-American artists. What would you say?

Mayhew: (Laughs) Oh, it has to do with Native-American and African-American artists heavily involved in the beauty of color, feeling, mood. Someone said to me, "What do you see as purple and this blue?" So I took him out in the landscape and said, "Look."

(Laughs) That's what it looks like.

Mayhew: (Laughs) And there it was. California and the Southwest — big oranges and bright yellows and different changes of patterns. Here in California it's phenomenal — the color constantly changing. And green becomes a bright green and then it changes to an orange and gold, different colors. And the sky out here. When I was in Europe I was looking at the different sky effect. It had to do with the density of the atmosphere and how it reflects the light from the Earth, causes difference in the color of the sky. I was walking along the coast of France; the sky is purplish orange, and he said, "What do you mean, purplish?" And I said, "Take a look! Look! The density of the atmosphere and the cloud cover and that kind of reflection creates that kind of color difference. The color is part of the expression of the warmth and sensitivity of my culture. That's it."

It sounds to me as though you're talking about an incredibly complex layering of things. Your eye as it perceives the landscape, your Native-American heritage, your African-American heritage, the association of all of those things together ...

Mayhew: Mmm-hmm. Well, how much all of this — trying to live in that state of creative expression is not easy. Especially the way they work is very intuitive and spontaneous. Mmm-hmmm.

And maintain a certain spiritual truth.

Mayhew: It's very surprising, the reaction of the public or my peers embracing and seeing what I'm doing. In a sense I'm not as aware of what's happening, because it's taking place ... [in an] intuitive and spontaneous technique. I don't really see my work until it leaves the studio as an exhibition and I see it for the first time. They say well, writers, after the book is published, they reread their books and say, oh! (Both laugh)

Do you ever get tired of people saying, "Rick Mayhew, African-American art?" Do you ever think, I should be with the landscape people?

Mayhew: Most of the group in Spiral were completely abstract. Romare Bearden, Norman Lewis, Hale Woodruff, Charles Alston — most of these master painters were abstract. They're involved in painting their personal sensibility. And Norman Lewis always challenged; he said, "I'm doing African American art." I said, "What is African American art? Is it an image, of just painting black subjects?" That's not true. It's the gut and feeling of the sensitivity of this person which is African American. And so this is what Norman Lewis was — one of the staunchest spiritual abstractionists, how much he argues the point, he says the artist has the right to paint any way he wants to, not to the dictates of the art market, which is involved [with the issue of] "this is black art, and this is not black art." They are talking about black art being Romare Bearden and Jacob Lawrence because of the symbols and painting of black subject matter. And that was completely contrary to the reality of what African-American artists are. This constantly is being rehashed over and over again. Only the media always dictates, this is what African-American art is, and this is what it's not. But that's not what the African-American artist thinks. Some of them that are artists are abstractionists, but they're painting their sensitive symbolism, like Hale Woodruff was painting symbolic images. You have to realize he was one of the greatest of muralists, which is being lost. You hear about Jacob Lawrence, but Hale Woodruff painted the murals of African-American culture, subject matter and history long before Jacob Lawrence started painting his subject. And murals were all over the country, historic murals. In the later years he painted abstract subject matter based on African sculpture and forms and symbols.

His Card Players *is pretty well known still.*

Mayhew: Oh yeah, *Card Players* is not really — that's what the media shows, right? They don't show you murals, which are in Atlanta, on all the walls down there, and out here in California, and in the Midwest, and Indiana, and also Los Angeles — *Card Players* is really primitive symbolism, and he never painted that way. That was only one image. And this is what they dig up to show, this is Hale Woodruff? (Laughs) The media again controls.

Do you feel like there is anything like that that happens to you when your work is described?

Mayhew: For years they didn't know I was an African-American artist because I wasn't involved with those kinds of subject matter, right? And the landscapes were accepted on the basis of that, so I had problems with, well, he's not painting disruptive subject matter, which is a pain to our society. I had problems with that for a while, but many of my peers respected what I was doing, so I just continued to do it. It has to do with the sensitivity of my culture, my dedication. My dedication now is really helping other artists, and that was part of the whole group.

Your work feels primarily dedicated to the kind of outreach that is discussed in connection with Spiral. But it goes beyond that for you, when I see you lecturing in classes, or connecting with other artists—

Mayhew: Spiral was just a group that got together to exhibit together. A couple of the people in Spiral will say this is what it was. But that's not what it was. It was a dialogue, the group was involved in a dialogue, a concept in communication and evaluation of their time period, reacting to it. And that's another reason why it needed to stay together all the time, as a group. That the concept would continue, to be involved in the support of other artists, mainly, at the time, African-American artists, which is a continued concern. And also, the same multicultural concerns about art and our society, or what role art plays in society. Art is very important for the stabilization and functional existence, and without it the society stagnates.

Do you have some concerns now about cuts recently for the arts on the federal level?

Mayhew: It has to do with the grants and fellowships and the government supporting the arts. All the countries in the world are aware of this and they support the arts. Our government from time to time fluctuates back and forth on how important the arts is. Right now, the Bush administration feels their budget cannot contribute to the arts because other things are more important. That is a misnomer; there's a problem with that. First of all, it has to do with health and education. It shouldn't hurt education, but education is part of the arts, right? The university system also and elementary schools cut out the art programs in the schools, not realizing that is the backbone of education. And that has to do with the limitation of, the dictation of teacher education, and what are their priorities and which is important.

You have a fairly expansive definition of what art is. I wonder if you would include your community networking as part of the art that you make.

Mayhew: The National Endowment for the Arts is involved with arts and humanities, that's the program ... humanities is part of the community sensitivity of cultural development, and cultural development is the arts. Everything that one is involved with in the environment — their clothing, their housing, their furniture — is all part of a design concept that comes out of the creative process of the arts. And no one sees that, they always say, "Well, the painting on the wall, that's the art." Or, someone that's involved in the theater, or that's involved in music, this is the arts. Art is the whole cultural sensitivity of an area and people that's always being denied and not seen. When the arts are cut out, the great design concept of society is denied. What you see in the new cars ... look at the design of the car, how much it's changed all through the years. The engineering, the functioning of the car, the motors and so forth. It's all part of a design concept that comes out of the arts. And they separate this from the painting on the wall, or a music piece, or a book — right? That's art, and this is not art. And the whole thing, the cultural development is part of the humanities. The same thing is going [on] in the libraries, the concert performances ... which are not being supported.... I'm very concerned about that. I hope I live long enough to make a difference in that relationship.

Would you say that attitude, that perspective that you have, is one that is shared particularly by the African-American community?

Mayhew: Actually, it has to do with Native American and African American — art is a part of their culture. In Asia, in all the other areas — art is their culture. And when I was in Europe, it is a society that embraces and respects the arts, the artists, makes them feel good, their contribution. But we don't have that here. European heritage came to be denied that cultural heritage. African Americans and Native Americans are quite involved with the cultural sensitivity of the arts. They've always been involved with beautiful craftsmaking and developing. And, for years, in terms of African art being craft instead of fine art, that was part of the dictation of the media again, and the dictation of a controlling culture that says what is important and what is not.

⁂

Mayhew: When I came back from Europe, I started teaching at the Pratt Institute. There was this group being formed. The Civil Rights Movement. And the March on Washington. Philip Randolph called Hale Woodruff and Romare Bearden, and asked them to form a contingent of artists to be part of the March on Washington. And so Hale Woodruff, Romare Bearden, and Norman Lewis got together and called some other artists to come and discuss this. As it came together, it wasn't about just a March on Washington. It was the march of creative survival. We got involved in a debating exchange. I didn't join them at first. It was Romare Bearden, Hale Woodruff, Norman Lewis, and Merton Simpson. They formed the group, and they started calling others. So they got in touch with me. I brought in a lot of the younger artists at the time. Hollingsworth, Reginald Gammon — it was about five others that I brought in with me. So you had the youngsters and the older [artists].

And you were the bridge, in a way.

Mayhew: In the exchange of that group, at first when they met, it had to do with — some of them didn't know what the other artists were doing. But you find it was such a diverse group, everyone worked completely differently. Most of them were abstract! Which is unusual. Except for Reginald Gammon. And a lot were semi-abstract, some of the others, right. And then the exchange, the friendship grew out of this. I knew them casually; I never really got to know them [before]. Through this I got to know them fairly well. It was a kind of mind search, in terms of the creative process and thinking, and how they were involved with their careers. We got involved with examining a creative black aesthetic — how much was in music and writing, and how much was in the visual arts. They started questioning each other, in terms of their direction, and what they were involved with. In terms of, with subject and direction, were they involved with European influence, or was it ethnic influence, how much they were caught up in the game of copying what was going on during the time. So the exchange got very heated, examining the credibility of why one is painting, or why one was creating.

Who were you close to? Who were your closest friends?

Mayhew: I started bonding with all of them. Which is very unusual. Norman Lewis was an artist I was very close to. And Romare Bearden. And then later on, Hale Woodruff. Actually, I became very close to him, because he lived longer than the other two.

Can you tell me about your relationship with Romare Bearden?

Mayhew: Oh, Romare Bearden — he wanted to — this [Spiral] was a think tank, rather than a club. Ah, and we used to meet in the studio, and then we decided to shut up the storefront on the West Village, so it wouldn't be — whosever studio it was would be in command of what was going on. This way it would be an open forum. Ah, and one wouldn't have to entertain everybody else that way, right? This way it would be an open kind of thing, and everyone shared the expenses of this being set up. But, then, the exchange started examining what they were doing. And so Romare Bearden one time said, "Why don't we all work together? In a certain particular direction." And that's when he got involved with the collage idea. And wanted everybody to do this. Cutting out papers and so forth. A lot of them felt that wasn't their thing.

(Laughs) They didn't want to do it.

Mayhew: I started doing it. Romare was starting it, and, of course, I was sympathizing with what he was doing, and I thought it was a good idea, so I started doing some cutting out. But the one who was doing this before was actually Reginald Gammon! He was a graphic designer, and this is what he did!

Oh. Wow!

Mayhew: (Laughs) He was showing Romare Bearden how to paste up! And then, the Xerox machine actually made a copy of the collage. So the first time, it was a collage of the copy of the collage! It was just black and white! Near the end, when Romare Bearden was passing away, he did tell the story to Reggie Gammon. It has to do with pastes and glues and so forth, which is the last thing that would be permanent ... but Romare Bearden got so entrenched with this idea! He was fascinated by the challenge of what he was doing. And then he really got into it. (Laughs)

Were there powerful personalities put together?

Mayhew: Well, personalities, it was a conflict ... each one had ... Bill Majors was an artist I met when I was in Florence. And he's the one I brought as a youngster, younger artist, into the group. I met him in the Penzioni Bartolini, right on the Arno river, in Florence. And actually—I had my children with me on my grant. (Laughs) No one was doing that. (Laughs) So Scott [Mayhew] ran out into the lobby, and ran into Bill Majors. And Bill picked him up and said, "Who are you?" And I came out to retrieve Scott, and that's how I met Bill Majors, who was sketching the roof, over the Arno. (Laughs)

Mmm, nice story.

Mayhew: When he came back from Italy, he came and we shared a studio on Twenty-Second Street. So I got to know Bill Majors. He died very young. He was showing the art, he was a printmaker, showing all of the work for the artists, because he was a printmaker. So there was a kind of exchange going on of different ideas. They were questioning the integrity of direction. Some of the women would challenge the group, in terms of, there's no women in your group talking. There was Emma Amos, who was brought into the group. I think Hale Woodruff brought her name, if I remember correctly. And she was saying, "There's no other women involved." So we got in touch with Faith Ringgold, and Vivian Brown, at the time, and a couple of other women. They were discussing outside of the group, actually. They didn't come to the meetings. Actually, Emma Amos didn't come to all the meetings, so she never got involved with some of the scuffling that went on in terms of debating exchange. And they got hot and heavy sometimes in terms of the ideas of why one was painting the way they were. So they challenged the credibility of the integrity of what one was doing.

Did you have heated discussions about politics?

Mayhew: Well, politics, everyone in that group was certainly denied — there were only four artists, African-American artists in any of the galleries in New York — Jacob Lawrence, Romare Bearden, Norman Lewis, and myself. Those were the only ones in the galleries. So, this was a respectful thing, the fact that you were accepted in the galleries. But, for many of them, that the rest of the artists were denied — they were in the background. There was an article in the *New York Times* during that time — the doubt that Afro Americans were at the level of intellectual capability of maintaining a creative consistency. That was an article in the *New York Times* in the sixties. All right? (Laughs)

Unbelievable. How can you not be angry?

Mayhew: Anger is a self-destructive state. One vents their anger in a destructive way, in terms of prisons, or their own kind of denial of a functional existence because of their anger. One gets caught up in that kind of intrigue, which is self-destructive in many ways. Now, if you come back to disapproval and dissatisfaction with what's going on in a constructive way by dealing with what was happening, why, one would feel unhappy with the situation. That's applying a constructive contribution to how you feel about a situation, such as what was going on in the sixties. The whole segregation situation that was going on.

Well, let me ask you this as a teacher. It's one thing to say, anger doesn't get you anywhere. But how do you realize that as an angry person?

Mayhew: Well, you see, you're still thinking about one being an angry person. That person can think of themselves as a creative, constructive person. You're not caught in that pitfall of self-denial and destruction. Otherwise you find yourself involved with anger, psychologically, you're always involved with denial, self-denial in the face of accepting how you are being treated. And how one would feel, like this man who went in the store and kept his hands in his pocket ... they thought he was going to be stealing something! That's self-denial, right?

I'm sure you had artists, maybe it was Reginald Gammon, maybe it was someone else —

Mayhew: Reggie was very angry.

And so was Marlon Ross.

Mayhew: He was angry about it.

And so how did you interact with them about it?

Mayhew: Well, he, uh — Marlon Ross was very strange. He would have the most foul language you can imagine, right? But he'll cut you off and hug you. It's this mixed thing, right? And that whole group, when I came and joined them, I was so impressed by them. Because they came out of the Harlem Renaissance. I was accepted in that until Merton Simpson. But Hale Woodruff, Romare Bearden, Norman Lewis, Ernie Crichlow, all of them came out of the Harlem Renaissance. And Charles Austin. He had the workshop in the Harlem Renaissance. He was the only one. And Augusta Savage. They were the ones who had the school for —

Oh, Augusta Savage, did you know her?

Mayhew: No. She died before then. There was this group, that kind of element was part of the established group there, which was exciting to be associated with them. They were the top African-American artists at the time. And the association with them, what they thought, and how they felt, and how they created — ah, they were a serious body of people. It wasn't frivolous at all. And that was impressive. It wasn't a little joking little gang of artists meeting. I used to go — I joined other groups at the time. I went to the Educational Alliance group, the Social Realists on the Lower East Side in New York. I used to go visit with them and their group. Some of them were not involved with that same kind of dedicated, serious exchange of ideas. I went over to what was called the Club, the Abstract Expressionist group. And the Cedar Bar in New York, where all the artists used to meet. Greenberg and Rosenberg used to be in there, and [they were] orchestrating how they can take the lead and develop the movement in the art world, the writers.

And so they did!

Mayhew: They did! Right. They kind of made us known — no, no, no. They kind of made the Abstract Expressionists, at the time, become famous.

Mm-hmm. Tell me about Greenberg and Rosenberg.

Mayhew: Well, I didn't get to know them very well. The only time I ran into them was in the Cedar Bar.

Were a lot of the artists and writers there pretty—

Mayhew: They were very arrogant. Very arrogant and also very egomanic, right (Laughs) But very bright! (Laughs) Very bright. So, what they said they were going to do, they did! Excellent. (Laughs) And that's true of the Pop artists also. They got involved in a group when they were there. Andy Warhol and that crowd. And what they were going to do, they did that, too! Which is still going on! And there was this media of the established culture that takes over, and this is what we were aware of. How we can challenge established culture. And how we evaluate creative development, and who is respected in that creative area, writing and composing and so forth. The men used to come to the group, some of the composers and writers and so forth. And some of the top writers came and discussed with us their new creative process in life! So that exchange was very serious. It was on the level of— it was recorded, which hopefully, every one of the younger guys could put a tape underneath the table in order to tape this. They didn't want any kind of recording, because of the constant furor over the exchange of ideas. And Norman Lewis, to try to make a point, he slammed his hand on the table, and the tape falls to the floor. (Both laugh)

Mayhew: He didn't want a tape, he took it and threw it against the wall. (Laughs)

That's great.

Mayhew: So, all of that should have been taped. It would have been fantastic. A very eloquent exchange of ideas and creative thinking, right?

It sounds like you were drawn to Spiral more than the other groups because—

Mayhew: Well, the other groups, they were involved with — certainly, the Social Realists, I think there was, maybe, one black who was involved with that group. But the Soyer brothers, I was pretty close to ... these were part of the group. And they were thinking about the creative process of depicting the social problems of the time. So I was concerned about that. Right. And the Abstract Expressionists, I certainly got close to them — de Kooning, Motherwell, Kline, and so forth.

There seems to be such an arrogance in that movement. Would you say that was true?

Mayhew: Well, they were [arrogant], because it was a movement of the fact that they were right, and everyone else was wrong. It was that kind of thing. This was the way to work, and what to think, and the whole process of that.

It also seemed like they had a poor attitude toward women.

Mayhew: Well, maybe de Kooning. (Laughs)

And Pollock.

Mayhew: And Pollock. Yeah, right. Right. And also, what's his name, one of the Pop artists, were particularly involved with that. Right. Andy Warhol. Right. So you have this kind of attitude. Because the women at the time, like Faith Ringgold, were very aggressive about women's rights. And that got in the way of them as a creative person, because they were constantly challenging it on the basis of male-female situation, rather than being involved in creative exchange with the other artists. So that got in the way a little bit, right. I certainly championed their views because I invited them to a particular panel in the Art Students League. Most of the women of that time were on that panel. Right. Betty Blakely was one. I have a tape of Betty Blakely. She was involved with the Children's Caravan. She was teaching all these children how to paint and so forth, like that. And her whole dedication was to that! So as a result, today, she's not that well known! But her work, you have to see it, it's fabulous! And she was very active and prominent at the time. So, when it comes to inviting them to come to the meetings, fine, but then the exchange, in evaluation, such as Norman Lewis, what did you ever do? What are you involved with? What is your direction? So, not just the women, but the youngsters in the group. He said, they have hardly any years yet, in terms of creative development. Which is true, several of them, right. They were just discovering who they were as an artist. What do you think of being an artist? Woodruff was saying, "It is a creative dedication and commitment, completely involved with creative dedication and commitment. It's involved with the integrity of creative self-indulgence." So, excellent. Mm-hmm. So you had this kind of talk that was going on, which is fabulous, right. What kind of honesty and integrity in terms of the indignity of the African-American artist and what they were doing, right. And how one maintains that level. So each one coming there was challenged about what they were doing. Romare Bearden challenged us [by asking] "Why [not] get honest about what you are doing?" That's why he started doing the other thing. He felt he was kind of patronizing. His abstract paintings were fabulous, right.

Tell me about how you kept informed about political events.

Mayhew: The newspapers were not a help about what was going on at the time. They would watch what was taking place, just about the time we were meeting, right?

Were you involved in any events that were local?

Mayhew: Oh, we picketed the museums, right, and galleries. And Andrews and I became a separate group, involved with the Emergency Black Artist's Coalition. We were the ones who challenged the museums and galleries and so forth. Romare Bearden was very conservative about doing that. They felt that wasn't the way to go. They felt they could approach it in a more intellectual way instead of challenging the media, and challenging museums by letters and so forth, like that.

So you made signs and …

Mayhew: Oh, yeah, we went out and picketed. The Sullivan museums and galleries, the Metropolitan Museum, the Whitney Museum, right? But the Whitney Museum has not emerged out of that yet. You can check their collection and find how many African-American artists are in their collection. Their show came out here to the Museum of Modern Art. And they had their big show of Romare Bearden there? They

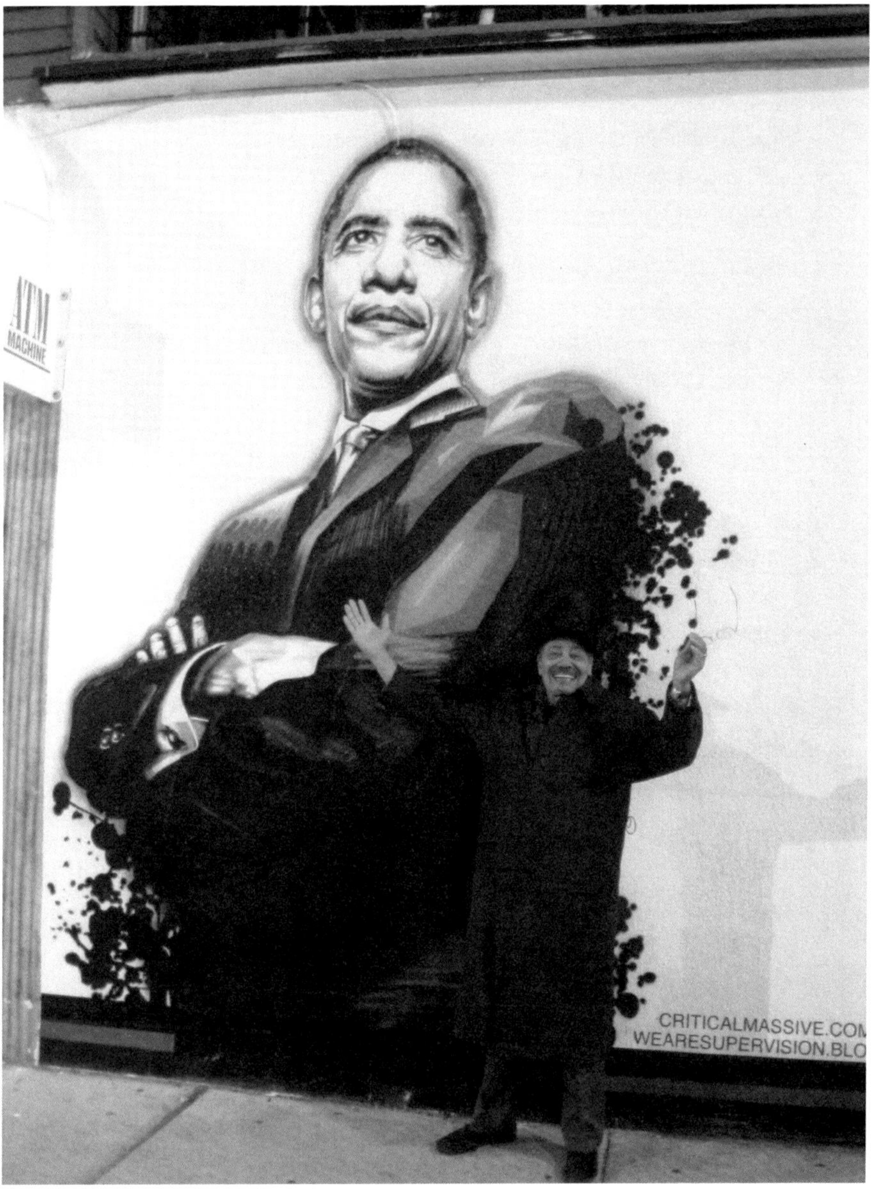

Richard Mayhew in front of a poster of Barack Obama, New York City.

keep him out of their collection. (Both laugh) So it still goes on in the dominant culture, and how much we're involved with a multicultural society. We are very aware of the multicultural society emerging, the Latinos and Asians, and the one group that's always left out — Native Americans. They were never included, in terms of those who were part of groups which were denied and omitted.

It almost seems to me as though you fought that battle early on. And you continued it, because you were involved in [the African-American] Civil Rights issues. And now, you've [directed] more of your attention to the Native-American struggle.

Mayhew: Oh! I was always involved with the Native-American struggle! It's constantly denied! No one hears what you're saying. No one's interested in what you are saying. And it's not important because there again, the dominant culture invades one's sensibility of thinking and functioning. The African-American culture is certainly involved in terms of slavery, and what was going on — actually, the African Americans championed the causes of sitting in the back of the bus, or, sitting in a [theater] balcony — which now people want to be in the balcony. (Laughs) You have to be a minority just to be in the balcony! Not in the orchestra! Ever! Right? I remember going to these movies, I had to sit in the balcony!

Really?

Mayhew: That's right. (Laughs) And then the uniform, when I was in service, I had to sit in the back of the bus with my uniform on. Okay?

I don't understand how that can't make you angry, and—

Mayhew: Well, as I said, you can internalize anger, and you get involved with alcoholism, drug addiction, and anger, which you lash out about something and end up in prison. Which happens to many. It ends itself that way. It just attracts people on the basis that the hate is so strong. And, it's self-defeating, in many ways. And also Malcolm X [who struck a more confrontational tone than Martin Luther King].

I don't understand how you can be so gentle and kind.

Mayhew: Well, in order to be inventive and creative, as I said, there's a spiritual element. We discussed it briefly. I think I discussed it more with Hale Woodruff than I did with Romare Bearden. Because Norman Lewis was great, very bright, very brilliant. But he was very angry. He would vent his anger in communicating with people. Someone come to the door and right away he'd say, "What the hell are you doing here?" Slams the door, right. Then open it. (Both laugh)

So he was soft underneath.

Mayhew: There was the reaction of defense. Right? And then opening up. So there's that kind of problem, right? Many musicians I used to work with were involved with insecurity [due to] the lack of respect [they received] for what they were doing.

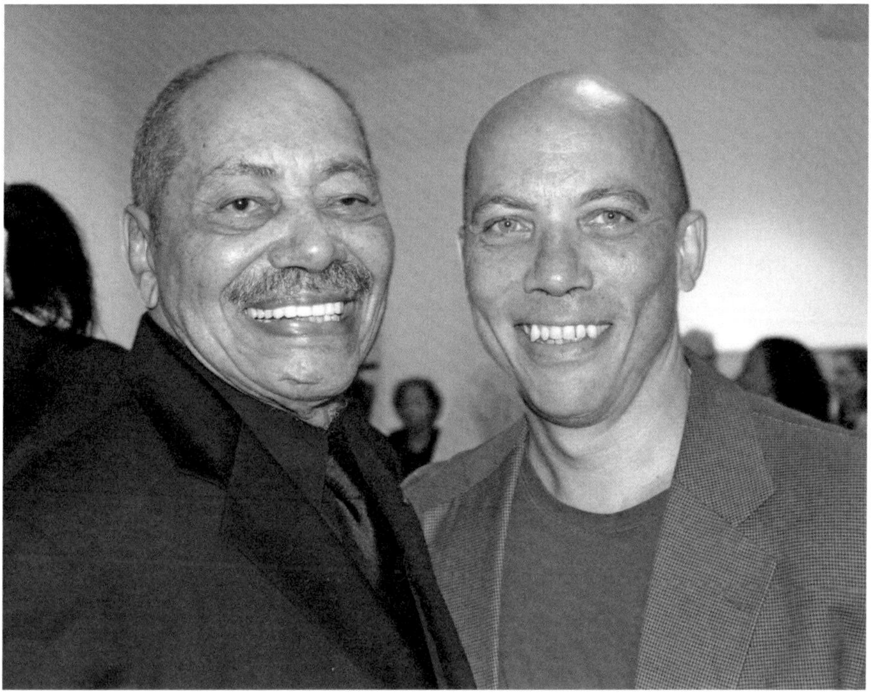

Richard Mayhew and his son, Scott, ca. 2000.

What do you say to your students who come to you [in frustration]?

Mayhew: Mm-hmm. How much you paint angry paintings and problems. Ernie Crichlow did very well. I don't know if you know his work.

A lot of people don't.

Mayhew: He did the beautiful children, beautiful girl in this white outfit hanging by her neck.

Oh!

Mayhew: But I'm just showing you … unbelievable. Right.

What did you think of that work?

Mayhew: Well! He was very clever. He was very bright, very clever. And a master draftsman. Some of the artists were good, but they couldn't execute images the way he did. Right? He did representational, beautiful figurative forms, depicting African-American figures. And also Jacob Lawrence!

Right.

Mayhew: Charles White? Beautiful interpretation of African figures, right? Ernie Crichlow. Reginald Gammon's early work was like that. So, you find there was this other area, the anger was involved with creating beauty. To show that there was something here besides.

Ah.

Mayhew: My doing is in terms of landscape, that's involved with spiritual sensitivity, involved with, people involved in religious commitment.

Were there other artists who felt that spiritual commitment?

Mayhew: Ah, not that I know. I got some of it from Reuben Tam. Reuben Tam was a Chinese Hawaiian. Very brilliant man. I think one of the most intellectual persons I encountered, other than Hale Woodruff. And I'm sorry [I did not see him] in his last years; I wanted to go to Hawaii to visit with him. After he was retired. He always taught at the Brooklyn Museum! Excellent teacher! Fantastic man. When he retired, he had, off the coast of Maine on Monhegan Island, a fantastic house that he built there, right. And it was on the basis of Hawaiian background, I think, the way he built the house. So when he retired from the Brooklyn Museum, and was moving back to Hawaii, he disassembled the house and shipped it to Hawaii.

Wow!

Mayhew: (Laughs) So there was a strange kind of intrigue of people like that. He had that kind of mystical, spiritual sensitivity. I got a lot from him. And also from Edwin Dickinson. It wasn't so much that spiritual thing that Reuben Tam had, but it was credibility. He was very dedicated to creative honesty. Wow. It was hard to live with. And Hale Woodruff was the ultimate at this, right.

You teach creative survival. How was it that you and your friends survived creatively at that time?

Mayhew: It had to do with creative dedication.

I mean literally. Did all of you teach?

Mayhew: All. Romare Bearden was a social worker. Even while he was still doing the work! And then Hale Woodruff was one of the great teachers of art education. One of the great ones. Right. Mm-hmm. At NYU. I think he was the first African-American teacher in a major white institution. I don't know if you've ever seen him, but [he is] a very statuesque man.

Oh, really? (Laughs) Well, you have that quality.

Mayhew: Very, very, you know, very astute in manner, right. And it's like a respectful gesture right away when you see him, right.

Mmm. So it really was your passion, you really did have to make your living in other ways.

Mayhew: Oh, yeah. I was an illustrator. Recently, when I was in Washington at an exhibition, a man came to visit because it was a one-person show, at the gallery in Washington. And this man came over to me at the end, he says, "I've collected all your books on illustration." He says, they're online! I said, "You're kidding! But they're out of print!" He said, "But they can get them for you!"

How wonderful!

Mayhew: (Laughs) I think I did about eight books. One was on tools, mm-hmm, and was for children, right? The origin of tools. And guess where they came from? Africa. Can you imagine, when I went to the library looking up the origin of the pulley, the scissors, the pliers, anything you can imagine, it came from early development in Africa! I said, "Oh, no! This is the kind of thing someone is putting us on, right?" (Laughs) No, it was there. The block and tackle, you know? (Laughs) So that's me. I did an illustration of that, and I illustrated a book on the circulatory system, which was the Medical Library in New York, studying the circulatory system, which was [in] my hobby — one of the doctors in England that discovered the circulatory system in terms of vessels and capillaries and so forth, and arteries. So I illustrated that. And Tristan and Isolde — I also wrote a book on Tristan and Isolde. The opera? (Laughs). And Michaelangelo. Those are all children's books now, right? (Laughs)

Every time I talk to you there's something else.

Mayhew: So there was this man came in and he got all my books! I said, "What?" (Laughs) Because I don't have them! I should go online and find my books! I even forgot the titles! (Laughs) That was part of survival, doing illustrations, right? Also I was a ceramic decorator! That's how I met my first wife! She was a ceramic decorator. I used to work in Cambridge China Design.

Do you still have any of your ceramics?

Mayhew: (Emphatically) No. (Laughs) I don't have any of it! I don't have any of my own paintings! (Laughs)

I understand.

Mayhew: That was another world. A complete and other world. I used to work there and then go home and paint! Right?

Mm-hmm. What were your painting hours? You painted at night.

Mayhew: I painted at night sometimes, weekends — different times. And when I was teaching, during the whole summer and mid-winter breaks, I paint. But while I was teaching, I was teaching two and three days a week, that was it! The rest of the time I was painting.

Did you have your own studio always?

Mayhew: Yeah! Always had a studio. It was always in the home.

Mm-hmm. But that smell—

Mayhew: Separate, it was separate. Oh, no, I just shut the door and closed it off. The room was separated from the — so you didn't have that. And then I had a separate studio on Twenty-second Street.

So you had both.

Mayhew: Well that was — yeah. I had both. The one on Twenty-second Street was a special studio. It was a third-floor walk-up. Everyone did sculpture, but they had to carry this stuff upstairs, and I didn't do that. (Laughs) It's easier to be a painter, right? (Laughs)

(Laughs) That's right.

Mayhew: And then I had a little school, which is on Sixth Avenue. Right near Twenty-second Street. There's a church right now, still there, and the studio was next door to that church. On the top floor. One time I went in there late at night, because sometimes with teaching I had to go in my studio and paint, and I had little classes up there for people. Mm-hmm. Mostly dilettantes used to come. (Laughs) I forgot to close the door downstairs, and the police, they go around at night checking all the doors. This is a building right next to the church, it's a brownstone. The storefronts are right in a part of that. So the police are going around checking all the buildings and the door was open. They came upstairs and I was in there, and they said, "What are you doing here?" Right? Rrrr.

(Laughs).

Mayhew: Well, this black man in that area, you know, they questioned me, and I said, "I'm an artist, this is my studio, and I teach." And they said, "Well, the door is open downstairs. You broke in."

Oh.

Mayhew: I showed him the key, I had a key; they didn't expect that. So, one of the officers … so while I was talking to him I was sketching.

(Laughs)

Mayhew: He came over and he says, "Oh, wow!" (Both laugh loudly)

Great story! Is that true?

Mayhew: Right. No, it's a true story. They kind of backed off with suspicion. I want you to know that. The suspicion was still there.

Right. What a story.

Mayhew: (Laughs) There's this prejudice — it's always there.

Tell me about your relationship — when you dealt with galleries. Was that a problem?

Mayhew: Well, the galleries that I went with, the first gallery was a little gallery in Greenwich Village. Morris Gallery.

The Morris Gallery?

Mayhew: Morris Gallery.

Just a little one!

Mayhew: Yeah, it was a little gallery, in Greenwich Village.

Just a little one.

Mayhew: Right. And then, I had a show with him. And he liked the work. So, the *New York Times* reviewed this show (laughing).

Of course they did!

Mayhew: And the very first review, by Canaday, the staff writer for the *New York Times*! (Laughs) So in this little gallery, wow! (Laughs) It was [written up in] the *New York Times*.

I guess you celebrated about that one.

Mayhew: So then Atchison, which is [in] upper Madison Avenue, saw the work. And he wanted me to join his gallery. It was on Seventy-second Street and right off of Madison Avenue, right? Mmmm. In the great area there, right? So I became part of their gallery! That was before I went to Europe. And while I was in Europe, [the gallery] supported me. Sent money, for several paintings — sometimes, he just kept the paintings and gave me money for them.

What about in the years following? What's your relationship like with your galleries?

Mayhew: Well, I develop a rotation; it's a respectful kind of relationship. That became involved with creative survival — how artists and writers function and survive. I got to know the gallery — because there was a group in the gallery, the whole thing, in New York, and everyone got to know me and I got to know them. Then I went to Midtown Gallery, and dealt with [them for] twenty years! They were very supportive of everything I was doing, and the other artists in the gallery, we became a kind of clique in supporting one another, right? Elizabeth Bishop was in the gallery, a woman artist whom I had great respect for, and she was very supportive, right? And then I was elected to the National Academy! Which was unusual at the time. I think there was only — what was it, Charles White, and ... I can't think of the other one right away, the only African Americans that were in the National Academy. And I became another one! Most of them were in their seventies and eighties that become members of the Academy. That's years of accomplishment; you get the respect and support of your peers. That's the relationship of the academy to your peers! It's fantastic. So, when I became a member of the National Academy, then there was the support of the gallery, the fact that you were an academician, one of the highest honors one can receive in the visual arts. I didn't know at the time, right? I didn't realize it was like, wow! (Laughs) And no one even knows where the National Academy is, most people. That's one of the oldest art schools in the United States! You know where that academy is? (Laughs) Next to the

Guggenheim on Fifth Avenue. (Laughs) Across the street from the Guggenheim. Good location! (Laughs) The oldest art school, and the National Academy was founded by Samuel Morse. Who invented the telegraph. He was a portrait painter. And the telegraph, right? He was going to England to paint the royal family, on the boat. And he needed some way to communicate with his wife. He said, "There's got to be a way." That's when he started, he invented the telegraph. On the boat. Then when he came back, in the basement of NYU, he set up the stretcher frame. His apparatus for the telegraph was set up on the stretcher frame in the basement of NYU. I did the book. (Laughs) A children's book on that. (Both laugh)

How do your galleries now, or how have they in the past, marketed you?

Mayhew: Well, they never did enough. The book, right? They never did the book.

Right.

Mayhew: And, how many brochures? They never did lengthy brochures, right?

Mm-hmm. But you've shown me some—

Mayhew: Yeah, but not necessarily from the gallery; it usually was recent galleries. I haven't been satisfied with the brochures that were done. Really.

How is it that people—that your galleries show you to the public? What is it that they say you're about, and do you agree with that?

Mayhew: Well, there are all these writings now, in terms of being a member of the academy, and being involved with Spiral group, and—involved with spiritual development, they've become aware that that's what I'm doing. So that would be projected, right.

Do you feel like there's something more that you wish they would—

Mayhew: Write a book! (Laughs) I was looking at books on Motherwell, and Kline—ten, twelve books out there, right? (Laughs)

Part of my struggle in writing a book about you, has been that people say you're going to have a very difficult time putting him in the context of other Modernist painters because your subject matter isn't angry, political, overtly—

Mayhew: It is. I'm painting "Forty Acres and a Mule." That's the political connection. I'm painting the treaty land that never honored these Native Americans. Which is still going on. Okay? Civil rights, that was working very well, in terms of Afro Americans and other ethnic groups. But never Native Americans. They're still on the same space they were before. Because of the land rights! And their claim on this country! It's still there, right? I don't know if you've gone through that book … you can see, well, the holocaust! Literally. Right.

But why should you have to—

Mayhew: This is the only image—[there are other] images where the Indians are being attacked, and the Native Americans are being slaughtered, and so forth—it doesn't get to the point. The spiritual connection—I guess one looks at the painting and gets a spiritual feeling about it, but they don't know the source of it, right? A couple of brochures that I had were involved with why I'm doing paintings. Explaining the fact that it's involved with spiritual sensitivity. As I've said, there's others who've latched onto this, and they want to write a book about dying unafraid. Because of the spiritual uniqueness of being able to deal with any situation, even death. Which is internal sensitivity.

Why do you think a critical audience would want to engage with African-American and Native-American artists that showed struggle against oppression, but they wouldn't want to look at works that showed the spirit itself?

Mayhew: This is the other side of the coin. You've got the head and the tails, right, and how much you're involved with the other side of the coin, which is the spiritual inner self. You have the face. This inner self is not visible. Even though you, when you look in the mirror, you don't see yourself. Who are you? Who am I? And that's the inner self, which no one can ever touch but you! You're the only one who ever knows! One gets married, but they'll never know that person inside. Really, ever. And so there is that uniqueness which is the beauty of human existence. It's the intellectual internal creative existence. Which is always there striving to get out. (Laughs) And really be constructed, right?

Mm-hmm.

Mayhew: I guess I was hoping to live long enough to see Native Americans get their due in society. African Americans have reached some point of some respect for who they are, and not enough, it's still a problem. They've risen to a level. I went to a meeting in San Francisco. There were a lot of African-American women [who had] become head of corporations. And men involved with head of corporations. No Native Americans. Not to say that they're not brilliant enough, right? Some great minds, great teachers. But they don't accept them on that level, because of that one thing, still there. Land rights. The attitude is that this is a colonial government, which it is. Colonialized government. The Native Americans gave it up — they came to take over their land. They said it would be hard to allow them to do that, and they didn't allow them to do that. They fought like mad. Even the stories still haven't come out how they battled, and the colonial control in this country, which is still going on.

What I think most people see in your work, is very peaceful landscape. Now I'm starting to see it as a statement. This is the land, this is what's being denied—

Mayhew: I painted figures, like in the sixties–that's been ignored! It's being ignored. How many paintings do you still see? Angry torturing in paintings that were done at the time, which was excellent, fantastic! But I felt there was something more here that needs to be done! And that's why I was involved with this internalized sensitivity. Hale Woodruff started to realize what I was doing; he says, "Tell me more." Right. Because this is how he worked, from his internalized feeling in the painting. And all abstract painting is based on internalized creative expression. Guts. That's what Norman Lewis said to me. He said, I'm putting my guts on my canvas. True. It might seem a crude kind of way of saying it, but that's it, right. All Abstract Expressionist paintings are involved with that kind of sensitivity. It's not a visual image you can hold on to, but it's the internal feeling that they're expressing.

But there is that remnant of landscape in your work.

Mayhew: Well, landscape is part of an environment which is really sensitive. Every time I look at the landscape out there, it's saying things. What it's really saying is, it's internal. It constantly replenishes itself. Constantly reborn. One season after season, keeps coming back. And it's changing. Which is a reflection of the human existence. That you can be just like nature, constantly rejuvenated and rebuilt and redeveloped. You don't die.

That must be why the book you told me about, and the nursing homes have—they draw so much from your work.

Mayhew: Well, they're saying that, some of the doctors, they don't know how someone has a severe cancer where one dies, and this other one survives it! It's an internal kind of struggle, like, the child is born, wants to live. Wants to live.

It reminds me of the time I went to visit you in the hospital, and the nurse said, "Well, he should be here!" And she said, "I guess he left!" You just walked right out of there.

Mayhew: (Laughs)

I went to see you and you had said, "Forget this!" About five years ago. I went to see you in the hospital and you had said, "I'm outta here." (Both laugh)

Mayhew: When I was at Penn State, I was involved with internal medicine. There was a whole group there that was talking about it, how people can cure themselves, right. And it has to do with the circulatory system, right. It's very strange; I was involved with that whole thing, and I did a book on the whole circulatory system, and I had this blockage in my artery! I said, "Oh, wow!"

Everything's coming together!

Mayhew: Amazing, right? (Laughs)

I want to ask you about some of these early childhood experiences, and the teachers you had, and the artists you knew, and those influences. But first, why do you think your story, your art, has been omitted? You said when I had the title "Forgotten Genius," you said, "Oh no, it's not forgotten."

Mayhew: Yeah!

Why has your art received perhaps less attention than Faith Ringgold, or Romare Bearden, or—

Mayhew: That's the media. They select not only African-American artists, but any artist. They're involved with a certain selection process of who's in and who's out. It goes back to the Medici family: who's in favor in the court! It's the same thing now — that hasn't changed. It has to do with, in the society of today and the art world — I was just reading that journal on contemporary art in the national paper. It talks about who's in favor at the time, and a particular society, in a particular area, just like who's in favor in Europe right now. Because of what's been going on with the whole development in the arts in France, in Germany, and England, and Italy — the selection process there is not involved with the power element that was in the past, who established the Impressionists or opposed the Post-Impressionists. They weren't in favor at all. It was the Salon! Now how much the contemporary Salon in the United States, and who's in favor — the Abstract Expressionists were in the '50s and early '60s. That started to change!

One would think that—your work has been compared to Helen Frankenthaler's.

Mayhew: It all has to do with if you're placed in the category in which that happened, in which you mentioned; African-American artists are like a separate element, not in terms of the American artists, they're African-American artists. And, as a result, who they select in that category, you get involved in Romare Bearden, and Jacob Lawrence, and no other. Right?

But it's that category.

Mayhew: It's a category of discrimination, right? Isolation. Omission. Denial.

Let me give you my theory.

Mayhew: Mm-hmm.

I think there's a narrative element to Faith Ringgold. Jacob Lawrence. Romare Bearden.

Mayhew: What do you think of Faith Ringgold's art?

I like it.

Mayhew: Why?

It's very colorful; it tells stories, right?

Mayhew: It's primitive! And that's part of it. It's a primitive form, and also folk art. So you're involved with, she's in favor with the court, because part of the acceptance of an African-American woman is doing folk art. Again, the media! Who selects whom? There's Betty Blaton. Which you have no idea who she is. See that? She's fantastic. In the early '60s, long before Faith Ringgold reached any recognition, she was involved with the Children's Caravan in New York. Showing all the children of New York, mainly, you know, minority students, the arts! Introducing them to the arts. As a result she neglected her input into the art market. She was a fantastic printmaker, and painter, right? And then there's Vivian Brown, also a prominent painter in the '60s!

You're embarrassing me. I don't know them.

Mayhew: Well, no! They weren't in favor in the court! Now Faith Ringgold is in favor in the court! She's very aggressive, very ambitious, and she's a folk artist! I'm just saying, her acceptance is fine. But she's in the particular category which is accepted by the media.

I wonder if all of those artists—I know you're talking about Ringgold differently, but Faith, and Jacob Lawrence, and Romare Bearden—those are perhaps the most popular right now, African-American artists. Why?

Mayhew: Because of the selection of who's in favor in the court! And this is the new court!

But could it not be that it's because all of them have, to some degree, this quality that you mentioned, that narrative genre?

Mayhew: No. No different than, uh, Hale Woodruff, Charles Alston—

But they're much more abstract! Their work is much more abstract.

Mayhew: So was Romare Bearden! Until 1963.

But no one looks at his abstract art.

Mayhew: No, this is in terms of the category: what is African American art? So they classify it in this area. So it becomes important. Not in terms of American artists, but African-American artists. Which is a denial of their contribution as an artist! It separates them from the higher level of acceptance, really. It characterizes them. Which is my objection. It's Romare Bearden's objection. Jacob Lawrence also says the same thing. The idea, the patronage of him on the basis of what he was doing. And this is part of what still goes on, in terms of Civil Rights Movement in the '60s, it's still going on.

When I gave a lecture on your work, on your activism and your work, everyone after the lecture raised their hand. What is the pain that he's painting from?

Mayhew: The pain?

Pain. I said, I don't think he's painted from some kind of pain. Although if he had had it—

Mayhew: It has to do with denial. I was talking to friend of mine; he was a white artist, he was completely not accepted because of the way he works, you know. So it's in terms of how artists fall into a certain category in terms of acceptance in the loop. And, again, no matter what artist is out there, African-American artist, and Native-American artist, [they] fall into one category. Because Native-American artists — fantastic painters!— they, like the African artists, are considered, you know, craft. (Laughs)

Which is why I'm asking you this question. I don't think you'd ask a lecturer who's talking about a white landscape painter's work, "What's the pain that he's painting from?"

Mayhew: Well, it has to do with, you're talking about music and the blues. The pain of the white musicians singing the blues! How much they were involved with the pain of why African musicians sing the blues! It's from pain, and suffering, which is a mix of love and hate.

I know you've had a lot of pain in your life, but I don't think that's where you paint from.

Mayhew: Well, it's not, no. I came from a dual culture. I just discussed this recently in a lecture in New York. The dual culture is the fact that Native Americans, African Americans, are completely denied. Native Americans are completely denied today, so there's a pain there of seeking acceptance and respect for the natives of this country! They — they're not on — you never see them on television. The only time you see them is [in] Westerns. (Laughs) How much they are involved with the secondary role. They were never in any leading roles. Or you never see them being interviewed on television. And those who were commentators on television, you don't know if they're Native American! So you have this denial which is part of my heritage, not so much African-American denial, as Native-American denial! I have a great pain in terms of the suffering of that area. And it's not so much pain, it has to do with the dual culture that I came up in, and an aggressive necessity to survive. No matter what. So the dual culture is a very powerful kind of unity, in terms of creative ambition, functional ambition. Creativity to me has to do with the natural joy of functioning.

Exactly!

Mayhew: That's right.

There is a Native American artist, Rick Glazer-Danay. An interviewer asked him, "Is this appropriate Native-American art?" When he was painting about things that weren't "Native American."

Mayhew: Yeah, right. That's it.

And he said, "Everything I paint is appropriate Native American art." I wonder if your omission, perhaps to some degree, is coming from the fact that you're Native American.

Mayhew: I'm more prominent than most African-American artists. And very recognized and well known. How much the others who were denied has to do with the fact that it came because I've been very aggressive and very ambitious about it! And challenging the system. In academia

I was constantly involved with the challenge of the acceptance and rejection, right? Of minority artists, right? And there are lectures all over the country, I do them constantly, on creative survival. And creative survival has to do with all the arts, but it has to do with those who were mainly denied, because of their particularly unique creative direction, and commitment. It gets involved with how much the writers also get caught up in this too, because they categorize, again. And isolate. And how much this artist has been denied because the quality of the work doesn't measure up to the quality of the established acceptance.

But no one ever says that about your work.

Mayhew: No, no, but this is the attitude! Even though my painting had fallen in a category which they can't define. They can't fit it in this category, can't fit it in that category, they write about it as a metamorphic form, right.

Do you get attention from Native-American scholars and critics?

Mayhew: Well, I'm a part of the National Association of Native American Art. That's a powerful group!

Do you feel you get more attention for being—

Mayhew: Oh, more attention because I'm accepted in the art market, and Native-American artists are not accepted in the art market. Okay? So within the society itself, there's a support relationship, which allows them or supports them to continue to create. Psychologically, it's very important for the needy to have some kind of recognition and support.

Do you feel you get more attention being categorized as an African-American artist and Native-American artist?

Mayhew: The main thing is to be accepted as an American artist.

Oh, I know.

Mayhew: Yeah, I know, but again, it's how much emphasis is placed in accepting one or the other. If you say you're a Native-American artist, there's no acceptance at all! African American artists have been accepted, but in a separate category. Hale Woodruff constantly talked about [this]. I have part of a letter he wrote to someone else about me. The fact that I was a credible person had nothing to do with being an artist.

Mm-hmm.

Mayhew: But being a person could have also — having this from one of your peers! The acceptance had to do with how much one is honestly involved with creative credibility. That's how much one is Native American, right? How much is constantly being denied. In the media, Greenberg, Rosenberg, the writers made a difference. The writers supported this particular direction and individuals. They were part of a media, and then the art market picked up on this, you know? How many writers today are doing this? If you read any article about what's going on today in the arts, how much you become the power of the kind of Greenberg or Rosenberg. And no one's taking this on these days.... They were involved with the, what do you call that — hype! Constant racial hype, of the time. And now the writers today are doing that. Very clever. Very clever. They made the Abstract Expressionist movement. Writers, now. The written word became the power there ... writers have a lot to do with it. The media, how much is involved, it becomes a — public hype. Helen Frankenthaler. I knew Helen Frankenthaler!

You know everyone.

Mayhew: No, not really.

Some people say that she was with Greenberg, and that's why she became very well known, and perhaps — you weren't with Greenberg, as far as I know! As far as I know, you weren't Greenberg's lover.

Mayhew: She was on the inside track of colleagues, okay? Which support each other. This is all their work.

The question is, why this one Abstract Expressionist canon? Is this a false direction? To try to figure out, why not Mayhew? I'm curious about today, at the MOMA. I wonder why this man is not as well known. It's in the canon, but it's not quite as well known. Maybe it doesn't matter why.

Mayhew: I don't know if you've looked at many. If you're talking about Ed Clark, a fantastic painter! He's still not at the level of success he should be.

No.

Mayhew: Right? And he's internationally known! He's known all over Europe, and in the United States, and he's in all the prominent collections, but he still doesn't have the accolades he deserves.

Perhaps — perhaps it doesn't really matter.

Mayhew: Well, it really matters. It matters in terms of the contributions society will accept as inspiration and stimulation and functional creative consciousness.

The public desire for some kind of destructive ...

Mayhew: Public desire ... the public is controlled by the hype! Conceptual art form, performance art — which I did for a long time — it's a whole procedure. And also in academia, those involved with the whole thing, the combined art element — it's integrated study. Of the arts.

The music, and having dancers ...

Mayhew: It started on the Lower East Side of New York. I could get more involved in that, but the way you're questioning now, it has to do with acceptance, and how much any artist is accepted, because of the media or direction of the time. Actually, conceptual art has faded out; it's been fading for quite a period of time. When I did a lecture in the Middle East, they didn't understand why the different directions of art forms from every decade keep changing. Their culture remains consistent. And so the change is not there. They couldn't understand why the constant changing, from Realism, Surrealism, Abstract Expressionism, Impressionism, Magic Realism — how much the constant changing, and computer art, and conceptual art, and performance art — they didn't understand the change. I said it reflects society at the time. Now, how much it's a reflection of style today, in our society, is projected in some degree — that it's involved with a certain decadence! And the decadence is reflected in the art form! Which is excellent ... it's in writing, it's in music, [it's] in all different areas.

I have to find a way to determine why you were omitted to some degree.

Mayhew: Because it's up to a historian to categorize a particular artist! And this is what's been going on all the time! What historian or writer of the time would be involved with making the point about this particular artist in this particular direction, or the contribution of this, or the importance of this, or the denial of it. Right?

I think — my theory is, it's racism, pure and simple. It goes back to what you said about Faith Ringgold's art.

Mayhew: Right. Oh, I respect her for what she's doing. And also Jacob Lawrence. They were only accepted by the media, and this is what African-American art is. That's where they put it! African-American artists. Now Faith Ringgold was considered an African-American artist.

That's racism to some degree, and I think that's why critics have trouble with your art.

Mayhew: Well, the dominant culture is involved with maintaining the status quo, and if they start accepting the power of the subculture as being equal to their culture, then they start to lose the foothold control in terms of the dominant movement of thinking and ideas. All the books in academia about mathematics, about science and so forth, it's always leaning to the area of the dominant culture, in control. And so, as a result, the sensibility of the so-called minorities or the so-called subcultures never reached a level of equal development. I hope I live long enough to see multicultural government involved in multicultural creative consciousness of society.

As a woman, I feel the same way.

Mayhew: Well that's it! Actually, as a woman, all over the world, maybe this society is the only one that has women reaching a point of some kind of credibility in level of functioning. Because all the women wearing gowns and covered heads and so forth, goes back to medieval time, medieval society! Women are involved with a subservient kind of society! In every society! No matter how much the United States and parts of Europe where women have been liberated to the point where they're able to reach a level of equal functioning as a person. Not in terms of women or a man, but as a person. In our society, it's still, mmm, and in academia, the woman gets less money than the male, in the same subject. How come? How is that controlled? How is the art controlled? It's the same thing. Who controls this? Has to do with the women in our society, and how much a woman becomes the president? If a woman becomes the president, is she still a male president? You're not a feminist [if you have that power], right? Which are more concerned about society than males are, because of their kind of dominant thinking, and mannerisms. I'm wondering, they're talking about a woman becoming president, I said, women have become president in other societies! In India, and also now in South America. But they're completely controlled by the male dominant thinking. Women in this society have become prominent top artists. Who is the prominent top woman? Helen Frankenthaler. The media makes her the prominent [one]. Right? (Laughs) And she goes back to the late '50s, early '60s. Right.

I want to talk about your childhood influences and your teachers, and some other artists who might have influenced you. You've mentioned that your grandmother had an affect on you.

Mayhew: Well, actually I wasn't aware of it then, but the influence certainly was a part of it. She was encouraging what I was doing. I was drawing and sketching all the time. Even my schoolteachers, my elementary school teachers were curious about what I was doing. Very interested in it, and supportive of my scribblings, right? And then my grandmother used to give me books and magazines —*Apollo* magazine. Which is still published in England, an art and antique magazine. Right. So I used to browse through these and see different art forms and inspiration there.

Do you remember anything in particular?

Mayhew: Looking back ... it has to do with creative ambition.

Mmm.

Mayhew: And to make things, and do things, right. It was part of that creative activity. It was like a nervous desire, almost.

Sure.

Mayhew: Right. She used to save the brown paper bag because I could draw on it. I like it now, that paper's fantastic! (Laughs) To draw on. And the media works out; you can work on it very well. The print on the page was nothing but print — no pictures or anything on there. And the graffiti of the print would create a certain grayish background, and I used to work into that! That was fun. I know Kline did a lot of his black-and-white paintings on newspaper. He had this background effect along with the black scrolling and the graffiti, right? (Laughs)

What about ... is there a connection between you and Hudson River School landscape?

Mayhew: Well, in the summers the Hudson River painters used to come to the Long Island coast, and paint by the water. I used to go and sit and watch them, right? I was curious to see them! Dipping their brushes in the paint and the images showing up on the canvas, the magic wand. You know?

Yeah, yeah!

(Mayhew laughs)

How old were you?

Mayhew: Oh, thirteen, fourteen, I guess. Twelve, you know. And then, one of them, because I was sitting there so much, watching — I think it was out of patronage — he said, "Oh, I'll give him a brush, see what he does," right.

(Both laugh)

Mayhew: So they, there's some talent here! Yeah, right? So he wanted — so in summers he would take me on as an apprentice, so that was good. I don't know whether there was any prejudice involved. But the artists didn't seem to have any, right? They were just encouraging this young man to do this. And also medical illustrations — I have done medical illustrations! He was a medical illustrator as well as a Hudson River painter.

Who is this?

Mayhew: James Wilson. Later on I found out it was James Wilson Peale. It was just the summer association, and drawings, and so forth.

How could you be doing medical illustration when you were fourteen? Is that later?

Mayhew: No, that's what it was, the books made a mistake that this was very much later, in the '60s. It wasn't. It was very early.

I brought some images of your work. Those are drawings.

Mayhew: Yeah. Full-length drawings.

That's gorgeous.

Mayhew: Right. Mmm-hmm. That was included in a drawing book: how one is involved with certain techniques, right. Mmm-hmm.

It's beautiful. My first question relates to things that critics have said about your work.

Mayhew: Hmmm. Confusion. (Both laugh)

Absolutely.

Mayhew: You're right. Right. They don't know what category to put me in. Whether I'm an Impressionist, and whether, in the early years, they said I was a reflection and involved with the Barbizon school, right.

Right. And an American Impressionist. Ryder.

Mayhew: Yes.

And then Inness, right?

Mayhew: But I feel that the comparison to Courbet makes a lot of sense, because of his social orientation.

There's also how much direct [plein-air painting is involved], because none of the Impressionists worked direct[ly] in their subject matter.

Mayhew: Well, I respect Impressionists. That's why I went to Europe, to study the Impressionists. Because of the association with that sensitivity. Right. Also, after they broke from the Salon — the dictation of how one had to work at a certain time. I was related to them in the sense of being rebels. And somewhat independent, right … [with respect to] the work they wanted to do. It reflected the era, right.

And it seems to me that in Courbet's work there's an acknowledgment of social inequality. But it's not explicit.

Mayhew: Right.

And that's what I see in your philosophy.

Mayhew: I was a still-life painter for a while. But this I thought you'd like to see.

Oh, wow! That's fantastic. Johnson's Dying Unafraid, *based on people with terminal illness. Wow.*

Mayhew: And this is the author. She's a good friend. (Laughs)

Wow.

Mayhew: I'll show you some of my influences. Right here. American Impressionists! Right here. William [Harnet]. Trompe l'oeil. He paints on the wall, but contemporary, like wire hangers, and pieces of paper of the time—

That doesn't seem like your work at all.

Mayhew: But that's the way I painted! It actually was like this! Things hanging on the wall … a brick wall, peeling and cracking, and so forth, right?

You were looking, you were observing very closely.

Mayhew: Well, it was mainly involved with memorabilia. Like Betye Saar? Only I was using things of that time. It was early. And there's another one, Piko, but he's not in here.

What do you make of Betye Saar's work?

Mayhew: Ummm, aaah, folk art.

All right then.

Mayhew: Here. My influences.

Albert Ryder. I can see that, very clearly. Sure. Ryder.

Mayhew: And Blakelock. Ralph Blakelock.

Absolutely, I can see your work in Blakelock.

Mayhew: So there was an influence there. And certainly Inness. George Inness, was really.

George Inness, absolutely.

Mayhew: He was my mentor, in a sense, right?

Sure. It almost seems as though — it's ironic to me, it's surprising and ironic. It almost seems to me that you draw a distinction between fine art and what you describe as primitive or folk.

Mayhew: Mmm-hmm.

That surprises me, that you do that.

Mayhew: Well, you say primitive — you have to define that, because that's been [a] misnomer for years — well, you see Bannister.

Oh, yes. Bannister. Absolutely.

Mayhew: It came out in the text. It came out in the fact about why they put him in there — well, anyway, I won't get into it. (Laughs) How many African-American artists were accepted in the early years, right? Oh, here's George Inness. This was really my mentor. (Laughs)

Oh, my goodness. Yes, I can see why.

Mayhew: Not so much that, but his later work, which is more mystical.

Ahh. Especially this, Sunset at Mt. Claire.

Mayhew: And the later years, right. Mmm-hmm.

Sure. There's an echo of Love Bush *right there, in* Red Oak.

Mayhew: These are American Impressionists! All members of the National Academy, which was shocking! (Laughs)

Your work has also been compared to that of Monet. What do you make of that?

Mayhew: Oh, yeah, well, there is that, yeah. All of the Impressionists, and how they executed their work. Monet was involved with, never [a] real direct intake of the subject. It was this kind of mystique. And it's actually related to that, more than anything else.

The mystique of it. Some critics have described your work as like Tanner's, because of the quality of light.

Mayhew: Oh, Tanner. I would have liked to have gotten involved with more Tanner work. Because he worked impasto. Very thick application of paint. The control of that is quite unique.

Did that draw you to Tanner?

Mayhew: The uniqueness of it, and the impasto control of application. I was concerned about technique. And I was impressed by his control and illusion. Because if you look at his painting closely, there's not much detail at all.

Critics also describe you as a superb technician. What do you make of that?

Mayhew: No, no. It's [to] some degree because I started working with a palette knife, and no one [painting] looks like I've been working with a palette knife. So that's, there must be some master control of the technique—

(Hess laughs)

Mayhew: Not necessarily, right. (Laughs) Because I work with the brush and the palette knife, combination. It is involved with impasto application. I've worked more direct[ly], like Tanner did. He worked directly right in with a heavy thick impasto paint, not like I do. I kind of underpaint, and then I build up, right. He did it directly. And I've always admired that. (Laughs)

Did you feel it was difficult to go against what seemed to be the norm of Abstract Expressionism and do landscape?

Mayhew: That's the dictation of the media and people of the time. They said, "This is the way you should paint." And I was so caught up in trying, with my Native-American influence—they didn't realize how heavy it was, Native American and African American. Recently I did a talk about that: the combination had become one. It's one culture, in terms of the dedication to the earth, and the sensitivity of nature. It was subconscious that I got more dedicated to this and challenged by it, driving across the United States six times. Three over and three times back.

And each time I drove, I felt it wasn't enough. Because I really didn't understand until the next time I went over.

So you had to do it.

Mayhew: And what I saw, observing, the feeling of nature. Phenomenal. The neglect of the dedication of people who are involved with this. The treaties — the more I got involved with Native-American culture, all this land, it's respected and supported by Native Americans, but they get no credit for it, or no respect for it. The fact that, this is their land! But it's no longer their land because it's owned by others (laughs). And so there's this feeling in going through the Rockies, in going through the desert, and that's why I adopted California, because it has everything.

(Laughs) It certainly does.

Mayhew: It has all the possible terrain factors, right. Mmm-hmm.

It sounds like you didn't necessarily feel criticized or excluded because of the landscape.

Mayhew: No, I didn't mean to be avoiding your question (laughs); it's that this was a dedication that haunted me. I wanted to master it in some way. My paintings became very abstract, in some way. And this was part of the nature that was involved with this very free feeling. Right? But then I found that it was depicting, sometimes, the mystique of what was going on. It was maybe sometime avoiding the mystique of the foliage, and the feeling of that. Like the shadows in the trees, over there. It's the mystery about what's going on in there. Right. And then, uh — because I, I went to uh, one of the plantations in the South.

Oh.

Mayhew: And I was looking at the foliage in the trees around the place. I said, "Whatever happened in that spot over there?"

Mmm.

Mayhew: Right.

Mmm-hmm.

Mayhew: And, uh, so, I got involved with a very haunting kind of mystery kind of feeling when I was there. The ghost of the past was plaguing me. So I had to leave. I left. I didn't stay there.

Mmm.

Mayhew: But then again, that's my subconscious feeling was that. Thinking, right?

Mmm-hmm.

Mayhew: And the fact that this was a plantation which was involved with a lot of oppression.

Horror. A lot of horror.

Mayhew: And so that was the identity that I had in terms of being there. So across the country I had to deal with all of the feeling of nature. Traveling around Europe, it's bland compared to the United States! Unbelievable. Actually, three countries is the size of one state! And couldn't imagine it! Because going across France, it didn't take that long. But going across Pennsylvania or Ohio, that's longer! I said, "Oh, that's strange," feeling about this, right? (Laughs)

[Asks question about a statement on Mayhew's work from Henderson and Bearden]

Mayhew: How does one make statements, you know? I've made statements that I've regretted. Several times, right. And regretted it on the basis of the fact that sometimes [they] were taken out of context. And that wasn't the full meaning, right?

No, that's actually why, in my [first] book, I quoted you verbatim … there's a danger when you begin to—

Mayhew: Mm-hmmm. When you are narrowing it down. Right.

There's a danger that … anyway! Henderson says that you experienced a kind of visual homesickness when you moved from Long Island to New York. And that may have been part of this issue of landscape.

Mayhew: When I moved from Long Island?

To New York City.

Mayhew: Oh. Well, I was very young, extremely young. And that is misinterpreted with the fact that I was involved with medical illustration. I was involved with medical illustration when I was fourteen, fifteen, sixteen, seventeen years old. Not twenty and thirty years old, which they associated with me, that's not true. Because I studied — he died before I was in my twenties, when I was working with him.

So there's not really a sense that you moved toward landscape because you were homesick.

Mayhew: No. I was a still-life painter!

(Laughs) Okay.

Mayhew: A portrait painter! I was a commercial portrait painter. I painted the Grossinger family, and also Neville Hotel, I don't know if you know about the borscht circuit. And the Grossingers. That's the borscht circuit, you don't know? That's where everything happened before Las Vegas.

Is that in the Catskills?

Mayhew: That's right! So I went and I painted a family up there, also I sang up there. I was part of a whole thing. Right. Painting portraits. Which was part of— just in painting the faces, it was more of a spiritual connection to the person. Like my friend does. Nelson Shanks. He's involved with the spirit of the individual when he paints. Then I did still life! I was fascinated by, what Betye Saar is involved with. Memorabilia. All the things around that particular time, the things my grandmother used to have on her dresser, or something like that, I could make that, right? Especially things like a wire hanger, contemporary, right? And I had rags and cloths hanging from the wire hanger. And I painted a hammer and chisel hanging from the wall. It was like in a workshop, right?

What happened to all those paintings?

Mayhew: A couple showed up recently on auction. One was I did, it was, the first ... an old boarded fence, and a chicken had laid eggs in there, right? (Laughs) That showed up at auction, a friend of mine [Ed Littlejohn] bought it. (Laughs)

Wow. What did it sell for? A lot?

Mayhew: Practically nothing! (Laughs) Because no one thought that was my work. He called me, he said, this is your name, is this your work? And I wrote back and said, "Yes." He said, "Oh really?" (Laughs) He got it for a song. He bought it! It was worth, like, $10,000; he got it for $300. (Laughs) I said, you gonna sell it to me? He said, "Yeah, for the right price." (Laughs) But he said he would give it to me. Right. He has one of the best self-portraits I've ever done. I did the cover of his book. There were portraits of all the judges and lawyers that he did a book about. In Michigan. I did the cover with portraits, right? (Laughs)

That's a thread in your work. Henderson says that your training as a medical illustrator, when you had an internship, restricted your creativity.

Mayhew: I did a book on the circulatory system.

Well, he said that that confined you, it made it difficult for you, in your work.

Mayhew: No. Who said that? Bearden, no. Henderson, maybe.

Right. Henderson. I'm just trying to clear it up.

Mayhew: Being a medical illustrator made it difficult for me to paint? No.

(Laughs) It didn't sound right to me.

Mayhew: That's an assumption, right? How would that make it difficult?

Because it was so rigid, and—

Mayhew: Oh, no, that was what I had to break away from in the beginning. I was working as an anatomist. I can draw a figure upside down backwards right now. I can close my eyes and do a figure. Much early control over anatomy. And I taught anatomy at the League for a while.

But did that restrict your creativity?

Mayhew: No! It broadens your sensitivity. And why I stopped doing figure painting — it wasn't spiritual enough. It identified in a particular moment of a particular thing and a particular image. So I broke away from that and a rigidity that I didn't want to be involved with. But I still love to do it because it's so facile, so easy for me to do it. I can make up a figure, right now. With models I've seen long years ago. In fact, I have one. I just did one to see if I can still do that. (Laughs)

The March on Washington. 1963. All of the literature about you goes back to that, and Spiral's founding. I wanted to ask you to reflect on what that meant for you. In Bearden's text, he says that the two critical questions that you felt Spiral was about, were how relevant is what we're doing to the struggles of black people, and how honest is what you are doing. What does that mean?

Mayhew: He said the struggles of black people, and how honest one is in terms of creative sensitivity. How much they're involved with creative aesthetics, right? How much they're involved with honest internal sensitivity, which comes out of their cultural background. And how much they identify with the reality of who they are. Instead of mimicking what is fashionable in the market. And how much they were Abstract Expressionists based on the Abstractionists of the particular era. Their education came out of a European education salon, right? Some of the ones I studied with were students of the Royal Academy. Easel painting is European. As opposed to other cultures.

But that's what you do.

Mayhew: Right. Well, that's easel painting. It's a matter of having it involved with a smaller context instead of doing a tapestry, or a weaving. Things like that, or painting on skin. Which Native Americans did.

And also Africans did. Right?

Mayhew: Mmm-hmm.

Mmm-hmm.

Mayhew: So this is more contained, which can be moved around, from one place to another. Which is part of the European thing. Which seems very practical. Ah, and also the fact that, it became a commodity — right? Which in the early years of the others it wasn't a commodity, it was a ritual thing they were doing, right? So how much one is involved with their contemporary influence, based on their background, and mine was a combination of the two, which I felt became one. Native American and African American for me became one culture. Somebody says, African American is based on African heritage. African after five hundred years became a new tribe.

African Americans. And how much you're involved with a whole other sensibility, because of that. Even though their ancestors did come from Africa. But after five hundred years, involved with a whole other cultural sensitivity, and functioning, very close to Native Americans, native to the land. Very dedicated to the land. And survival. Much involved with creative survival. So how much is coming from their works, and each of these artists, how much they are involved with doing this. Norman Lewis, he was really, in his abstractions, was very close to that kind of sensitivity, even though some of his work was based on music. But there again, it was based on jazz, in a sense.

What does this have to do with the Civil Rights Movement, and the March on Washington?

Mayhew: Well, there again, that's narrowing it down to a limited thing. The Civil Rights Movement goes back to when these people were born. You're thinking just the '60s, that's the Civil Rights Movement.

I'm thinking about Spiral's beginning.

Mayhew: But Spiral — these people, as I said, get involved with the aesthetics of reality. Who they are is not just the '60s. It was their whole life as an Afro-American.

So Spiral was not a sense of, let's form a movement that responds to Martin Luther King and the Civil Rights Movement.

Mayhew: No. It was a concept, intellectual consciousness of who they are as a creative person. That's it.

But why then do all of the books link the March on Washington in 1963 to your involvement in Spiral?

Mayhew: Because of Martin Luther King.

Why?

Mayhew: Not Martin Luther King's march! It was our march.

Ah.

Mayhew: And so a lot of that — completely false! Erroneous, right?

So you would not say that the March on Washington was this watershed moment when Spiral said, we must respond to this.

Mayhew: Well, Phillip Randolph called Hale Woodruff, whom he respected, and also Romare Bearden ... would they form a contingent of artists for the March on Washington? That's what it was all about. So what'd they do? They called each other to get together and talk about this. As a contingent. Now that had nothing to do with just the Civil Rights Movement, in a sense, but in terms of coming together, and when they came together, they realized they were involved with a challenge of aesthetics and the creative process of African-American artists. So they got involved heavily in terms of the consciousness of creative thinking. Who are you as a creative person? Are you mimicking European culture because you've learned the technique and process? How is that reflected in your art? This is what Spiral was ... it was the challenge of the creative process.

Could you discuss the fence, the paintings from the fence in 1959?

Mayhew: Well, it was Jacob Lawrence and Ernie Crichlow, and myself. We exhibited on the fence, in a little park in the center of the area right there [Bedford-Styvesent]. On the fence, to communicate the art of the African-American artists of the community!

And you've always done that!

Mayhew: I've always done that. But not only that ... my painting, I felt, was a self-indulged joy of living. I felt that that was the communication I wanted to give to the community. So I went, and I was involved with several activities, such as an outreach program like a Center for the Arts for the community. When I came to California, I helped establish the Creative Center for the Arts and Science in Marin County. And several other special projects I've been involved with in the community. This was the activity other than my self-indulged joy.

Do you feel that this interpretation of Spiral members, as thinking about how they wanted to be like African artists, is wrong?

Mayhew: They were involved with creative aesthetics and the creative process. And how much in terms of being black, or being white, is how much the white artists were reflecting their cultural background! And their influences! African-American artists, they felt, had to really deal with the reality of what are you doing. Are you mimicking? Or are you truly involved with the commitment of yourself?

But it's not, let's be like the African artists in working with others.

Mayhew: No. It wasn't about — it was really dealing with aesthetics.

Okay.

Mayhew: Well, you have all the heavies there — I mean, these were the great mentors of African-American artists! These are great people! That came out of the Harlem Renaissance. The youngsters that came in, such as myself— there was also, which is neglected sometimes, Hinds! One of the greatest conservators! He was the head conservator for the Hirschhorn Collection. Belworth Hinds. Fantastic artist. He was a great American artist. But he never exhibited his work very much. That was his indulgence, right? Self-indulged, creative process. And his work was as a conservator. But he always wanted to be known as an artist, because most conservators are technicians. I'm an artist, right? (Laughs)

Right.

Mayhew: I did a lecture, and I didn't know he was in the audience, and I was talking about Hinds, one of the great conservators and so forth, and at the end he grabbed me. (Laughs) "I'm a painter!" [he said.] "Remember that next time!" (Laughs) And he became one of my closest friends. In terms of technique, I was learning about application of paint, and the technique. He was a hard-edged painter, and the paintings were so smooth, and the edges were clean without him even putting tape around it. How he could do that! Right? And the paint was so flat and smooth! How — what kind of medium was he using, you know? (Laughs) And his studio was immaculate. No dust. (Laughs)

How did he do that?

Mayhew: Well, a conservator, right? (Laughs) But he was of a great mind. Very brilliant man. Very dapper. Right? Very distinguished manner, right? Always composed. Never down, being foolish or anything like that. He was always right on. But so was Hale Woodruff! Great respect for them, right. Also, you know, there's Emma Amos, and Merton Simpson! Merton Simpson was part of the original group, right? And they forget about him! Fantastic painter! He's a composer, and a saxophone player, great one. He composed music for the eulogy of Romare Bearden. The memorial.

Interesting how there's this thread of music in Spiral.

Mayhew: It's part of the nature of African-American culture! Native-American culture has another kind of sensitivity. Not necessarily based in music. But the African American is involved with that, right. It's part of— it was also part of slave survival! They could sing songs and the white slaveowners didn't know what they were talking about. Right? It was part of a freedom! The gospel music was part of that, right? Like that song, "All God's Children Got Shoes?" "When we get to heaven we're gonna get shoes/gonna dance all over God's heaven?" That was Canada. (Laughs)

Henderson talks about some of your different community efforts, and one of them is Ramapo Mountain. You told me once that that really didn't work out in the end.

Mayhew: Well, what happened — it has to do with the power of control of the dominant culture. Dictation. After we went there and we set up the whole program and activity, going on and going off into the community and getting them involved with their own [Iroquois] art, we built a cultural center in a geodesic dome, very modern kind of form there, right, which was their cultural center. Then we went back — it was filled with cement and sand. Never used as a cultural center. Because it drifted back into the way they were! A completely divided community. Which is part of the oppression of the dominant culture — divide and conquer and control.

Does that discourage you? Does that mean activism doesn't work?

Mayhew: No, it's just how dominant the control of the dominant culture is, in terms of African Americans and Native Americans. Native Americans, you know — you're not an Indian unless you, uh —

Right. One-thirty-second, or —

Mayhew: Hmm?

Unless you're one-thirty-second —

Mayhew: No, no, it has nothing to do with that at all. It has to do with the government giving you a card, the fact that you are Native American.

Right. You're registered.

Mayhew: If you're not registered Native American, you're not Native American. All these people are Native American, not half Native American but Native American, but cannot claim being Native American because if they do that, they can claim land rights. That's the reason. And that's the reason why normal media is controlled, and you never see them in the news. You never see them in any other area. Not in the movies except in the Westerns, right? This history … you have to realize, within five hundred years, Native American and African American have become one. When I did a lecture, I think I talked about that, at the Smithsonian; half the audience was black. I was talking about my cultural background, Native American, that I'm actually more Native American than I am Afro-American. But in fact, I said, how many in the audience, African Americans in the audience, are Native Americans? Everyone put up their hand. Everyone. I said, how come we don't know about the history of how this happened? There is nothing written about it. And it's always squashed.

Why?

Mayhew: Property. This land right here is Native American land. That you're sitting on.

But if you're one-thirty-second Native American, you can register.

Mayhew: Yeah, but you're talking about blood drops. That has to do with the fact that you have a casino which is more successful than Las Vegas. (Laughs) And they're part black. Fifty percent. And then the Seminoles, okay? The Cherokee! And the Crow! There are hundreds of tribes which were part black. But also, Afro-Americans. We want to know, where's the history? How does this happen? And it has to do with the secret passages and helping each other back and forth through the years, the early years. They used to actually shelter slaves, and hide them, and African Americans helping Native Americans fight battles. Even though they had a group that fought with the French and English against the Indians. Which is a part of the controlling factor that went on earlier. But the wedding together of the support of this, the cultural background was close. It's the land. The forty acres and a mule they never got. (Laughs) And the treaties which have not been honored. Like the end of Long Island. The Montaugs. Or the Hamptons, right? (Laughs) Native-American land. The treaty rights, the fact that all of the end of Long Island belongs to the Indians. But the property is owned by neo–European culture. They can only get the tax from the land that they're on. But that's not going to happen. (Laughs) This is a part of the cultural background — it's how much one is constantly involved with dealing with a reality. You're talking about civil rights. The civil rights of Native Americans and African Americans are wedded ... but all you hear about is African Americans. You never hear about Native Americans. Because, you see, there's not that many. There's not that many that they register, right? There are millions of African American and Native Americans. Millions. You can't imagine that. (Laughs) Did you ever see the map of all the tribes of the United States?

You've shown me a map. It's amazing.

Mayhew: Oh yeah. They're still here. (Laughs) The ancestors are still here. And those coming across the border. Okay? Native American coming home. There's a tribe that lives on the border, on both sides of the border down there, that they've blocked now for them coming back across the border. You know, because this is part of their family, back and forth, right? They've blocked them now, when they come across the border now, they're considered Mexican. This is the history that I live with. And it's part of the cultural thing when I'm painting the landscape. There's a mystique here, of a special spiritual mood and form, space and subject. Each tree is like images of these people. Each little pattern and form and shape. There's a spirit here that goes on with that. Spiral was involved with an analysis of what was going on. They're questioning each other. Really brilliant conversation used to go on. Mmm-hmm. And sometimes you get involved with this mediocre kind of dozens playing. Which is natural. (Laughs) But then it gets down to basics, the importance of why we came together.

Well, if there's this kind of blending, what is African-American art? If it's indistinguishable from Native-American art, what is African-American art?

Mayhew: What is African-American art? You want to define it in terms of Romare Bearden and Jacob Lawrence. Right, now think about it! What would you think is African-American art?

Ah … art made by African Americans.

Mayhew: (Laughs) Would you think of them being American artists? You would put them in a different category? Putting them in a separate category, they don't consider them American artists, the African-American artists.

But you gave a talk called, "What is African American Art?" or something of that nature, so that's why I'm asking you that.

Mayhew: What is African American art? It is based on those individuals, in terms of—what is White art? What would you say, what is White art? That's what I talked about in my lecture.

The art of the dominant culture.

Mayhew: That's right. And the dominant culture is not necessarily involved with their cultural heritage. This is what we were pointing out. We had this discussion with several contemporary artists — de Kooning, Motherwell, Kline — right? Well, I had one with Motherwell. He was [a] very brilliant man. He was talking about how much they're involved with the decadence of contemporary society, and you reflecting that. Whoa. (Laughs) That was a great summation, right? The fact that you're reflecting and projecting, because art does that. It reflects and projects the time. And how much it was going through constant changing, development, in the '60s. Actually, '40s, '50s , '60s. In the '70s it started to change. Right.

Mm-hmm.

Mayhew: Computer art was then, and social realism was always there, but magic realism started during at that time. And that's part of the hard-edged painting, a cross-section from the '60s into the '70s, right. Again, reflecting the constant change in society. He defined it, it was how much [one is] involved with the positive element in society — also the decadence in that society.

That would be the African-American artists?

Mayhew: The decadence: No, no, he was talking about white artists. He was talking about the white artists.

How would you define African-American artists?

Mayhew: African-American artists are in the middle of a massive culture, right? They're defining their own sensibility, but also influenced by the dominant culture at the same time. It's hard to divorce yourself from your environment.

Of course.

Mayhew: So it's part of their environment. We were dealing with that reality. Excellent discussions. Sometimes, whew! (Laughs) Way over your head. And then, all of them were over their head. Bring it down to a reality of some sensibility of what's happening, was how we thought, right? This was in the '60s–'62, '63, '64. And then we started separating.

Was there some title for these talks, or?

Mayhew: No.

You just hang out in the bar, or?

Mayhew: No. We had a center, on the West Side. At first we used to meet in all of our studios and have these discussions. But then they got down to aesthetic realities: Who are you? Why are you painting the way you paint? And that would pin people down; they'd say, "Well, I'm, I'm, you know—" (Laughs)

(Laughs) Right.

Mayhew: You have to think about, why are you painting the way you paint? What were your influences? Is it a special technique? Who'd you study with? And so forth. I studied with a lot of people! Well, there again, there's a myth. I didn't study with Hans Hoffman and Max Beckmann. I visited their classes. I monitored their classes, let's say. And that was good, to see that. I wanted to see what they were doing and what they were thinking. The whole German thing, and the exile, and also the oppression, and, how he was thinking, and how he painted. Also Hans Hoffman; he was part of some of that background influence, and how he was working. And his abstraction. And Joseph Albers, also. What he was doing with his work with pure color and emphasis on illusion, right. All of that became part of my sensibility.

Okay.

Mayhew: So that's part of your thinking, is what these artists are thinking and what they are painting. And I was involved with the Educational Alliance, Lower East Side, which is part of the group of social realists down there. Soyer became very close friends. And looking at my work, you kind of understand what I was doing. I knew what he was doing. And his influences, his social comment, right?

You're harder to figure out.

Mayhew: This [is] where I started to break away from just being a painter. And the Educational Alliance. I went there and I was doing a lecture, with slides, to a group of students in the area. And they came to hear my lecture and they were bored to tears, with, you know, slides, lectures, like, "Oh-ho" … Like, "Oh, big deal."

(Laughs)

Mayhew: Next door to me was a jazz group playing, on the other side was a rehearsal place down there, where you could use the center, a dance company rehearsing. I brought the dancers in, and I brought the musicians in. And that was the beginning of my multicultural development in the arts. I started teaching that at Hunter; I taught it in California at Sonoma State. It was a design class in multicultural art form.

You ran away. You stopped doing it. Why did you stop teaching there?

Mayhew: Because they didn't accept it. When I went to Penn State, it was the culture of the arts and science. Not just the arts.

Did you have trouble doing your work when you were teaching at the university?

Mayhew: No. Well, this is what Hale Woodruff told me. He said, "Be careful. Teaching is a creative process. Don't let it interfere with your art process." And I have never forgot that. He said, "You pull a curtain between your classroom and your art, you've made it. You can't — you're in trouble."

And you managed to do that.

Mayhew: That's what Woodruff told me. And I remembered to do that. So I was doing very well — I was creating very well, and functioning — I was the only one at many schools who was exhibiting outside the university. I was part of the loop; they were not. I never thought of it that way, but when I went there — that was the reason they accepted me as a professor at the universities, the fact that I was involved with this outside area, right? Not at Sonoma State. I was a threat there.

What about department politics? What about academic politics?

Mayhew: Academic politics has to do with the dominant culture! The dominant culture is in control of all the books. Someone said, "Why don't we have all the children go see the books in the library?" One day I told the students that and they looked at me and said, "Whoah!" (Laughs) Because they said, it's a dictation of a limitation of a certain culture.

Why are you talking to me then? Because I am a white academic.

Mayhew: You are a white academic, but you understand the broader concept. That's the difference. Those in academia certainly have to adhere to the structure and format. I was on a lot of doctoral committees. A Native American, she was writing about the aesthetics and sensitivity of Native Americans. I said, "There's no books to validate what you are doing, you know?" This is how much academia controls that concept. It doesn't allow for the subculture to become part of stronger academic and literary contribution.

But where does the white academic have a role in that?

Mayhew: Your government. Say, the government, don't say academics. How much your thinking can challenge that system. Which you do, you are doing it, really, in many ways. If you're teaching African and African-American culture, that's challenging the system. And you finding other insights which are not in the books — if you're just doing it from the books and how they talk about African art? And African culture, then that's white historians doing that. But if you were a little beyond what they're writing about and what they wrote about, that's making the difference. And eventually you would get into the curriculum or get into the books in the libraries. But not now — it's not there. I was on one of the committees to read over some of the books in terms of inclusion, right? And I looked and they just changed the paragraphs around. (Laughs)

People will say, "You're white. You don't know what you're talking about."

Mayhew: Well, they're only saying that you're coming out of the dominant culture, which dictates what they're thinking. And how much you're able to bridge that gap. It's hard, because I know a lot of white historians and white artists who have crossed over. They know. But they can't influence the larger picture. So when they look at you, they look at you as the dominant culture. How much you can convince them is hard, the fact that you are beyond the norm of the dictates of the dominant culture.

But do you think that effort would be better spent trying to live — to help — trying to extend help? Would that be a better use of time?

Mayhew: Well, it's a matter of being able to do that. You know the bridge. You might be able to walk across the bridge; you end up in the center of the bridge. To be able to cross over, then you're the rebel. Right? (Laughs) Once you cross over, you're the rebel. But if you're in the middle of the bridge, you come bouncing both sides, placating, you see, both sides.

Mm-hmm. I think I'm in the middle. (Laughs)

Mayhew: You have to be! In academia, this is what my problem was, right? I was a thorn in their side, always, right? And also teaching interdisciplinary study of the arts and science! They were not ready for that! They didn't even understand what the hell I was doing! I presented the program to staff it, they understood, what they were saying was, they didn't want to bring anybody in from the outside to teach this. They wanted internal. I said, "Okay, you do it internally, and give me credit for contribution to it." They wouldn't even let me do that. Okay? Because there again, it's the Afro-American influence. Making it different in terms of their concept. If I can write about this, it'll make a difference. All the teaching was — I was constantly, the last in control. At Hunter, what I was teaching there was interdisciplinary study of the arts. It has to do with theater, music, dance, individualized. And I used the — my class, I took it out of Hunter and took it to the Manhattan Theater Club. Which is about three blocks away. On the East Side. And I met with Moses [unintelligible], the famous black actor, he died recently, close friend. And he helped me over there, in terms of the mindset, right? Of image illusion. Of gesture and illusion, right? Also, I studied with [a] French mime master. He was in my studio. I have a studio here and he brought his studio in, and I heard something banging, and gesturing. I went down and saw him, and he went [makes a face and laughs]. Didn't say anything! And I'm entrenched with the mimes! So I understood the illusion of gesture and movement, right? Which is part of illusion — visual illusion. That's part of my cultural development. And that's part of why I got involved with — I'd like to do performances. Like I used to do, dancers and musicians.

You're a great lecturer.

Mayhew: That's fantastic to do that. And I kind of live there, right? So my visual art, as I said in my discussion, that's my personal indulgence! (Laughs) It's a selfish indulgence! And so those people ... well, the fact that you share with others, that's part of the joy of painting, is you can share it. Right. (Laughs) Or writing, same thing.

Right. Sharing it. Or music, right.

Mayhew: Right. Theoretically, you're sharing it. (Laughs)

(Both looking at images painted by Mayhew)

That's Forty Acres and a Mule.

Mayhew: *Forty Acres and a Mule.* After I painted it, I felt that this is part of the land, the treaty rights which were never honored, and the forty acres and a mule that African Americans never received after Reconstruction.

This intense purple here — what's that about?

Mayhew: It has to do with the shadows as part of the mystery, that subtle area of sensitivity which is never really revealed and ones of hidden feelings of thought.

Mm-hmm. Right.

Mayhew: Like the shadows in the trees over there.

Mm-hmm.

Mayhew: What's going on in there? This is part of the sensitivity of that, right. It's really in there.

And this light blue, to me, or this violet?

Mayhew: It has to do with a feeling of space, and it creates a certain sensitivity of space. But I do it more in relationship to color interaction. What's happening here, and the color there. How much it ended up in terms of landscape feeling, but it's a constant play on color all the time. And shapes. The shape here becomes important to me — each area, shape is important. It reveals a certain feeling. Sometimes the shadows on the face becomes it, right?

Mm-hmm. Okay. Thank you. What about Serenity*? It's very abstract.*

Mayhew: They are responding to it as an abstract shape and space.

Well, it does seem very abstract. Were you thinking of landscape when you painted it, or were you thinking—

Mayhew: Mood.

Mood. It's your mood.

Mayhew: Feeling. Space. Shape. That's more than sensitivity. And, also, the patterns in here, it's a certain mood of space that goes on with that. A certain feeling of time.

Mmm. Okay.

Mayhew: So it's time and space and the feeling it gives; certainly the color's not true, but you can see a little bit of it, right?

That color contrast, between the red and the blue, is quite dramatic.

Mayhew: Right, right.

It's quite — I wouldn't say angry, but—

Mayhew: Yeah. It has to do with the mood of feeling, and the gesture and sensitivity of that. And the shapes of that too, right? You can see the different sensitivities of shapes.

This is called Sacred Path. *Can you tell me about this one?*

Mayhew: It's an area, you see a lot of worn areas where people travel on these spaces. And they leave their mark by doing the path, but not knowing where it really goes. So there's a mystery about the future, right? How much what's happening here is part of an experience in the past, but the future's over here.

You know this darker purple? This is just me, but this darker purple seems—

Mayhew: It all has to do with the color, again. I—always involved the color which creates a certain mood space—how colors interact with each other. There's a certain feeling right there, right.

But it's hopeful to me, here.

Mayhew: Yeah, right.

It's hopeful. But not so much here.

Mayhew: No. It has to do with the shapes here, and—certainly that shape there really turns me on.

(Laughs) Nice.

Mayhew: It's that worn spot where people walk, and gesturing—but then where does it go?

And this emerged naturally, as you painted it.

Mayhew: Right.

You didn't plan that.

Mayhew: Nothing is planned when I paint. You have these tree forms over here, but nothing is planned.

Mm-hmm. But you must start to make a tree, when you are painting.

Mayhew: Mmm, no, I put color on the canvas, see it thinning in and out … it completely changed. The mood evolves, at the moment. So that path dictates a certain feeling of what's happening with those tree forms.

This one is called Indigenous Spring, *and it has a path as well, but it's quite different.*

Mayhew: Yeah, it's different. And it's not so much a path here, as it is a feeling of time. And space. And the mood of early spring. It's not a late spring. It's early. Really early. Almost like now.

It's a large, open space there. What's that?

Mayhew: It has to do with, again, that mood or feeling, which, in spring—nature is constantly evolving, changing, changing. Constantly reinventing itself. And that's part of the change of space. The change of time, in spring. It's the beginning! Since I'm an Aries, that's the beginning of Aries. (Laughs)

(Laughs) Do you see — to me, there's a dialogue between the top half and the bottom half.

Mayhew: No, it has to do with the feeling of time and space again — there's distance and the beginning of a particular mood. I don't think about it. After the fact, I feel it. It's not a planning thing. So when it's finished, I live with it.

To me, it seems that this is the ending of a path, and up here is a more transcendent space. Does it matter what I — do you accept that?

Mayhew: I feel it very nicely ... suggests things to different people. Remember the two women in the exhibition? They were looking at the painting, and didn't know I was standing behind them, right? (Laughs). One woman was talking to the other one and she says, "The scenery, it's just like England! The northern part of England!" And the other woman says, "No, that's Oregon."

(Laughs) That's a great story.

Mayhew: So it was an emotional encounter, experience! Their experience, right? (Laughs) They put [in] their own experience. Like you, just what you said: it's *your* experience. Or your identity with what you see.

And you accept those different experiences.

Mayhew: Yes, fine. Whatever turns you on. (Laughs)

Scarlet Noon. *I love these.*

Mayhew: It has to do with a certain time of day. And the feeling of that. *Scarlet Noon* — it's like — the middle of everything. The middle of the day. It's like — the middle of life. The strength and the power of that experience.

But there's something to me — Love Bush, *there's something almost erotic to me about these.*

Mayhew: Well, that was the intention, too. (Laughs)

Was it?

Mayhew: Sexual.

Because I see that, absolutely.

Mayhew: (Laughs) No, that's part of it. *Love Bush* is part of it.

Yes. Exactly!

Mayhew: (Laughs)

Can you put that into words? I mean, what—why is it that you would want to put that kind of eroticism—

Mayhew: Well, in the beginning, it was this color underneath. And then I thought that worked so well with the yellow, and the feeling of that. So it created a certain mood. Then when I started building on it, I underpaint with a brush, and then I build with a palette knife. I scumble and skip and scrape and spat and it creates a certain texture and feeling.

So that was the red.

Mayhew: It even adds to that power of feeling. It soothes moods. But also shapes. These shapes become very important to me. And that shape right there is important. Even down here. Each pattern becomes important to me. Right. And creates moods.

To move from Scarlet Noon *to* Blue Breeze*—this is really abstract!*

Mayhew: But the reproduction is not—there's more character in here than you see in the reproduction. More contrast and change, right.

Even still, it's very abstract.

Mayhew: But the silhouettes have feeling. The orange and blue are complementary colors. (Laughs) Creates a certain mood. It's a certain time space. You put red next to the blue, it's another thing. Orange next to the blue, creates another time feeling. And distance. But I don't think about it when I'm doing it. It just happens. The shapes in there. Look at that. Really, shapes, I love it. That's what I love to see happen (laughs). It's got this moody feeling (laughs).

Yeah, oh, yeah. It looks to me like a person.

Mayhew: It's like water down here, you see, up that side there and that feeling in there? But these patterns are part of it. And it's the mood … it certainly could work that way [upside down].

Mmm, sure. I prefer it that way. Here's one that's almost totally abstract [no title]. And yet I could see trees here.

Mayhew: Oh, yeah, it's just a mood of nature. But I like it this way, too [upside down]. (Laughs)

Is this a watercolor? I love this one. It's upside down.

Mayhew: You like moody stuff.

Well, that's me.

Mayhew: It's real moody stuff. (Laughs) But that's part of what I like to do. It's a mystery. It's a mystery to me. These are mysterious feelings … what happened there? What happened in the past in that area before these trees grew? Or what happened even after they grew?

This one reminds me of the story you told about being in the South [referring to a set of abstract images].

Mayhew: That's right.

Did you have that in mind in this picture, or no? But it makes sense. Oh, this is gorgeous.

Mayhew: People are copying these over and framing these, and I went to their house and saw them on their wall, she says, "I have a Mayhew," and I said, "Where'd you get them?" (Laughs) She got it off the internet! (Laughs)

Now this — this is something. That's totally abstract!

Mayhew: Not if you look at it. It's a mood, a feeling … how do you like that one?

It's abstract still!

Mayhew: (Laughs) Yeah, but — not necessarily abstract. You look at nature, you just look at the trees and you don't look at the whole area, you just look at the trees that are right there. Or that hillside up there, which I like, there are certain little changes going on up there.... But you don't include the sky; you just see the trees. So it's not really an abstraction, it's very natural, made after nature.

It's so assertive, this painting to me is so assertive.

Mayhew: Right. Yes, it is.

And I don't know what you're saying to me, but I love it.

Mayhew: (Laughs) It's sexual.

This one?

Mayhew: (Laughs) Yeah.

Really? Okay. Well, figures.

Mayhew: This one even more so.

Oh, I love this one! Wow!

Mayhew: (Laughs) Right.

Purple trees in the background—That's amazing!

Mayhew: (Laughs)

It surprises me. You are such a gentle, really warm, kind person, and yet this painting is so intense!

Mayhew: It's part of that feeling. (Laughs) Even there, you can see the shapes in the image, become very, very important feeling. Right.

You, as a man, are more like this top half, gentle, here. But this I'm not familiar with that side of you.

Mayhew: Oh yeah, that's, that's my, really my erotic side.

Oh, I see.

Mayhew: (Laughs largely) It's really there.

I see.

Mayhew: (Laughs largely)

Well! There's that, then.

Mayhew: (Laughs) This is a little mystery feeling, right? Kind of like what's in between the trees, the same little spot over there, right?

It's like Love Bush *meets* Sonorous, *or something, over here.*

Mayhew: Right, right. This is more musical to me, right.

You know, this top half of this landscape almost reminds me of your view here [at his home].

Mayhew: Right.

Is there any influence?

Mayhew: Any straight line creates distance. So if I want to create a mode of distance, I just use a straight line, if I want to get more depth. A straight line gives depth right away. Also, in order to keep that from going back too far, you put warm colors in and it comes forward.

You mean like a pink?

Mayhew: That's right. Because it doesn't go back that far.

This almost looks violent to me down here.

Mayhew: Which I like, yeah. A little shock. (Laughs)

Now this is an inferno.

Mayhew: Right.

It's upside down. But it's an inferno. What is that?

Mayhew: It's really — I like it this way better.

I do, too! I agree; that's why I put it that way.

Mayhew: But this is — the watercolor is no bigger than this!

This is an all-orange inferno with green at the bottom.

Mayhew: But it's really no bigger than this [reproduction in a book].

Oh, really?

Mayhew: Yeah! (Laughs)

Wow, it looks enormous! It has a lot of power. Oh, God, that's gorgeous. It reminds me of Rothko.

Mayhew: Yeah, right. Right. Mm-hmm.

Anyway, it's beautiful. And this one is another watercolor.

Mayhew: Mm-hmm. Right. But it's upside down, right.

It almost appears to me as though you started to do a landscape rather like this one, but then, you just took over at the bottom half, and—

Mayhew: Well you know, it does it itself. When I—you ought to see me do watercolors sometime. I just paint it, and then we'll go away and go back, and it does its own thing when it dries, right? It changes! Because I sprinkle salt on there, and—

Salt! Really!

Mayhew: And different water—sometimes I use ocean water, it has minerals in it, creates a different effect with the paper. So the pigments will dry differently. It creates another kind of mood. I like the reproduction of these pictures!

That purple, there, really—

Mayhew: That's part of their mystery. And then the yellow comes into there—

Whoa!

Mayhew: Because that's its complement, right? But it creates another mood, right away—that's great. And then what's going on down here, right?

It looks like blood, or—

Mayhew: So when I finish the painting, I said, "Whoah! Wow!" It's a shock.

It's shocking!

Mayhew: A little shock. Yeah.

Beautiful. Now here we go, to something more—

Mayhew: Your reproductions are great on here! Wow.

Mm-hmm. Mm-hmm.

Mayhew: The color you've got. That's good. So there's a kind of mystery here, too. The watercolors, because when you're using salt in there, it does its own kind of—this stuff's taken [on] its own mystique.

When you were painting this, you weren't thinking, I want to make a bush, or I want this to be mysterious, or—

Mayhew: No. Zen painters. They go into a trance and do a painting and after finishing come out of the trance and look at it and, ooooh. (Laughs) Art is almost the same thing. I only just recently found out one of the artists I respected so well — I was just looking in the book I got from the National Academy, that Chin See died. He was a man I admired so much. (Laughs) With this big, long brush. He would use while he's painting. (Mayhew makes an explosion sound)

(Laughs) Wow.

Mayhew: [unintelligible] Has some teeth! Then it was about an hour later and we'd go back and look, when it dried, oh. I couldn't believe what I saw. He says, "Now we look! Now we look."

(Both laugh)

Mayhew: He was a little man, very gentle. Gentle man, right. Chin Shee was — a master watercolorist. Unbelievable. So I'm learning from all, learn from all these people.

I guess you know I like this one.

Mayhew: Oh. Yeah. The *Love Bush.* (Laughs)

It speaks to me, it's so powerful, and—

Mayhew: You know what's going on with all the subtle changes, right.

It's sexual! That purple—that purple is—

Mayhew: Oh, yeah, that's it. It comes even more, that reproduction brings all these colors out, right? This is mystery stuff.

It's also quite literal. What interests me is the fact that you don't turn to one of these and say, "Now I'm being representational."

Mayhew: I don't think about that. I just think about mood, and feeling, and the color. Color is my whole thing — it just keeps me intrigued.

It's like you're moving toward this place here.

Mayhew: They say, "How could you put a pink in?" I said, "Well, why not?" (Laughs) It creates the same feeling, right away.

What does pink in a landscape mean for you?

Mayhew: Just the mood of color, subtly — actually, the value level is very close to this. This value and this value and this value are the same. It's red, or in the red family — it comes forward. So it creates a certain kind of distance right away. It upsets the distance, really. And then what's going on here, the blue. There again there's a mystery in there. (Laughs) It's full of people. There's a mystique you don't know about people. There's a hidden person. When people marry, the fact that there's always that little secret corridor and no one ever knows. You never know that person.

Whenever I show this slide to audiences, they all say, "Ooooh." (Laughs)

Mayhew: They all have that strange feeling, right. It has to do with that red, and how much this form becomes a certain reality. And the shape takes on a certain mood. It takes on a certain mood of gesture, right.

Is there any statement that one can draw from this painting? To me, it says something quite angry, or dramatic.

Mayhew: Maybe dramatic, but not angry.

Angry is the wrong word, but— something strong. Something very strong. Power.

Mayhew: Right. Because that's the strange thing in my nature — I don't think I ever really got angry. Frustrated. And maybe sometimes confused about things that I don't accept. It is much more subtle, and the colors in here.

Oh, it's gorgeous. This section down here could be—

Mayhew: Right. Well, there's that mystique again, down here. The shape in itself creates a certain gesture and mood. With people, it's a kind of issue. There's a kind of isolated mood of, of individualism, that's a part of this. Right.

Yeah, it is quite — a little bit — solitary.

Mayhew: Mm-hmm. Right.

What do you think about the way that, that you're portrayed here, in this photograph? [Referring to a brochure photograph]

Mayhew: The photographer did this.

But what do you think about the way that you're being portrayed there?

Mayhew: Well, it's true to me, really. It's pretty close to me as a person.

Do you think so? Because this is not how I see you.

Mayhew: I know, but this is pretty — pretty true. Someone heard me lecture, and they said, "I couldn't tell it was you."

You look so lonely and sad and — like a loner.

Mayhew: I am kind of a loner.

I didn't know that. You're so social.

Mayhew: Well, there's a special kind of mystique in the world that people live in. It's hard to live there in that kind of existence. It's an internalized inner life. Right. You have to see the core that no one ever sees. But you. No one will ever know but you!

But what is that core?

Mayhew: (Laughs) It's kind of, I guess, a spiritual inner self.

What is it for you?

Mayhew: Well, that would be in terms of religious, kind of, sensitivity. The spiritual inner self. You see that portrait, everyone sees me that way. You see that.

Are you sad? Is this unhappiness that I see?

Mayhew: No.

It's not unhappiness.

Mayhew: No, no.

Okay. Okay, let's look at that picture.

* * *

So, this has got to be my last interview, for now.

Mayhew: The last? It's only beginning! It's just starting! (Both laugh)

Interviewers are always saying, "Where did you grow up? Who influenced you? What's your earliest memory? What were your parents like? What was where you lived like?"

Mayhew: My early memory is my grandmother. In terms of encouragement to being an artist. Right?

Do you remember a big window, or did you have a little dog, or—

Mayhew: Well, there was a house … a large house, a farmhouse structure. It was very nice.

Was it on the water?

Mayhew: No. And then there was the community in Amityville, right?

Right. And it was you and your brother?

Mayhew: My brother.

Just the two? And—what did your brother end up doing?

Mayhew: My brother is amazing. My brother—anywhere you'd go, he'd take over. Unbelievable. He went to the airline corporation that was manufacturing planes as a worker, right? Soon became a foreman there. And then, one of the men who was involved in electronics was working on one of the planes and he couldn't figure the wiring system. And my brother got in there and put the wires. Matched the colors.

Oh, wow.

Mayhew: So he was always really amazing. And then he became the technical engineer. He retired recently. And he became the commissioner for the elderly in New Haven, Connecticut. Everywhere he went, he was just—he excelled. Even though he had problems and was a wild young man, right?

Right.

(Both laugh)

So were you close? Are you close?

Mayhew: He was in New Haven. Right. He just retired from that position.

But when you were growing up, were you two close?

Mayhew: No, we were not. There was sibling rivalry

Sure, I understand. What about your mom and dad?

Mayhew: Well, they were separated, right. Back and forth with separation. I lived with my father sometimes, and my mother sometimes, and I lived with my grandmother. My grandmother was the one — I don't like that being part of the history, because that's not my concern. My grandmother was the one that encouraged me to be honest. Without even knowing it, really. She used to bring home different drawing materials because, you know, I liked to draw. So that was the beginning. I liked to draw. Right. But there was no encouragement, really, even though I became an apprentice to one of the artists, Hudson River, in summers. But that wasn't really a support situation. There was no one along the way. It just had to do with this strange, creative ambition. Creativity was a challenging thing ... I just need to draw, I need to make things, I need to be involved with doing that. I was constantly involved in that, rather than just playing baseball or football, even though I did excel at some of the other sports.

Oh, you did? What did you play?

Mayhew: I was a barrel walker.

A barrel walker? What's that?

Mayhew: You can walk a barrel. And when it rolls, you can walk on it. You can walk several blocks on the barrel without falling off.

(Laughs) Wow.

Mayhew: Not just a flat barrel, now. These are the ones that are curved barrels. Right. (Laughs) And what it is, is strengthening of the legs as a result of that.

Oh my God, you've done everything.

Mayhew: I used to bike ride a lot. I haven't done that in recent years — that was a joy of mine. It used to be I'd ride miles and miles and miles every day, right. After school. So the beginnings there, it has to do with, that was the African-American, Native-American community. The cultural development that came from that was very supportive. And it was excellent because of that. Creative survival was involved in that kind of instinct. Which I wasn't aware of until recently: how many people come out of that background, and then fail completely because the conditioning was very oppressive until they learned to accept the two cultures. Being able to live the two cultures. I have lived completely within the two cultures. A Native American with black skin. (Laughs) You know, that's almost a part of it. Mm-hmm. The consciousness of that kind of development and creative thinking — only later I became aware of. My brother and I both excelled. Coming out of an area which was very oppressive to African Americans and Native Americans. Especially the Native Americans. African Americans could get a job, and Native Americans could not.

Tell me, what was your dad—

Mayhew: Well that was the environment, right. My father was — he never left that town of Amityville. That was his whole life. And — he was a painter. A contract painter, but he couldn't get the contracts because they wouldn't give them to a Native American. So he had to get a white person to get the contracts for him, and then he could do it. To get the job, right? He was also a letterer — he could paint letters on a store without controlling the lines and measurements and so forth. He was very sensitive; he could build cabinets and things like that, right? I raised chickens, so he built me a chicken house, and things like that.

(Laughs) Wow.

Mayhew: He was a very sensitive man. And, uh — very vulnerable, because of the conditions. And I didn't want to — in watching him, I didn't want to fall into that pitfall, which was a product of that kind of heritage. How easily one could not excel because of being psychologically oppressed. But he was a very statuesque man, very tall, very handsome.

And involved with a — survival kind of instinct, even though he was in the middle of this oppressive situation, right.

Do you feel like he was discouraged, or cynical, in a way?

Mayhew: No. Very proud man, even though he was living a mediocre kind of existence. Wasn't extremely poor, but low-middle income, right. He made an existence, a living as a painter, you know — house painter.

Do you feel like you were close to your dad?

Mayhew: Oh, yeah. I had great respect for him. And also my mother. She was a very sensitive woman. She never wanted to live in a small town. She was a city girl. So there was a problem with her. She kept escaping and going to New York. She always wanted to be in the theater and stuff like that, right? That never happened, right. A very strong personality. Both of them had this. This kind of stature, no matter how oppressive things were, they were survivors. So some of that rubbed off on my brother and I.

Oh, I can see that.

Mayhew: She was very ambitious. And functioning. But [for me] in a weird way when I was a youngster. Mmmm. We got involved in a lot of things. But anyway.

I won't ask.

Mayhew: (Laughs) Right. So I used to escape to the areas, and [was] involved with my art. Strange. I never, in later years, try to imagine how I got involved with that situation as a youngster. And then — actually going, as a teenager, going to museums and so forth, on my own. Not really aware of the whole existence of being an artist. I had no consciousness of that.

I remember you said once that you had met Jackson Pollock, all of this, and your brother's situation — do you feel lucky that you didn't end up drinking, and all that— was that all around you?

Mayhew: I wouldn't think in terms of being lucky: it's a matter of my — when I left that town, I still had the pitfalls of one who had lived in that existence. And I needed to get out of it. I needed to leave.

Yeah.

Mayhew: I didn't want to be involved in the limitations — where my father — really — never left that town. The mediocre existence because of oppression. The oppression is unbelievable. Right. And complete denial for any kind of functional reality.

Would people say — did you — did your father experience blatant racism?

Mayhew: Well, of course. An Indian was not respected, you know. Even though they functioned in the community. I once witnessed a very disturbing thing, this is not what happens, just a very disturbing situation. I went in a shoe store and he was getting a pair of shoes.

Uh-huh.

Mayhew: And so he's trying on different shoes, and they were too tight, and set 'em over there. And they said, "You bought 'em."

Wow.

Mayhew: Because he put the shoes on, and it was like, no. Anyone else can't put those shoes on. So I remember later I saw he cut the toes out. The ends of the shoe out so he could wear them. Which he could only wear when he paints houses or something. But, uh — that was embarrassing. And I saw him — he was humiliated, but he didn't want to show that, you know, to me. So he — he bought the shoes, and we left. But I can see that kind of, uh, that's just one small situation. Or the fact that he couldn't get a contract because he was an Indian. Right? And so, that kind [of] psychological thing, and I saw the whole town of these youngsters. Where were they going to go in the future? I never thought about the future. I just had to get out of that limitation of that kind of existence. There was a dead-end street, right?

Did you go stay with your mom, in the city?

Mayhew: Yeah, I went to stay with my mom, because that's where she wanted to be. That was after my grandmother died.

Did she work there?

Mayhew: Yeah, my mother worked in the library; she [also] worked as a television operator. Pushing the buttons. (Laughs)

Wow! Okay.

Mayhew: (Laughs) And then I think she was a day laborer. Right.

And so you and your brother would stay with her sometimes.

Mayhew: We would go back and forth. He [my brother] really got trapped into that lifestyle. He worried about it for that reason. Because there was a doctor, he was at the hospital, and there were no attendants around to help him. He had to do an emergency operation — he was working as the attendant. And [the doctor] made him come in to help him. And the doctor realized he had fantastic talent. He asked if he would like to send him to medical school. And, he didn't — oh, I don't know.

Oh, no.

Mayhew: He said, "I don't want to do that." And then he went in[to] the service. He was going to become a pilot. (Laughs) He was a fantastic runner, swimmer, as an athlete — he even tried out for — at the time it was the New York Giants football team. As a kicker! He could kick the length of the field, right? But [when] he went in for the tryout, he had a hangover.

Oh no!

(Both laugh)

Mayhew: You have to understand that community! That oppressive, how it affects your psyche. And I — I needed — subconsciously — I had to get away from this. It wasn't part of something I wanted to live with.

How old were you when you left Amityville for good?

Mayhew: I was about eighteen.

Mm-hmm. And you moved to New York.

Mayhew: Yeah. I was in New York. I don't tell the other part because I don't want to identify with it. I was an officer in the Marine Corps.

Oh, wow! You don't want to talk about that.

Mayhew: Right. (Long pause) And because I was opposed to the whole thing of the service, they put me as a sergeant, a first sergeant. (Laughs) So anyway, that's, uh —

That's another life.

Mayhew: Which I hated, the whole thing. And, uh, I had to sit at the back of the bus with the uniform on in North Carolina. So, I said, "No, no, no."

Maybe not.

Mayhew: Unh-uh.

How long did that last?

Mayhew: A couple years. I went to the South Pacific. I was an artillery — the head of an artillery outfit. (Laughs)

You've really done everything, haven't you?

Mayhew: No, well — yeah, I've been there and done that. (Laughs) But then — not necessarily a pleasing situation. That was oppressive because of discrimination. Now, it's integrated service. Back then, it was an all-black unit. Which was very bad. When I came out of the service, I applied to art school.

You went right in.

Mayhew: Mm-hmm. And while I was in [the] service, I used to paint all the pictures for the soldiers! I drew all the women on their tanks. (Laughs) And they all said, "No!" You've got to cover them up!

(Both laugh)

Mayhew: That was very astute, as a lesson in drawing, right? Because I could draw anything, right? (Laughs)

And you knew what people wanted! So there it is!

Mayhew: (Laughs) So, when I came out, I wanted — I needed to go to art school. I needed that training. I went to school, and I applied for grants and fellowships and Macdowell Colony — that was very encouraging. Because there were writers and painters and composers, right? Very creatively stimulating, talking to them. Haven't you heard of it? It's the most famous colony. One of the most famous colonies, right. So I went there, and that inspiration, of all those creative people, it was unbelievable. I was just a youngster. They allowed anyone to come there, no matter what level, if you had some kind of promise, that's why they accept[ed] you.

So you sent them your paintings, and they appreciated them.

Mayhew: You can go there for three to six months and just do your own. Like the composers who were there, and so forth. [Leonard] Bernstein was there when I was there. These were people who were at the place. Prominent writers were there. And the exchange — it was very open. Even though the level that they had reached, there was no attitude of supremacy in manner or attitude, which was excellent. They respected you even though you were a beginner; it was great respect (laughs). I loved that whole idea, this whole milieu that I had no idea, right. So I kind of bathed in it, accepting that as a way of life, right?

How does this fit with your career as a jazz singer? How do those go together?

Mayhew: Well, it just kind of happened. After the Macdowell Colony, I applied for grants to go to Europe. Meantime, I was married and had two children.

So, where did you meet— what's your wife's name?

Mayhew: Dorothea.

Dorothea. Where did you meet her?

Mayhew: I met her because when I came out of the service. I had to get a job, so I got a job as a china decorator. And she was one of the people working there. (Laughs)

And the rest is history!

Mayhew: Right. Right. And then, you know, with the Cambridge china, doing painting on glass, china, vases. (Laughs) Right.

So, you lived in New York, and you had your children.

Mayhew: I was working at these china shops, and then going to school.

Mm-hmm. How did the jazz come in?

Mayhew: Well, early there, I was singing. Because that's what I thought I really wanted to do. I wanted to be a singer. Or involved with the theater, because that was the ambition of my mother. I thought that was the way to go. So I went some place in terms of dancing—people learn how to dance and sing and so forth. Then I took voice lessons. The voice I have now actually came out of that.

What's this dancing thing?

Mayhew: Later on I realized about dance. The whole creative functioning of movement. Because when I went to the colonies I met people involved with theater and dance. I got involved with understanding what they were doing. The whole creative existence in that. Movement has a lot to do with how one physically functions. So dance is part of that.

Did you ever try dancing?

Mayhew: Mm-hmm. I'm a good dancer.

(Laughs) Of course you're a good dancer!

Mayhew: (Laughs) I'm a good dancer. But then singing, someone said, "You have a good voice." I said, "All right," so I took voice lessons. So, I sang professionally for about four years.

Unbelievable. Where did you start singing?

Mayhew: In New York. In clubs. In New York.

Did you have a band you always sang with, or—

Mayhew: No, I just freelanced. You'd get a gig with a group that's playing at some place, and then Grossinger's, [in] upstate New York. I went and sang with his clubs, at night. Painted portraits in the afternoon. (Laughs) I painted the Grossinger family. And at Evely Hotel, which is also part of the borscht circuit up there. I sang out there.

Did you have a favorite club?

Mayhew: In New York? One of the jazz clubs at the time was the 5 Spot, and things like that in New York, right?

I see. Where was the 5 Spot? Where's that?

Mayhew: In the village. Greenwich Village.

So you never sang up in the Harlem area.

Mayhew: No, I didn't — in little clubs there. I just — when you're a singer like that, you just go wherever, who you work with, whatever.

Absolutely.

Mayhew: I sang with a lot of bands once, right?

You told me a story once about climbing out a window?

Mayhew: (Laughs) Yes, that's in New Jersey. One of these rattrap places, right?

(Laughs) And I was singing there, and a guy pulled out a gun and was shooting up the place. (Laughs) We ran in the bathroom to get out that way, [and] the drummer was trying to get his drums out of the bathroom window. I said "No, forget it, get out yourself!"

Those poor drummers.

Mayhew: (Laughs) But really, mmm, those rag tag places. Anyway, got a little job for the night.

So, so you went to school, you were a jazz singer, you were painting portraits —

Mayhew: Right. And then actually, china decorated.

Then what?

Mayhew: Well, then we had two children. I took them to Europe with me. After Macdowell, we applied for grants! Once you [were accepted] in the one place like that, it's easier to get other grants. So I got a grant to go to Europe. And I took the family! No one takes their family on a grant! (Laughs)

Where did you go?

Mayhew: Florence! I studied in Florence, Italy.

Where did you live in Florence?

Mayhew: Well, first the Penzioni Bartollini, which is a famous hotel right across from — it's right on the Arno. And the room that I was in later — I was involved with a larger room because of the family. Then the family had to go back. Because my wife developed pneumonia. Very bad.

Oh, dear.

Mayhew: So — had to send them back. I stayed over. But the room where I stayed later was the room where *A Room with a View* was written.

No, it's beautiful, really? Wow. Of course!

Mayhew: (Laughs)

I'm not surprised.

Mayhew: A small, little room in the Penzioni Bartollini.

Wow. And it had a view!

Mayhew: Right. Of the Arno. (Laughs) And the Uffizi Museum, also, you could see right down the Arno. I was right there. Right. So each one of these were … inspiration. Macdowell Colony was one, being aware of that whole existence. And, actually, my wife was very supportive of what I was doing. Very encouraging about it, right. So that was good. She was very supportive.

So that was a long marriage.

Mayhew: Right.

What kind of work were you doing in Florence?

Mayhew: Well — actually I was involved with the process of learning how to paint. I was studying the masters there and so forth. And I met a lot of artists who were there at the time. Red Grooms was there at the time. So this kind of milieu: American artists that were there also, at the same time, right? A lot of American composers, young composers, were there, combining things in terms of creative thinking. Constantly involved with motivational, creative sensibility. Which was not a conscious thing [for] me, but I was getting more and more involved with that kind of life, internally.

What other artists did you know when you came back to New York City? I remember you told me a story about Jackson Pollock, and how he wasn't very friendly —

Mayhew: No. At the Cedar bar. All the Abstract Expressionists used to hang out in the Cedar bar. So you would meet them. Klein, and Motherwell, and de Kooning … they were all in the Cedar bar.

Were there any of them that you liked, especially, or disliked?

Mayhew: No, just people you meet —

Say hello. They just hung out there.

Mayhew: They weren't famous at the time. (Laughs) They were just other artists! They had semi-fame, because that was the movement at the time, and they were the ones, because of Greenberg and Rosenberg. Also, there were writers in there, used to hang out in the Cedar Bar. I used to hang out with them. But then I used to hang out with different groups. The Socialist painters I used to hang out with, the Soyer brothers. When I came back to Europe I started teaching at the Brooklyn Museum. But before I went, I studied at the Brooklyn Museum, with Reuben Tam, Edwin Dickinson, Max Beckman, Kunioshi — these were the people who were teaching there at the time. Back and forth, between the classes, meet with them. I didn't really study with Max Beckman, but I used to go visit his classes. He liked the idea that I would come in there. Right? So that was great. That was fun.

It sounds to me as if you have this incredible energy.

Mayhew: Thinking about it, yeah, I was doing all this, but it was part of that creative environment that I was seeking, right. And how I got involved with the performance art was also part of that. How innovative I became — I was doing a lecture on the Lower East side, because that's where the Educational Alliance was. And they have studios where different groups come to rehearse. I had one of the rooms — I was doing a lecture, a slide lecture. And when giving a slide lecture some people get bored, right? (Laughs) So on one side there was a jazz group rehearsing, and on the other side was a dance group rehearsing, in the other rooms, right? I went over and said, come on over and stimulate these people. What I wanted them to do, I was projecting slides on two big sheets. I took the sheets down and gave them to the dancers to use as a screen, and moving around, with them moving. And they projected on the screen. They wanted to work improvisationally from the musicians that was playing, which was orchestrating them — the dance was orchestrating the musicians, and the musicians were choreographing the dancers!

So you really have a sensibility for the music, and movement—

Mayhew: Well, it's putting things together. That was part of that. Uniting things. It's like, different paints together, and mixing and stuff, right. With the theater, that was part of my thing, right there. I took it on the road after that, right? (Laughs) That kind of performance, that combination of slides, and dancers, and musicians, right.

What do you mean you "took it on the road?"

Mayhew: When I went to university I did it at Sonoma State. In a giant inflatable [space]. It's a new challenge. I'm looking for new challenges. Like you are a challenge. (Laughs)

Mm-hmm. I don't know about that, but—

Mayhew: It's a creative challenge, right. And how inventive that takes place. I get bored otherwise. When I'm reading a book, I'm bored. I jump to the end and see how it ended. And if it seems exciting at the ending, I'll go to the middle.

(Both laugh)

Mayhew: Otherwise, I get bored!

That's cheating.

Mayhew: I drove across the country six times. Three over and three back, right? Once with my son, once with a friend of mine, and once by myself.

Oh, by yourself it's hard.

Mayhew: No, I loved it! Each state I went through is like a new world. And each time I drove across the country, I was seeing it for the first time! I grew, intellectually, about what I was doing, what I was seeing. The first time I was just driving across country. Next time, when I was driving back, I started realizing the difference in the States as opposed to Europe … the terrain in Europe of one of their countries is like the size of one of our states! I didn't know that until I was driving across country and realized it's enormous, and also in the middle of the United States nobody is living there!

Well, I used to live there.

Mayhew: In the cities, you lived in a city, right? Nobody's here! (Laughs)

A little different from California.

Mayhew: Different from Europe! Right? There's a mass of the states with nobody living.

Do you find that big space inspiring?

Mayhew: It has to do with the whole sensitivity of nature. The way nature constantly resolves itself, constantly renews itself. Through the seasons, comes back renewed, and different! Actually the Zen painters say, "Watch a branch on a tree each season, from year to year, and see what happens." So I've tried to do that. I was watching that, and the leaves would come out a different angle. Up, and down, and around. And the branch would change direction … it recycles every year that it goes. Life never stops in nature.

How much of your work now involves trees?

Mayhew: In the beginning, there's a little, but [it comes out] completely abstract. No volume, no structure. It's just color and shapes. It may be suggestive of landscape, but that's all it was.

Mmm-hmm.

Mayhew: In the street sometime I'd see [something I wished to portray] … but the mystery wasn't there. So I started adding some of the sensitivities and feelings of nature. Like the shadows in the trees, and shapes. There are going to be shadows, the mystery of that. And who lived there, and what was that years ago, and how did those trees grow, and the nature and development of that. The shadows become important, really. And the light beginning to form. It was the mystery of that ... speaking to the sensitivity of time and space and form.

Does it matter what kind of trees you look at, or are you thinking about that?

Mayhew: No. Each one has its own personality. I did the whole series painting trees, different types of trees, and the shapes, and so forth. I used to work directly from nature, in the early years.

Right.

Mayhew: Learning more about it. It's involved with the whole sensitivity of African Americans and the land. And Native Americans. And the trees, of the land. And the mystique of that. In Native-American culture, nature is celebrated, completely.

But what does that mean, literally, when you're painting something? Obviously you're not painting something thinking, "Oh! I'm Native American!"

Mayhew: That's a natural instinct. An internal existence. If one feeds on that, it comes out in creative [ways]. I learned this from Norman Lewis. [I would ask him,] "What are you painting? Is your painting abstract, or some kind of pattern?" He said, "I'm painting—that's my guts on the canvas. It's my unique identity." I can paint figures upside down and backwards. It's easy. Easy for me to do that. And the mystique's not always there. Sometimes you just paint for the mystery of the people. There's a mystique about each person. It's an internal instinct in the person that no one else will ever know. Only that person.

You have some really beautiful—what are they, drypoint? Sketches in pencil.

Mayhew: Oh, pencil, yeah.

Pencil. Well, they're amazing.

Mayhew: But there again it's more of a feeling, an emotion into sketching. When I did medical illustrations, I went to the medical library in New York, and I was looking at the drawings, because they didn't photograph anything; it was all done by artists! Sketches of the vessels and capillaries, and the muscles and tissues and internal things. These sketches ... too emotional! Unbelievable! Beautiful things ... it's not exhibited anywhere. It's in the medical library. I started imitating the pen technique; I learned about more about it. Not easy to imitate it. I started using a crow quill pen, on a rough surface, on watercolor paper. And sketching on that. The challenge of the surface in using a crow pen on that — if you make a mistake it will just scatter! (Laughs) And with mistakes, you can use those scatters as part of the design.

Why did you move away from that into this amazing color?

Mayhew: It had to do with ... when I was in Italy, I was very close to the Barbizon School. I didn't realize that until I started studying the American Impressionists. When I was in Europe, part of my grant was to study color. In the archives, I had a grant to study in the archives of the museum, right? And no one else could go down there but me. It was a very strange experience.... I went where the books are down there, and things which can never be exhibited, can only be there, and I was opening one of the books, and the pages fell apart. I was holding it in my hand and the conservator walked by while I was doing it, and she said, "That's all right. Just close it." She said, "We can restore that." I couldn't believe what she was saying! She took me, and showed me pages that I had just — looked like that and how they restored them. I said, "You people are amazing!" I was surprised she spoke English! She was a scholar ... she spoke Italian, German, and English. She was a guest conservator there, right. All these kind of connections, they have to do with this unique world of creative sensibility, and a specialized existence. That amazed me. To live in that kind of environment. Right.

But still I don't understand how — these crow quill drawings are so beautiful. I don't see you do it later.

Mayhew: That's only part of the sensitivity of doing that. I didn't have the patience of doing that. It's a time situation. Great intimacy when you're doing that. I had no intent when I started to do it. It just evolved into painting. It evolves. And this is what I got involved with. In studying the Eastern paintings … it got involved in internalized creativity. This is what I got more and more involved in. That's what happens to the paintings. When I go to the canvas, there's no intent what's going to happen. All the paintings here, they just started with a splash of paint on the canvas.

I've noticed your latest work is larger, it's more intense, reds and purples. What is that about?

Mayhew: Emotion.

But why now?

Mayhew: All my passion, into the painting! (Laughs)

You need another outlet.

Mayhew: That's right. (Both laugh)

But I don't see it so much in your earlier work.

Mayhew: It has to do with—it evolves. Stagnation is distressing for me. You have to move on to another space. I was watching as I moved around, watching nature.

You were just talking about passion with your painting lately.

Mayhew: Through the years, this constant sensitivity is changing. It's watching nature's constant changing from one space to another.

Do you feel like your passion is for, let's say, your romantic interests, or—

Mayhew: Well, it's there too, but if you put it all in the painting, it makes it easier having to explain it outside.

I don't understand what you're saying. If you're involved romantically, you're more likely to—

Mayhew: You don't have to be involved romantically—it's how much that passion of what you're doing romantically, and while you're doing your creative process, that same sensitivity gets into that area.

Oh, okay. It doesn't diminish.

Mayhew: Right. It's a matter of transference. It's part of the continuance.

How did the people you were involved with support your painting?

Mayhew: Well, your peers, you have the respect for that. I went to an exhibition and there were a lot of artists, and Romi and they were talking about, they say, "Well, what do you paint?" And I said, "I paint for the creative challenge." They laughed.

(Both laugh)

Mayhew: They didn't understand what I was talking about. They had no idea what I was talking about. They paint just what they want. I don't paint for that reason.

That's why you're such a success! When did you meet your current wife? When was that?

Mayhew: That was recent, right. That was about ten, twelve years ago.

Let's go back then to when you came back from Florence. And you were teaching.

Mayhew: Right. I got more involved in the exhibition world. A little gallery in Greenwich Village, called the Morris Gallery. (Both laugh)

How did you get connected with the Morris Gallery?

Mayhew: They were looking for someone to show, right?

It's usually not that easy!

Mayhew: It's a little dealer, right? And so I exhibited with him. I didn't know what I was doing, oh my God. Because I was naïve about it, too. I wanted the show bad, right? And so, the *New York Times* reviewed that show.

And it was a good review.

Mayhew: [John] Canady reviewed the show, the famous writer at the time, the *New York Times*.

And you got a good review.

Mayhew: Yes!

Well, that didn't hurt.

Mayhew: [He said I was] a neo–Barbizon painter here, rather unusual in this town. (Laughs)

Did you sell some work then?

Mayhew: Oh, yeah. The gallery got publicity — the whole gallery, it was, oh my God! (Laughs) And from then on my career started developing. I got involved with another gallery, the Issacson Gallery. That was before I went to Europe! And the Issacson Gallery supported me while I was in Europe.

Where are they? In New York also?

Mayhew: They were on Madison Avenue. Sixty-seventh Street! (Laughs) And he liked — when he saw it, he liked the work! He asked would I show with him, and I did. He was the one who was very inspirational and supportive of me in the early years, right. When he couldn't sell a painting, he'd buy it himself.

When did you start moving to other galleries?

Mayhew: Well, he had to close his gallery, because he just didn't want to be in the business any more. A really frivolous and, at the same time, a very bright man. He died recently, which was very stressful [for me]. And he gave his paintings to the curator of the Metropolitan Museum. That videotape of me? That man on there, from the Metropolitan Museum, that was the one Issacson gave the paintings to.

Oh. Okay. Are you unhappy about that, or are you—

Mayhew: Fine.

Well, it's in the Met!

Mayhew: Right, yeah! Because Issacson is the one who really motivated me to continue. When I left, when he closed his gallery, the Dorlacher Brothers took me in. The Dorlacher Brothers is one of the top galleries in New York. One of THE galleries in New York. Dorlacher Galleries is very special. And then when the Dorlacher Brothers closed, because the family didn't want to be in business any more, because the elder of the family died, and the children didn't want to have it, and

Askew was the master curator, of any gallery, in the world, but from Europe, right? When the gallery closed, he died. He was, like — this was his life, right? Isn't that unbelievable? That can happen to somebody? Wow. So when that closed, the Midtown gallery was there, he was very interested in my work. And so he took me on. And I was there for twenty years, in the Midtown gallery.

You were teaching in New York—

Mayhew: I was teaching at the Brooklyn Museum. When I came back from Europe, I started teaching at the Brooklyn Museum. And then at Pratt Institute. And then the All Students League. I was teaching at all three. (Laughs). I loved it! The challenge is fantastic. Very innovative, you know?

Did you ever teach students who went on to have really successful careers?

Mayhew: Well, most artists — people in the arts don't become successful. In the arts. They go out in other areas, though. Like Hunter, New York City University. Some of the students there, they take electives in the arts. Many of them become very successful because it's just creative stimulation. If you're involved with that creative, inventive existence — that's the world and mindset that I live in. And how that's passed on to someone else. That's what it's all about, in terms of creativ[ity] — has to do with survival. Not just creative survival, but human survival. It's involved with the same kind of motivation and sensitivity. And how one can move on from one thing to another. Like from teaching to law or something else.

(Both laugh)

Mayhew: And be successful at it. Because of passion.

At Santa Cruz, I saw you doing that with students. When you gave a lecture, I saw how you inspired people, and I wonder, where does this energy come from?

Mayhew: It comes from different experiences, like the Macdowell colony, and seeing these fantastic people. The inventive existence they have. And very humble!

I've met people with so much less talent than you, who are very arrogant.

Mayhew: It has to do with insecurity. Sure. These people became so confident, some of the great writers were there, they were so humble about it. Right? That was beautiful. Right.

Because they know they're good.

Mayhew: Yeah. You don't have to talk it. And if one is insecure, what are you doing? You've got to flaunt it.

Right. (Laughs)

Mayhew: Yeah, some of them have that attitude. Creativity is very humbling. Extremely humbling. Doing a painting is, how much this is going to arrive at a certain end. Those paintings will change three times before they're finished. You constantly change everything around. The mood is not there. The mystique is not there. It's a mystery of feeling and time.

Do you ever find that people don't take you seriously because you're humble?

Mayhew: No, no. Someone says, "You're a famous artist! Why are you so humble?" I said, "If you create … it's very humbling." You don't know from one moment to the next, that creative element that you're involved with, if it's successful. Not to anyone else, but to you!

But I've never seen you say to someone, "Oh, I'm Richard Mayhew."

Mayhew: No, no. They'd say, "I don't know who you are anyway!" (Both laugh)

Right. But, still, I remember telling the TV man, "This guy's famous!"

Mayhew: He was like, "Right." (Both laugh)

He didn't believe me!

Mayhew: Famous in what, yeah, right. Being patronizing, right. (Laughs) Those people that you'd know very well … oh … Motherwell. I was teaching, and Motherwell was a distinguished professor at Hunter College when I was teaching there. And in order to abide by his position there, he had to go to different classes. He said, "Can I come talk to your class?" So, [I] talked to him about that. Very brilliant man. He was brilliant. Very sharp. Very intelligent person. And he said that the creative process is very humbling. You don't really know who you are. The outside world sees you one way, you see yourself completely differently. You don't see that person you look in the mirror, that they are talking about. And it's true! I look in the mirror and I say, "Oh, yeah. I see a thirty-year-old when I look. (Laughs) Like in that book I showed you. Did you see that young man in that book?

Yes.

Mayhew: (Laughs) That's who I think I should be seeing in the mirror.

Well, you're better looking now.

Mayhew: (Laughs)

So did you ever know famous artists who were full of themselves, and so you avoided them?

Mayhew: Pollock. Pollock was very insecure.

Insecure! So there you go!

Mayhew: Very talented. Very insecure. There was that kind of attitude right away when you're insecure! You've got to prove yourself all the time.

Mm-hmm. When did you come out to California?

Mayhew: Well, I came — I was on sabbatical from Penn State. I came across country and I used different places on my sabbatical to stay, right? I went into New Mexico and started teaching at a Native-American school there, and I used their facilities. And I went to Arizona and I used their facilities there for a short time. And then I came to UCSC — I used their facilities here to stay. I went to the art colony in Woodside. And I used their facilities when I was on sabbatical.

Why did you choose Capitola?

Mayhew: I didn't choose Capitola. When I came here, I made an arrangement with the university for me to use their studio. As part of my sabbatical, right?

But how did you eventually end up here? You were working at Santa Cruz, and then you went up to Sonoma County. How'd you end up back here?

Mayhew: That was before I went to Penn State. I was teaching out here in California before that. And I was teaching at Hunter, and they didn't tenure me at Hunter, [so] I had to go look for another job. Now City College wanted me to come there, and I didn't go to City College. I'd always loved California, so I came out here, and there was an opening at San Jose State. And I went to teach there. Right? And the kids, I was trying to get them to come out here, and they weren't interested [in coming] to California. All their friends were back there, and their high schools were back there, and the whole thing, just when they were teenagers, right? So, I wanted to teach out here. I couldn't get interested in them going back and forth. So I taught at San Jose State, and Sonoma State …

Why did you keep moving?

Mayhew: Well, they weren't giving me full positions there! It was half-, part-time positions, right? I wasn't used to that. These part-time positions, mmm. I wanted to be involved in interdisciplinary study. When I went to Sonoma State, I did that whole thing. They weren't ready for that! "That's not regular design class," [they said]. I said, "Yes it is!" They didn't understand it was a design class, right.

Of course now they would understand it.

Mayhew: Now? Mmmm. Of course academia is really different now. They weren't ready for me then. San Jose State, I did that at San Jose State. They gave me a hard time! I built a geodesic dome out of cardboard with my students. (Laughs)

Do you miss teaching at all?

Mayhew: I miss the challenge! The mystery of living. Otherwise you stagnate.

I understand that. Ah, I appreciate that. How is it that you don't get lonely?

Mayhew: I do get lonely. And that's the passion in the painting. Okay? It gets into the painting.

It's such a solitary life.

Mayhew: Yeah. It all has to do with, my wife is not here, she's in Seattle, teaching, and comes down here, and we see each other maybe once every two months. So, as a result of the friends around here, as I said, there's no intellectual exchange. And that's the problem. They're living in a completely different world than I ever lived in. There's no exchange.

But you don't want to move to Seattle. Why don't you move to Seattle or New York?

Mayhew: Well, New York is another life. I love the beauty of this area. All of the ocean —

It's peaceful.

Mayhew: And the seclusion here is fantastic. It's very creative and motivating. But it does get lonely.

Mmm. You're choosing that.

Mayhew: I adjust to it.

But you're choosing it. You could live in Seattle.

Mayhew: Well … Seattle. Have you ever been to Seattle?

Yeah. It rains.

Mayhew: (Laughs) It rains, it's cloudy. It's a different mood, different feeling. There's lakes up there but not the ocean. I grew up on the ocean. Amityville is a half a mile from the ocean where I was. This is not that far from the ocean.

What do you want to do with the rest of your painting career?

Mayhew: Just let it happen.

Right.

Mayhew: That's what I always did. I didn't intend to teach. I found myself there, teaching.

So you don't have any objectives for the future.

Mayhew: Just the next challenge, whatever that might be.

What are you struggling with right now? Or do you not see it as a struggle?

Mayhew: Well, the struggle is where I want to be, in the studio or the building. Do I want to stay here, or buy the place in New Mexico …

A studio space! Your studio is very tiny.

Mayhew: Yeah, it's too tiny.

It is too tiny!

Mayhew: Actually, my creativity would improve if I had more space.

Chapter Seven

Mayhew on Selected Topics, 2012

In 2012, Richard Mayhew and I sat down at Barbara's Bakery in Capitola, California, and conducted our final interview for this text. The conversation ranged over many topics, and the following excerpts are arranged by these topics, which at moments extend comments from previous interviews.

On Racism and Religion

Mayhew: It was implanted in me as a youngster, not to submit to the oppression and destruction of your heritage or yourself.

I'm sure that every once in a while you encounter racism.

Mayhew: Oh, it's there. It's always there. It's always there. The genocide, psychologically, is there.

How can that not make you angry?

Mayhew: Anger doesn't help, you know. If you become angry, it's self-destruction. That's not part of Native-American thinking. You poison yourself. This is part of creative survival, and it's part of don't get caught up in self-destructive denial. I've been around a lot of African-American artists who've become angry about being denied. Norman Lewis is a perfect example of it. He was just very bitter, very hostile, because he completely ignored what he was doing. Great artist. Completely ignored. They wouldn't buy his work, you know? Publicize his work? He ended up driving a cab, in New York. Brilliant teacher. But there was this constant denial of who he was. If one wallows in the existence of despair and hate and anger, it's self-destructive. And that's part of Native-American culture. If one can live in a pure state of lack of hate and fear and insecurity, then one can survive.

But so many people do.

Mayhew: Yes. Because of the oppression of society that lives that way, it's involved with a competitive destructivism. And war — to me, war is futile. Nothing is really accomplished. Everybody dies, and nobody really wins. Everybody's dying, but nobody's winning. No one won in the war with Korea, no one won in the war in Vietnam — everybody died. Thousands and thousands of people dying. I have problems with the youth of the world going to war for the political aims and ambitions of their elders. They sacrifice these young people in a war in which they have no idea what they're fighting for. Because they're so young and naïve, and the dedication of their particular state of existence or society, that they sacrifice for their elders' politics.

Are you religious?

Mayhew: Well, internally, it's almost Native-American religion; it's involved with respect for others. All the things that other religions preach, Native Americans actually do that. And want to do that. And sometimes are forced to become contrary to that, right. So there's this natural instinct to be spiritually sensitive, and loving, and supportive.

Do you feel that your ancestors are with you in some way?

Mayhew: Oh, yes, right. That's part of that. That's part of that Native-American thinking, which is involved with respect and support, and any anger or hostility is self-poisoning.

Did your grandmother tell you about this?

Mayhew: Yes. Mm-hmm. She was a powerful woman in the community. When people needed information and so forth, they used to come to her. And when they were sick she would go and help them, and things like that, right. So there was this kind of heritage, and not just from her, but it was an inherited state that I found myself in. Some of it is pretty close to Buddhism, in a way.

Do you meditate?

Mayhew: When you paint, you meditate. When you write, you meditate. When you compose, you meditate. I found out, that's my religion. I did a lecture at San Jose museum, and there was a lecture on Jacob Lawrence. When I came, they said, "Was he a religious man?" I said, "We never discussed that. But I feel that he was involved with, when he was in his studio, a religion." They resented my saying this. Oh, yeah. You have to realize that a lot of artists are involved with this. There's a special state of spiritual creativity, sensitivity. Right. A lot of musicians, when they're playing, it's just like another world of joy, and distance, and love.

What do you surround yourself with now that supports that?

Mayhew: I used to, in New York, you can meet the people there, and talk to them. I don't have that here, so I feel very lonely and isolated. It's not here. No one to talk to. And the artists you talk to, they're very commercially oriented. They talk about how they're painting or sculpting to make money. And I say, "I don't do that." And they say, "Oh, yeah yeah, you don't do that." I said, "No, I never painted for — I paint for myself." That's why I say self-absorbed joy, a creative inner lifestyle. It's a spiritual lifestyle. Like one going to church, or synagogue, or temple, and praying. It's a special kind of religious metaphor.

On Spiritual Sensitivity and Ego

I'm seeing a spirit that I never understood before. I think that underlies a lot of what you do.

Mayhew: Mm-hmm. This internal self-religion is part of all religions, really. It's how much it's an internal situation. To do right, and survive within oneself. When a child is born, a baby, it is trying to survive, one is born that, but all of a sudden, it becomes oppressed along the way. And they start losing that natural instinct to function and survive. Even a child about three or four, they know everything. They really know. It has to do with the retarding of that kind of knowledge and that natural instinct. It's retarded, and it's submerged into a regimental kind of functioning. In terms of the natural instinct of creative thinking and sensitivity. It's cut off! It's cut off on the basis of the fact that certain forms that one has to abide by deny that uniqueness, and one gets caught in the formula, is no longer involved with the creative sensitivity of self. They have to conform to a pattern of functioning which is sometimes denying who they are, or what their potential is. It's hard to identify that as some kind of intellectual, conscious knowing. And to evaluate that is sometimes difficult because it's so abstract, and has no basis of explanation. I live in that space. And that's a religion! The religions out there, every time I tried to embrace them, I found it completely false. I was watching some of these programs of preachers on television. It's completely nonsense! If that spatial sensitivity, who I am, comes out in the work, then I'm happy about it. There are a couple of hospital homes that are using the paintings for spiritual decoration. One can project that kind of sensitivity.

Do you ever plan the spirituality of the images that you depict?

Mayhew: I just keep on painting into it until it evolves to a feeling that I want. There is no fixed image of knowing what I'm doing. Sometimes it's frustrating. I used to go around the countryside and paint directly from nature, which is always frustrating because you don't really capture nature. It's so gorgeous out there. So fabulous. You might imitate some of it, but you never really capture it ... being an artist [is] a self-indulged existence. Very happy, joyful work, and I love to paint, I love doing it. Like when I was doing singing. I loved to sing! I didn't want to be paid for singing because I just loved to do it! I felt I was cheating on the fact that, I'm being paid to do this! Same thing I felt about painting. This is my joy! It's a pleasurable encounter. It was the same thing as an entertainer. It was a pleasurable encounter. But how much is this contributing to the needs of our society? [Some say] it's an inspiration and stimulating, motivational existence. So it's hard to think of myself doing that. For others, there's that ego trip that goes down. I never had that, although I know many artists that do, or those in the entertainment field. Very egotistical about who they are and what they're doing. It's hard for me to live in that state of mind because when you're painting, it's constantly a frustrating creative challenge. And no matter how much it reaches the ultimate beauty, you end up going to the next painting, because this painting is never finished … [for writers] the book that they just did, it's really the next book. Because the book that they finish, it just conjures up so many possibilities that they couldn't write in this one book! And there's part of that in all the creative areas.

Talk to me a little bit more about this tension between working alone, and wanting to be a part of.

Mayhew: [In entertaining] you're involved with people out there. And it's instant applause. As an artist, there's no instant applause. It comes much later. Or maybe [it] never comes. Creativity in itself is very pleasurable. It's like some kind of fantastic joy that's hard for you to imagine or evaluate. I told this story over and over, seeing Edwin Dickinson in the lounge of the Whitney Museum, his retrospective was there, and I was asking him about the show, and he says, "Oh, when you see yourself in retrospect, you'll find you haven't done a damn thing!" (Laughs) He's an older man! All the things he wanted to do, he can't do it, there's not enough time left, right? The teaching, and combination of creativity, is different. One can be a very creative, inventive person as a teacher. Just in teaching alone. [Teaching] is a special art, and a special creative activity. And some people really have it.

But where is your satisfaction? Would you say it's mostly in your work?

Mayhew: It's somewhat of the applause that one would get as a singer, or an entertainer. The fact that you get people saying they like what you're doing, or they enjoy what you're doing, and they're asking for your autograph, which I always was embarrassed when that was happening, that they felt you were a great innovator in the arts area. So that sometimes is hard to evaluate your feelings about that.

How do you feel about being well known?

Mayhew: Well, it's hard to imagine it because, as a youngster, being an artist was like something on the other side of the mountain, but you never get over there. Because when you get to the top of the mountain, there's always another mountain. (Laughs) You never reach the peak, really. That's just like, why some people climb the mountain to get to the top, right? But when they get up there, what have they done? (Laughs)

When you look at your life, do you think, Oh my God, look at all the people I've known, and all the places my work has been shown, and how much I've done? Or, do you think, Why don't more people know my work?

Mayhew: Many know of it, all of a sudden realize I was there, and who I was, right? But then it's hard to deal with that reality. Fame has its pitfalls in terms of your family and friends. They see you differently. They treat you differently. And I don't like that. All of a sudden you're different.

But you get treated better.

Mayhew: I'm like the same old scrubby youngster making drawings. (Laughs)

But you get a lot of respect.

Mayhew: I get a lot of respect, yeah. But then it's hard for you to live with that. You look in the mirror and say, "Who the hell are you?" You know, that kind of ego-ness I don't have. Others — maybe I would like to have that, that they have, they're really involved in this ego trip, how happy they are within themselves. But sometimes I wonder, Are they really? (Laughs) Because I don't have that, I don't see that kind of egomania, or the fact that all of a sudden I became famous. What contribution have I made at being an artist? My indulged, joyful existence, my whole life. What contribution was that? That's hard to deal with. That's why I got involved in different activities in the community. It's very meditative, because when I'm painting, there's nothing else out there. I'm inside the painting.

So you're able to then translate that to other artists and not have your ego take you forward.

Mayhew: Well, the ego thing is subconscious insecurity. That you have to reinforce yourself and support this thinking over and over and over again, right? Someone says, "You're really a star." And I say, "No, no, no, I live a very humble kind of lifestyle."

Discussing His Community in Santa Cruz

The more I get to know you, the more I feel my purpose in getting to know you is not just about the book, but in my life, you have such amazing insight and advice to give me as a friend. How is it that that gift you have for supporting people and inspiring them goes together with your reclusion, and the lonely existence of being an artist?

Mayhew: Right now, this is very disturbing to me, because I'm at this stage of being completely isolated. I get a lot of work done as a result of it. In New York there's always so much going on. I miss that. They're trying to get me to move back, you know. I don't like the weather. (Laughs) The human-support relationship is very important. There's a certain credibility there and intellectual development there that I miss. But people are not there anymore. All of these people died away! That's what's sad about this. I miss them.

So who do you hang out with?

Mayhew: There's nobody here. There's no one here.

Well, you must have friends here.

Mayhew: No. There's no one here. All the people here are dilettantes. And even the artists, they're so caught up in trying to survive, as an artist, that they sell their souls. Maybe I'm becoming too critical of exchange with people, but I was so used to this very credible encounter with people, that these people are not there. Peers are very important. It's part of the social functioning, which is living life in community, that African-American system of relationship. If you don't have it, you're isolated, you're on an island. So discussion like we're having here, that's very good, to have that.

Despite the loss of all these significant people in your life [Ed Clark, Ernie Crichlow, Reggie Gammon, Hale Woodruff, Romare Bearden, and others], you're constantly reinventing. Every time I come here and go in your studio, there's something else that's fresh.

Mayhew: Otherwise you're stagnant. That's why the paintings never look the same. [It's] because it's caught up in redundancy. I can't stand the redundancy. Sometimes I'm telling a story and I say, "Haven't I told this before?" (Laughs)

About Spiral Ending

There was never a closure. You never said, "this is over with." You just went on your way.

Mayhew: Spiral is a concept. It's like a multitude which keeps extending out, in all directions, and touching everything. There's no end to that. It's a beginning. Hale Woodruff was the one who coined the phrase of Spiral. Archimedes, the Greek mathematician. So this is a very unique exchange, which continues, even though they're gone.

On His Family

Mayhew: The poverty in this country. They show the poverty in other countries, the poverty in Africa is unbelievable. But the poverty in the U.S.—it's completely ignored! And my heritage which I ignore and which I have in many recent years started to deal with. I've always lived as an African American. I'm Native American. I'm two-thirds Native American, and only one-third black. So I've always denied my heritage. It has to do with my mother completely denying her heritage as Native American. She didn't want to know. And I think it came off a little bit from her. The fact that the oppression, and omission, and denial, and how Native Americans were treated and thought about—today, there's 250,000 Native Americans. There are thirty million descendants of

Native Americans in this country! And they're completely ignored. Never see Native Americans in the media. All the talk shows and everything, all the ethnic groups, and never Native Americans.

Why are you not involved with organizing Native-American shows?

Mayhew: I'm very involved with them, right. I'm a part of Native-American society. Actually, I met with them over in Marin county — there were about fifty Native-American artists. We met together to form a society, supporting one another. Which was surprising to many how different each one was. The artists there were involved with every direction you can imagine. But, wow, it's not like tokenism — they were really great artists. So I've been involved with special programs, and financial things, systems of talking to them, trying to help them, but sometimes it has to do with the psychology we've been talking about, which involves self-denial. Which is implanted, implanted genocide.

Wow, that's quite a phrase.

Mayhew: That's what it is. That's what it is. Right. The fact that you're not going to succeed. Which African Americans are quite involved with that. I know I met this [man who owned] land and properties and hotels in Detroit and we were discussing this. And he says, "When I walk in the store, I still keep my hands in my pockets so they won't think I'm stealing something." He's a millionaire, right? It's still affecting my head, the insecurity was implanted.

Your "Forty Acres and a Mule" show, the title itself, was alluding to something, and you told me a story about when you were in Louisiana, you were on a plantation, and you looked in the distance in the bushes and were imagining the figures there. To what degree does that show up in your work?

Mayhew: Well, it has to do with the shadows in the foliage and a mystique in what happened in that area. I'm sure those bushes I looked at now recently on the plantation didn't exist in the early years. But the identity and the feeling about the oppression of slaves that lived on that plantation, and how much one has the history of knowing how destructive it was to a mass of human beings, right. I was reflecting on the sensitivity of that kind of history, and looking into the bushes seeing, maybe, the images of that oppression that had taken place. I was very disturbed by the environment, even though it's being used now as a cultural art center. Ah, it's that old plantation, right. That sensitivity—it had to do with the whole religious thing, because many [slaves] were flogged and beaten at home if they didn't become Christian. And the association with the Southwest, the Native Americans were [subjected to fingers or hands being cut off as] an example for others who didn't become Christian. The feeling of that was contrary to the philosophy of the religion, really. Someone says, "Why do you hate religion?" I said, "That has nothing to do with it; it has to do with who practices it!" It's like the Ku Klux Klan; they practice the Christian religion, but that's completely a distortion of the reality of the philosophy! Right. Mm-hmm.

How much of this feeling, of this history, emerges in the work?

Mayhew: Well, it emerges into my painting because of the "Forty Acres and a Mule"—during Reconstruction the slaves were supposed to get forty acres and a mule. And they never got that. It's a whole land thing. Which was completely denied them. And Native Americans, it has to do with all the treaties that were supposed to be given them, which has never been honored. I think there are one or two or three treaties around the United States that's been honored, which is the tokenism. And it has to do with also the casinos, which is reparation, really. But it's a kind of distortion of the contribution that they really deserve. And never get. No other group has been denied their heritage on the basis of the United States gives them the right to their heritage, or who they are, right. So that's part of the paintings that I'm involved with, the whole spiritual sensitivity and concern, which becomes landscape.

Would you be happy if an audience for your work had a lot of history about this that you've just described?

Mayhew: Well, some of the recent shows, actually, there were texts describing why I'm doing it. I liked that. But it's how much they understood that. During the Civil Rights Movement, certainly African Americans have benefited to a great degree, but not to the degree that they deserve; Native Americans never benefited from that at all. So there is this concern how much I would paint like many artists which were painting protest paintings, putting up a fist, or involved with someone like Ernie Crichlow in terms of a little child being hung on the cross, right? How much that made a difference to them understanding what that was all about. How much I'm doing the landscape was based on this whole sensitivity and concern for the land, the spiritual kind of reflection of self in the painting, how much they understand that, or that I paint Native Americans being slaughtered by the colonial government.

Do you care if they understand? Do you care if they don't understand?

Mayhew: Well, of course. I just hope I live long enough to see that it's a multicultural government, instead of a colonial government, [of] European descent.

There seems to be a contradiction between the peaceful, meditative beauty of your work, and this violent—

Mayhew: No, the peaceful meditative beauty is part of the cultural, Indian religion. Which is very supportive, very sensitive, very honest, very committed to the peace and love of humans. Someone says, "You're painting this during the Civil Rights Movement. How come you're painting peace and plenty, when the other side of the coin is violence?" I said, "This is the side of the coin that is inside the sensitivity of African American and Native Americans. It's a beautiful, sensitive feeling of love and commitment and association. That's the side that I'm painting. I understand when people look at my work, they are feeling this peace and feeling of tranquility. Maybe it's coming through!

It seems to me you're giving a gift, in allowing them to experience that beauty without them necessarily even understanding the violent history.

Mayhew: Right. Hopefully that's what it's all about. But it's hard to live there. It's like living in a completely pure state of existence. And this is what many religions practice, if one is a monk. The ones that are really dedicated priests. Or any religion. One of the purest concerns of the dedication of humanity.

Why is it hard to live there?

Mayhew: Because of the pressures of a society constantly contradicting and challenging, and how one can resist all the arrows and spears that's coming at one. Always standing with a shield to protect one from the outside influences of destructivism, right? So it is difficult to live there. How to not get angry when one insults you, or when one is struck, how much one has to strike back violently. So that's very difficult to live in that kind of state of existence, but you have the purists that do live there.

It seems to me that you do live there.

Mayhew: Well, I was hoping it shows up in the work, and how much I can live in that kind of state. Sometimes in a painting I'm in that transcendent state. But outside of that, during the years, how much one regrets certain decisions and so forth they've made, not in a violent way. I don't think I've ever been involved in a violent conflict. It has to do with directions in life in terms of my pursuing a consistent, purist lifestyle. And how can one ever live in that kind of existence consistently, without being a freak of humanity?

(Both laugh)

Mayhew: As a child is born, it's completely pure of this — it's kicking its leg, and spinning its arms out; it's involved with surviving. Just the idea of surviving. But completely innocent until the oppressions of education, and society, close in on it, to the point where it becomes retarded, in terms of that natural sensitivity.

In African belief systems, in African religion, the elderly and children are very close in their sensibilities. It's the middle aged that get muddled.

Mayhew: Strange thing, after studying African art form, Picasso picked up on this. He said, "If I could have the sensibility of a child, and still do my art today, it would be profound." See, he picked that up by looking at African art.

I think that's in some ways what you accomplish. Your art is deceptively lovely.

Mayhew: Yeah, but that's hard to know that. It's hard to know that, within oneself, because you're constantly involved with the challenge of consistency of doing this. Maintaining that kind of purist state of creative thinking. The persistence of consistency, even though it's constantly evolving and changing, you can maintain that kind of sensitivity in the work.

Because you do change. Some of your work is very passionate and angry.

Mayhew: Well, it changes in terms of application of paint, in terms of color, in terms of form, in terms of space, in terms of mood. I'm constantly involved and concerned about mood, which is part of that kind of meditative state which takes place in the course of working, really. I'm completely lost sometimes. I don't know what day it is, what time it is, and if you get to eat, right? Which would be good to do that to stay slim. (Laughs)

On Materials and Framing

Mayhew: I'm working with a brush. I used to work with the brush a lot. And then I started doing a lot of palette knife [work]. But working with a palette knife I found that it was getting too far away from some of the subtleties that I'd like to use, which you don't always get with a palette knife. I like that mystique of not hard edges; with a palette knife you end up with a lot of hard edges. The mystery of the fact that the eye can't focus on the edges because it's so subtle, so it takes a while for the eye to see it, which is part of the mystery. Which is unique, and I like the idea. Oh, not only that — using subtle close values, which takes a while for the eye to focus on that and respond to it. That's part of that subtlety which is part of nature. When you look at it at first you don't really know what's going on there. I was trying to get that. The mystique of Native-American culture, is part of the mystery of the sensitivity of knowing and not knowing.

That experience of the viewer in front of those paintings is quite — I don't know if mysterious *is the word; it's challenging, certainly. Because one wonders, do I stand close to the work?*

Mayhew: You don't see it right away. You don't see it right away. If you have enough time to stand and look at it for a while, then gradually you start to see the subtleties of it. I was painting for all of the years with a palette knife. It's a little different. It doesn't have the mystique as doing it with the brush. So I work with a combination of the brush and palette knife.

Do you like your audience to stand very close to the work?

Mayhew: Well, that's up to one's response to it, right. At a distance they see it, when they get close they probably don't see it.

I know with color-field paintings, ideally you're right up there.

Mayhew: If you get very close to it, you miss some of the mystery. You back away, you start to see it.

But certainly, for me, when I look at your work, at about four feet away, I start to understand it. Three feet, one starts to get drawn in.

Mayhew: It might draw you in, but the fact that you lose some of it, back away [and] you see more. Most paintings, that's one way to really view a painting, not too close. It also has to do with hard edge, as opposed to soft edge. And the soft edge is not so much the edges of form, but all the subtleties of color contrast. Which is very close in value. If you use the red and the green at the same intensity, you don't see the value relationship. If you photograph in black and white, it will be one tone. It'll be the same.

I notice some of your work is framed. Some of it is not framed.

Mayhew: This frame, that's more of a frame you'd use on a watercolor. Rather than on the oil. I prefer just a small molding. Sometimes I put these elaborate frames on there and I found that they change the frame anyway, so I stopped bothering doing that, and then I felt that the subtlety of the molding is fine. The frame gets involved with, I guess, a decorating situation for one's décor.

Does that bother you when people do that?

Mayhew: No. That's their thing. (Both laugh)

What about your watercolors?

Mayhew: Well, watercolors should have a wide mat, and also a subtle frame. Nothing elaborate, right. But there again people want to decorate their area. Some of the galleries they get involved with, in order to enhance the painting for better sales, they put a better frame on it, but that's not my interest at all.

Early on, did you have frames on your work?

Mayhew: Just very simple molding. Just a little tiny edge molding. Back in the early years, I didn't frame at all because as a young artist couldn't afford it! We stripped it! Just put a little stripping around it. A lap. A lap stripping, which is fine. (Laughs)

On Growth and Reinvention

So how do you work? Do you just get into a certain mood, and then walk into the room, and begin, or do you sit up and plan it?

Mayhew: It's actually a challenge — I'm always looking for another challenge. And why I change my technique, use more color than I normally use, work with different surface applications, and different mixed in media — I never use anything out of the tube; I mix every color. I mix and mix and mix until I find some color I'm going to work in. So I'm not always happy with it. I have to just stop, otherwise I'll just change the painting. I'll work on it and keep changing, changing, changing. And so it becomes different moods, start to take over, and I go that way.

You don't sit up at night and think about—

Mayhew: At night, I might go to sleep and wake up and think about the painting I'm working on. And I can visualize what's going on with it, and whether I like it or don't like it. If it really bothers me I'll get up and go paint.

Do you ever sketch out what you're going to do?

Mayhew: No! I just start painting. If I don't like what's going on, I just paint over them. Not over them, but I'll change the part of the painting which evolves into something else, right.

Do you ever take turpentine or something and go backwards over what something used to be?

Mayhew: No, I don't take it off, no. I just paint over it. In the early stages I might wipe it off, but I do that more with watercolors. I can take a sponge with warm water and wash the whole thing off. I do that more with watercolors than oils, right. I just keep painting into it until it evolves to a feeling I want. So my work is very abstract on the basis of that. And, also, I don't work from subject matter, I work from the essence of subject matter, of nature, and so as a result of that, there is no fixed image of what I'm knowing and what I'm doing with it. Sometimes it's frustrating. But if I go back, in the early years I used to go around the countryside and paint directly from nature! Which was always frustrating because you don't really capture nature. It's so gorgeous out there. So fabulous. You might imitate some of it, but you never really capture it. In painting directly from it, you're constantly changing it anyway, right.

Sometimes looking at your work, one could say a major concern is the distribution of very large forms. Today we saw on the ground some water outside the beach restaurant, and it was spread out rather like the form of a tree that you are painting right now. And I see this certain set of distribution of these large shapes.

Mayhew: Well, this is a reflection of nature, which is constantly involved with replacing itself. Just a puddle on the sidewalk, after a rain, is just another reflection of thc forms in nature, right? And then the trees, [they go] through the cycle of the change of seasons; it's always involved with reinventing itself, each spring.

What about the winter? Have you ever painted the trees in winter?

Mayhew: They go through a cycle of sleeping and waking. Because they sleep and they wake up, right? Because even in sleeping they're still functioning sensitively. Right now, this is like part of winter, and I cut all my rose bushes back, but you can notice that they're regrowing already. In summer the cycle goes on, in regrowth. So from that, there's no end. Which has to do with religion, with everlasting life! Continuous. And then how much that part of nature, how much is that part of the human existence? When one dies, it's the fact that one is going to keep on living! It has to do with how much is the mind that continues, or the spirit continues, according to many religions. The body is destroyed, but that spiritual sensitivity is part of some of the philosophers in terms of energy and space. It recontinues in space. In anyone involved with germinating some continued form of sensitivity, it's part of the energy of space forever.

On His Age

Mayhew: Someone told me, you shouldn't be traveling by yourself, what are you doing traveling by yourself at your age? I said, I think I'm forty years old, what the hell are you talking about? (Laughs) It's a state of mind. I was with a guy, he says, hey, Mayhew, Mayhew, Mayhew! I was running at the airport. (Laughs) I was too late for the plane. I said get out of my way, I'm catching a plane. He called me, he said, man, I see you running through the damn airport! (Laughs)

So what is your secret?

Mayhew: It's a state of mind. If you think you're forty, you're forty. (Laughs) But I look in the mirror and say, who the hell are you?

On His Children

Mayhew: I was in a restaurant in Paris. And having trouble trying to order in French. And the waiter was giving me a hard time on purpose. And then Jack Bolan was at the next table, and when he heard me fumbling, he turned around, he ordered for me. He was an artist on a grant like I was; we met there, and we've been friends ever since! Also, my son was sixteen, and he was a rebellious sixteen year old, which is excellent. But there again, it was a certain impression, a consciousness, at the time, too. [Describes his son in the middle of the desert, driving at night, and waking up with the gas tank almost empty.] "I think we're going to make it!" and we did.

My daughter went to Purchase, Rockefeller's School for the Arts; she got involved in a theater group there. An experimental theater where [one] could expand and contract the stage, scrim, producing and directing, designing — became a construction designer. I'm proud of her, but also surprised! Really, because you can't anticipate that one would come out of a school system like that and be extremely successful. She has connections in Los Angeles and the New York theater, and studied with one of the top designers from England in opera design, so she helped design sets in New York in the opera. Now, she's a committed set designer and director. Her husband, assistant director for *Law and Order* and *The Sopranos*, said, "I love Ina, but she is so damn good."

Scott is also a shocking surprise, unbelievable. I gave him his darkroom and camera when he was fourteen years old and he took some great photographs as a youngster ... that [particular] photograph is just ripples in the stream in the backyard. He went to Purchase, was assistant to [a] prominent photographer, used to do shoot for *Mademoiselle* and other fashion magazines. But then it seemed a frivolous area, so he got involved with a friend who is a printer/trainer for New York Health and Racket Club. [He] wanted someone to do advertising and designing on computer. [My son] said I can do that, went to the library and read up on computers, set up their computer system. Then he quit! Because his design was so contemporary. So he set up his own operation, put an ad in the paper, [and during that] first week got ten calls. One of the first interviews he was stuttering and so on, and the manager laughed and said, "You sound like I was when I was a young man — you're hired." Ended up with twenty employees, representing a lot of top companies, recently got the Bill Gates Foundation website.

Isn't there something about growing up in this artistic environment?

Mayhew: It's not "the apple doesn't fall far from the tree," it's the artists and writers coming to the house, the environment. Traveling around museums, I remember carrying Scott around under my arm in the Louvre, standing in front of the *Mona Lisa*. John Cage, Romare Bearden, Harry Belafonte, Maxwell Anderson [coming to the house, my children] had this kind of exposure to other people. And my wife is an Apache filmmaker; she went to UCSC, got a master's at the University of Washington, now is a Native-American documentary filmmaker.

On Native American Identity

Mayhew: Unbelievable. How meditative that is! I taught at the Indian school in Sante Fe in 1985. I was on sabbatical from Penn State. These were youngsters from all across the country. I felt so comfortable with them. The completely comfortable feeling I had there, I don't know if I'd completely had it before, although I was certainly involved with searching for my identity. I identified with them without even talking the different languages they were speaking. It was very special. And the eagerness of them to learn to create was fabulous, it was almost natural, they wanted to do it. You didn't have to always show them, they did it automatically. Wow! (Laughs) If you ever go to Santa Fe, they built a new school, you've got to go see their school. You can't believe what they did! In the middle of nowhere out in the country in the desert, they built a beautiful school of Native-American art, an art school, which is involved with theater, and filmmaking, and mathematics, in terms of the technology of creative thinking, right? Wow! That was really a pleasure. With Native Americans there's a very spiritual connection. I went there and I found it. This ethnic kind of background shows up within me, I guess. Right.

You sound like you have more of an affinity with that culture.

Mayhew: Yes, because it has to do with being taught my heritage is in Africa and I have to reach to Africa to discover my heritage. And I never felt really sensitive to that, and I never realized what that was, searching for African connections, and actually, I realized I'm Native American, and this is my heritage, this is my culture.

You have both sides, in the sense of having a Native-American and African-American heritage … what do you feel about, there's a problem of addiction in your community?

Mayhew: Genocide. It's genocide! It's hard to escape it. It's everywhere! It's like being denied on television, no Native Americans — you never see them on television. That complete omission. So you don't exist. And you know what the reason for that is. Land control. Land rights. Property rights. And identity rights. Unless you can prove you're Native American, you're not accepted by the government as being Native American. Now, come on! Every other group can say who they are, and accepted, but Native Americans have to be certified by the government. On the basis of the fact that they can make claims to the land. So you can see how secretly they can cut this off. In terms of communication and identity. It's big business, right? The addiction is part of that. On Native-American reservations, there are whiskey stores everywhere. And drugs are very acceptably brought into the area. It's the same with the African-American community. You go into the African-American community, every corner has a whiskey store. And also, on the weekends, the fact that, in order to have some enjoyment, they get their pay, they go get a bottle. To get happy. To drown the oppression and disappointment. Which is kind of forced on them to do that. Try that, get happy! You know. And then all the movies and everything, you never see the real culture of Native Americans or African Americans. What do they show? They show the drug thing, the oppression … so you don't have any real images, of who they are — all the movies ever done, there's no real image of who they are. And Native Americans, the only time you see them on television is Westerns. And then they have whites playing Indians! (Laughs) Now there's more and more, like *Dancing with Wolves*. But who's the hero?

A white dude.

Mayhew: (Laughs) Right. But anyway, in terms of the drinking, that's part of the genocide, it is self-imposed genocide, which is implanted. All right?

How can you be philosophical about all this?

Mayhew: There is the creative survival instinct, in terms of just finishing a painting, how one can be deflated by the challenge, and being able to follow through on all the possibilities and being accepted by the public. How one becomes philosophical about it is the whole creative instinct. That's what salvation is.

* * *

It is evident from interviews with Richard Mayhew that, while his work displays no overt stylistic affinities with African and Native American art, the overarching principles of community engagement in these cultures, and the integration of art and life, permeate his art's sensibility. Mayhew's work can be placed in the context of these cultures, regardless of subject matter, because of his deep and abiding commitment to community concerns. His astonishingly luminous canvases suggest the spiritual depth of the artist, but it is in the context of artistic production and community reception that they truly emerge as African American, and in their emphasis on land and lucidity that they reveal a heritage of Native-American spirituality. Mayhew is deeply engaged in formal, aesthetic issues, but he is passionately concerned with creative possibility for those who are consistently denied it, and the integrity and "credibility" of engagement in the world. Mayhew's emphasis upon artistic integrity and honesty extends to his encouragement of the people he encounters to be original, without fear: in relating conversations with Hale Woodruff, Mayhew states emphatically, "Be true to yourself, and if you don't know who you are, you are in trouble." For those struggling with institutional or societal expectations, Mayhew urges, again, to hold fast to a creative vision: "[How does one] break away? You must have the feeling of something else."

Afterword

> I sat back in my chair. I felt my feet on the ground. I saw clearly. Things came together. It wasn't just her story she had wanted me to know. While trying to help her, while trying to trace her story, I traced my own.[1]—Greg Sarris

I will never forget the extraordinary moment I met Richard Mayhew, talking with my neighbor Mel Wong, the brilliant Merce Cunningham dancer, at my home near the ocean in Santa Cruz. I saw, watching him talk to my gifted and cherished Mel, Rick's astonishing warmth and capacity for friendship; for the first time, I saw his art, in the painting *Love Bush*. That moment—the brilliant conversation with these exceptional artists, the gorgeous vibrancy of that image, with its pink sky and purple horizon, green ground, and intoxicating—even hypnotizing—image of a scarlet bush—will be held in my mind forever.

Richard Mayhew and I were often out of touch, primarily due to my preoccupations. Yet his loyalty kept our friendship together. His delighted response to the sight of my ancient, brilliantly green car, wedged awkwardly by his tiny garage studio; his spontaneously offered singing as a celebration over the phone; his gifts of chocolates, a teddy bear, a brilliant watercolor in exchange for my own awkwardly offered painting—all of these things illuminate his joyful and generous attitude. Still, I did not understand why it was so important for me to pursue what became an extraordinarily difficult project, or why, again and again, Mayhew reached out and persisted in his friendship.

I now understand that Rick's statements about spirituality, meditation, and the lack of attachment to ego, as well as his perspective on authenticity, creativity, and humility, was intended, in part, as a personal message. Richard Mayhew, in the almost two decades I knew him, had been patiently demonstrating to me, through his stories, that the academic structures within which I had confined myself, and my single-minded focus on myself and on academic advancement, had led me to essentially miss out on my own life. The central questions of Spiral—"How relevant is what you are doing to the struggles of others? And how honest is what you are doing?"—led me to consider whether I was assisting others in the world, or leading a life constricted by the expectations, real or imagined, of others. Mayhew taught me the value of throwing aside "normal" structures and guidelines, and of being true to my most authentic and creative self, the landscape inside. Why did he take the time to show me this? Why did he persist in helping me, a frustrated, even troubled, perhaps egocentric and marginally successful young writer?

Greg Sarris, the Native American author and filmmaker, asked the same question of his mentor, who had been patient throughout his years of frustration in attempting to push her extraordinary story into an academic format. In fact, as he reveals, this rare healer was giving him back to himself. In answer to the question, "Why did you do it for me?" she answered, "[b]ecause you kept coming back."[2] For Mayhew, too, I persisted, and he was, therefore, willing to share his story. In doing so, he helped me find my own.

The last time I saw Richard Mayhew, outliving as he has his peers and mentors in Spiral, he did not have the boisterous energy he once had. Rick had difficulty hearing me. His memory seemed a bit less clear. I was moved to ask him if there were any words he wished to share, to summarize, for others, about his work and his life. After only a moment's hesitation, through the pain he must have been feeling, he replied emphatically, with a broad and beaming smile that conveyed enormous joy and power, "It was all fun and games."

Chapter Notes

Introduction

1. Richard Mayhew, interview with the author, Santa Cruz, California, 2003.
2. Romare Bearden and Harry Henderson, *A History of African-American Artists: From 1792 to the Present* (New York: Pantheon, 1993): 470.
3. Christopher Volpe, "The Spiritual Feeling of Space: Richard Mayhew and the Visionary Tradition," unpublished.
4. Henry Louis Gates, Jr., in Darryl Pinckney, "Big Changes in Black America?," in *The New York Review of Books* LIX, no. 9 (May 24, 2012): 35.
5. Richard Mayhew, interview with the author, Soquel, California, January 2008.
6. Ibid.

Chapter One

1. Bearden and Henderson, 470.
2. Richard Mayhew, interview with the author, Santa Cruz, California, 2003.
3. Erika Doss, *Twentieth Century American Art* (Oxford: Oxford University Press, 2002): 135.
4. Ibid.
5. Ibid.
6. For a broader discussion of the association between communal production and performance and African or African-American art, see Janet Hess, *Art and Architecture in Postcolonial Africa* (Jefferson, NC: McFarland, 2006).
7. Bearden and Henderson, 476.
8. Richard Mayhew, interview with the author, Santa Cruz, California, 2003.
9. Richard Mayhew, interview with the author, Soquel, California, 2008.
10. Amy Fine Collins, "Richard Mayhew at Midtown," *Art in America* (February 1988), quoted in Bearden and Henderson, 470.
11. Marsha Miro, "A Rich Sense of Color and Composition," *Detroit Free Press*, July 21, 1989.
12. Sharon Patton, *African American Art* (Oxford: Oxford University Press, 1998): 79.
13. Amy Fine Collins, "Mayhew at Midtown," quoted in Bearden and Henderson, 470.
14. Steve Turner, "Richard Mayhew: A Singular Vision," Steve Turner Gallery, Beverly Hills, California, December 2000 (Gallery reception announcement).
15. Collins, "Mayhew at Midtown," quoted in Bearden and Henderson, 470.
16. Bearden and Henderson, *History of African-American Art*, 470.
17. Sidney Tillum, *Arts* 34 (1959), quoted in Bearden and Henderson, 473.
18. Richard Mayhew, quoted in Hess, *Art and Architecture.*
19. Ibid.
20. Hess, *Art and Architecture.*
21. Ibid.
22. Lizzetta LeFalle-Collins, "The Spiritual Realm of Richard Mayhew," *American Visions* 15, no. 2 (2000): 20.
23. Quoted in Lizzetta LeFalle-Collins, "The Spiritual Realm of Richard Mayhew," *African American News* 13, no. 2 (2001): 16.
24. Mary Schmidt-Campbell, in Judith Maloney, "Improvising Nature," *Research/Penn State* (March 1992): 27.
25. Lefalle-Collins, *American Visions*, 16.

26. Ibid., 20–21.
27. Ibid.
28. Patton, 79.
29. Richard Mayhew, quoted in Turner.
30. Judith Maloney, "Improvising Nature," *Research/Penn State*, March 1992, 31–32.
31. Joy Hakanson Colby, "Getting Back On an Upward Spiral: Mayhew Vows to Rebuild 60s Activist Art Group," *The Detroit News* (June 28, 1989): 30.
32. Maloney, "Improvising Nature," 28.
33. Charles Fergus, *Research/Penn State*, September 1983, 9.
34. Turner.
35. Hess, *Art and Architecture*.
36. Colby, "Upward Spiral"
37. Maloney, "Improvising Nature," 29.
38. Ibid.
39. Lefalle-Collins, *American Visions*, 16.
40. Ibid.
41. Ibid., 17.
42. Maloney, 28.
43. Ibid., 29
44. Ibid.; Colby; Lefalle-Collins, *American Visions*, 17.
45. Maloney, 28.
46. Bridget R. Cooks, "Richard Mayhew: A Sense of Place," in Cooks, ed., *The Art of Richard Mayhew* (San Francisco: Museum of the African Diaspora, 2009): 36.
47. Maloney, 28.
48. Lefalle-Collins, *American Visions*, 17.
49. Maloney, 28.
50. Lefalle-Collins, *American Visions*, 17.
51. Richard Mayhew, interview with the author, Soquel, California, 2008.
52. Mary Schmidt-Campbell, *Richard Mayhew: An American Abstractionist* (New York: Studio Museum in Harlem, 1977).
53. Ibid.
54. Maloney, 33.
55. Richard Mayhew, interview with the author, Soquel, California, 2008.
56. Lefalle-Collins, *American Visions*, 17–18.
57. Maloney, 29.
58. Cooks, 39.
59. Richard Mayhew, interview with the author, Soquel, California, 2008.
60. Lefalle-Collins, *American Visions*, 18.
61. Cooks, 36.
62. Lefalle-Collins, 18.
63. Schmidt-Campbell.
64. Maloney, 29.
65. Fergus, 9.
66. Maloney, 29.
67. Lefalle-Collins.
68. Ibid.
69. Cooks, 47.
70. Richard Mayhew, interview with the author, Soquel, California, 2008.
71. Ibid.
72. Schmidt-Campbell, 61.
73. Lefalle-Collins, *American Visions*, 19; Maloney, 32.
74. Maloney, 32.
75. Ibid.
76. Schmidt-Campbell.
77. Ibid.
78. Doss, 135.
79. Doss, 150.
80. Ibid.
81. Schmidt-Campbell.
82. Lefalle-Collins, *American Visions*, 19.
83. Ibid.
84. Schmidt-Campbell.
85. Colby.
86. Schmidt-Campbell.
87. Floyd Coleman, "The Changing Same: Spiral, the Sixties, and African-American Art," in William E. Taylor, Harriet G. Warkel, and Margaret Taylor Burroughs, et al., *A Shared Heritage: Art by Four African Americans* (Indianapolis: Indianapolis Museum of Art with Indiana University Press, 1996): 152.
88. Maloney, 32.
89. Ibid.
90. Richard Mayhew, interview with the author, Santa Cruz, California, 2003.
91. Ibid.
92. Ibid.
93. Richard Powell, *Black Art and Culture*, cited in Hess, 162.
94. See Robert Farris Thompson, *Flash of the Spirit: African and Afro-American Art and Philosophy* (New York: Random House, 1983).
95. Sally Price and Richard Price, *Maroon*

Arts: Cultural Vitality in the African Diaspora (Boston: Beacon Press, 1999).

96. Suzanne Blier, "Africa, Art and History: An Introduction," in Monica Blackmun Visona, Robin Poyner, Herbert M. Cole, and Michael D. Harris, *A History of Art in Africa* (New York: Harry N. Abrams, 2001): 18.

97. Robert Farris Thompson, *Flash of the Spirit.*

98. John M. Janzen and Wyatt MacGaffey, *An Anthropology of Kongo Religion: Primary Texts From Lower Zaire* (Lawrence: University of Kansas Press, 1974): 34.

99. Thompson, *Flash of the Spirit*, 106.

100. Bearden and Henderson, 470.

101. Richard Mayhew, quoted in Maloney, 33.

102. Schmidt-Campbell.

103. Ibid.

104. Richard Mayhew, cited in Maloney, 31.

105. Bearden, cited in Hess, 168.

106. Schmidt-Campbell.

107. Mayhew, cited in Hess, 174.

108. Maloney.

109. Richard Mayhew, cited in Maloney, 30.

110. Richard Mayhew, interview with the author.

111. Powell, 13.

112. Richard Mayhew, in Eloise Johnson, "Richard Mayhew: Defining Moments," Stella Jones Gallery, October/November 2006.

113. Lefalle-Collins, *American Visions*, 21.

114. Richard Mayhew, cited in Maloney, 31.

115. Ibid.

116. Richard Mayhew, interview with the author, Soquel, California, 2008.

117. Schmidt-Campbell.

118. Ibid.

119. Ibid.

120. Richard Mayhew, interview with the author, Santa Cruz, California, 2006.

121. Ibid.

122. Richard Mayhew, interview with the author, Soquel, California, 2008.

123. *Research/Penn State*, 31.

124. Eloise Johnson, "Richard Mayhew: Forty Acres," Stella Jones Gallery (October 2003): 4.

125. Richard Mayhew, interview with the author, Santa Cruz, California, 2003.

126. Richard Mayhew, interview with the author, Soquel, California, 2008.

127. Richard Mayhew, interview with the author, Santa Cruz, California, 2003.

Chapter Two

1. Christopher Volpe, unpublished.

2. Hans Hoffmann in *Theories of Modern Art* (Berkeley, CA: 1968): 537–44.

3. Volpe, unpublished.

4. Bearden and Henderson.

5. Richard Mayhew, interview with the author, Soquel, California, 2008.

6. Ibid.

7. Cooks, 37.

8. Ibid.

9. Ibid.

10. Richard Mayhew, interview with the author, Soquel, California, 2008.

11. Cooks, 38.

12. Cooks, 15.

13. Richard Mayhew, interview with the author, Santa Cruz, California, 2003.

14. Volpe, 12.

15. Canaday, in brochure for the Sherry Washington Gallery, "A Living National Treasure: New Adventures in Oil and Watercolor," September 1991.

16. Mary Ellen Abell, *Subjectivist Tendencies in Early Modernist American Art: The Case of Edwin Walter Dickinson*, Part 4, Spring 1999 (online publication of the Graduate Center of the City University of New York), cited by Volpe.

17. Richard Mayhew, interview with the author, Soquel, California, 2008.

18. Ibid.

19. Ibid.

20. Ibid.

21. Celeste-Marie Bernier, *African American Visual Arts: From Slavery to the Present* (Chapel Hill: The University of North Carolina Press, 1998): 74.

22. Bernier, 73–74.
23. Bernier, 172.
24. Richard Mayhew, interview with the author, Soquel, California, 2008.
25. Ibid.
26. Bernier, 174.
27. Bernier, 175.
28. Ralph Ellison, cited in Bernier, 176.
29. Bearden and Henderson, 239–40.
30. Doss, 135.
31. Richard Mayhew, interview with the author, Soquel, California, 2008.
32. Doss, 120.
33. Doss, 13.
34. Richard Mayhew, interview with the author, Soquel, California, 2008.
35. Doss, 134–135.
36. Ibid.
37. Doss, 126.
38. Doss, 128.
39. Doss, 132–135.
40. Bearden and Henderson, 318.
41. Bernier, 164–65.
42. Bernier, 165.
43. Bearden and Henderson, 323.
44. Bernier, 165.
45. Bernier, 166.
46. Jeanne Siegel, "Why Spiral?" in *NKA: Journal of Contemporary African Art* 29 (Fall 2011): 84.
47. Ibid.
48. Ralph Ellison, 151–52.
49. Tala M. Hassan, "From the Editor: Remembering the Black Arts Movement," in *NKA: Journal of Contemporary African Art* 29 (Fall 2011): 4–7.
50. Ibid., 4.
51. Michele Wallace, "America Black: Faith Ringgold's Black Light Series," in *NKA: Journal of Contemporary African Art* 29 (Fall 2011): 61.
52. Jeff R. Donaldson, "AfriCOBRA and Transatlantic Connections," *NKA: Journal of Contemporary African Art* 30 (Spring 2012): 85.
53. Amiri Baraka, "The Black Arts Movement: Its Meaning and Potential," in *NKA: Journal of Contemporary African Art* 29 (Fall 2011): 24–25.
54. Ibid., 31.
55. Wallace, 52.
56. Ibid., 55, 59.
57. Faith Ringgold, cited in Wallace, 51.
58. Richard Mayhew, interview with the author, Soquel, California, 2008.
59. See, for example, Sharon Patton, *African American Art* (Oxford: Oxford University Press, 1998).
60. Richard Mayhew, interview with the author, Santa Cruz, California, 2003.
61. Doss, 119–137.
62. Courtney J. Martin, "Emma Amos in Conversation with Courtney J. Martin," *NKA: Journal of Contemporary African Art* 30 (Spring 2012): 107.
63. Faith Ringgold, cited in Wallace, 59.
64. Kay Brown, "The Emergence of Black Women Artists: the Founding of 'Where We At,'" *NKA: Journal of Contemporary African Art* 29 (Fall 2011): 120.
65. Richard Mayhew, interview with the author, Soquel, California, 2008.
66. Emma Amos, in "Emma Amos in Conversation with Courtney J. Martin," 111.
67. Cooks, 49.
68. Hilton Kramer, "Black Art or Merely Social History?" *New York Times*, June 26, 1977, 71.
69. Cooks, 51.
70. Richard Mayhew, interview with the author, Soquel, California, 2008.
71. Gwendolyn Dubois Shaw, *Seeing the Unspeakable: The Art of Kara Walker* (Durham: Duke University Press, 2004): 116.
72. Ibid., 4–5.
73. Ibid., 9.
74. Ibid., 13.
75. Mayhew, interview with the author, Soquel, California, 2008.

Chapter Three

1. Romare Bearden, as recounted by Richard Mayhew, interview with the author, Soquel, California, 2008.
2. Henry Louis Gates, Jr., in Darryl Pinckney, "Big Changes in Black America?," in *The New York Review of Books* LIX, no. 9 (May 24, 2012): 35.

3. Richard Mayhew, interview with the author, Soquel, California, 2008.
4. Richard Mayhew, interview with the author, Santa Cruz, California, 2003.
5. Richard Mayhew, interview with the author, Soquel, California, 2008.
6. See Gayle Fulton Ross interview in Chapter Five.
7. Betye Saar, cited in Shaw, 115.
8. See Gayle Fulton Ross interview in Chapter Five.
9. Bernier, 160, 175.
10. Lewis, cited in Bernier, 165.
11. Cooks, 41.
12. Cooks, 41–42.
13. Spiral, cited in Cooks, 45.
14. Cooks, 45.
15. Cooks, 49–50.
16. Cooks, 45.
17. Richard Mayhew, interview with the author, Soquel, California, 2008.
18. Janet Catherine Berlo and Ruth B. Phillips, *Native North American Art* (Oxford: Oxford History of Art, 1996): 209.
19. Ibid., 212–13.
20. Ibid., 217–220.
21. Ibid., 221.
22. Rick Glazar-Danay, in Lawrence Abbott, *I Stand in the Center of the Good: Interviews with Contemporary Native American Artists (American Indian Lives)* (Lincoln: University of Nebraska Press, 1994): 9.
23. Ibid., 59.
24. Elsa, "Jimmie Durham — colle di val d'elsa," *Associazione Arte continua* (San Gimignano, Italy): 10.
25. Ibid.
26. Kenneth R. Fletcher, "James Luna," *Smithsonian Magazine*, April 2000, n.p.
27. Ibid.
28. Ibid.
29. Richard Mayhew, interview with the author, Soquel, California, 2008.
30. Richard Mayhew, interview with the author, Santa Cruz, California, 2003.
31. Richard Dyer, *White: Essays on Race and Culture* (New York: Routledge, 1997): 2, 9.
32. Ibid.

Chapter Four

1. Richard Mayhew, interview with the author, Soquel, California, 2008.
2. N. Scott Momaday, *The Man Made of Words: Essays, Stories, Passages* (New York: St. Martin's Griffin, 1997).
3. Mayhew, interview with the author, circa 2006–2007.
4. Bearden and Henderson, 205.
5. Doss, 196.
6. Christopher Volpe, unpublished.
7. Taha, 59, 62.
8. Richard Mayhew, in Fergus, 33.
9. Gayle Fulton Ross, Chapter Five of this book.
10. Nashormeh N.R. Lindo, "Catharsis: A Personal Journey Back to Happy Valley," in Bridget Cooks, ed., *The Art of Richard Mayhew* (San Francisco: Museum of the African Diaspora, 2009): 14.

Chapter Five

1. Richard Mayhew, interview with the author, Soquel, California, 2008.
2. Lindo, in Cooks, 14.
3. Richard Mayhew, interview with the author, Soquel, California, 2008.
4. Ibid.

Part II: Interviews

1. N. Scott Momaday, *The Man Made of Words: Essays, Stories, Passages* (New York: St. Martin's Griffin, 1997): 27.

Afterword

1. Greg Sarris, *Mabel McKay: Weaving the Dream* (Berkeley: University of California Press, 1994): 164–165.
2. Ibid.

Bibliography

Abbott, Lawrence. *I Stand in the Center of the Good: Interviews with Contemporary Native American Artists (American Indian Lives)*. Lincoln: University of Nebraska Press, 1994.

Abell, Mary Ellen. *Subjectivist Tendencies in Early Modernist American Art: The Case of Edwin Walter Dickinson*. Part 4, Spring 1999 (online publication of the Graduate Center of the City University of New York).

Baraka, Amiri. "The Black Arts Movement: Its Meaning and Potential." *NKA Journal of Contemporary African Art* 29 (Fall 2011): 4–7.

Bearden, Romare, and Harry Henderson. *A History of African-American Artists: From 1792 to the Present*. New York: Pantheon Press, 1993.

Berlo, Janet Catherine, and Ruth B. Phillips. *Native North American Art*. Oxford: Oxford History of Art, 1996.

Bernier, Celeste-Marie. *African American Visual Arts: From Slavery to the Present*. Chapel Hill: The University of North Carolina Press, 1998.

Blier, Suzanne. "Africa, Art and History: An Introduction." In Monica Blackmun Visona, Robin Poynre, Herbert M. Cole, and Michael D. Harris, *A History of Art in Africa*. New York: Harry N. Abrams, 2001.

Brown, Kay. "The Founding of 'Where We At': The Emergence of Black Women Artists." *NKA: Journal of Contemporary African Art* 29 (Fall 2011): 118–127.

Brown, Kay. "The Weusi Artisits." *NKA: Journal of Contemporary African Art* 30 (Spring 2012): 60–67.

Canady, John. "A Living National Treasure: New Adventures in Oil and Watercolor." Brochure for the Sherry Washington Gallery, September 1991.

Chipp, Herschel B. *Theories of Modern Art*. Berkeley: University of California Press, 1968.

Colby, Joy Hakanson. "Getting Back on an Upward Spiral: Mayhew Vows to Rebuild 60s Activist Art Group." *Detroit News*, June 28, 1989.

Coleman, Floyd. "The Changing Same: Spiral, the Sixties, and African American Art." In William Taylor, Harriet G. Warkel, and Margaret Taylor Burroughs, et al., *A Shared Heritage: Art by Four African Americans*. Indianapolis: Indianapolis Museum of Art with Indiana University Press, 1996.

Cooks, Bridget. "Richard Mayhew: A Sense of Place." In Bridget Cooks, ed., *The Art of Richard Mayhew*. San Francisco: Museum of the African Diaspora, 2009.

Donaldson, Jeff R. "AfriCobra and Trans-Atlantic Connections." *NKA: Journal of Contemporary African Art* 30 (Spring 2012): 84–89.

Doss, Erika. *Twentieth Century American Art*. Oxford: Oxford University Press, 2002.

Dyer, Richard White. *Essays on Race and Culture*. New York: Routledge, 1997.

Elsa. "Jimmie Durham — colle di val d'elsa." *Associazione Arte continua* (San Gimignano, Italy): 10.

Fergus, Charles. *Research/Penn State*, September 1983.

Fletcher, Kenneth R. "James Luna." *Smithsonian Magazine,* April 2000.

Hassan, Tala. "From the Editor: Remembering the Black Arts Movement." *NKA Journal of Contemporary African Art* 29 (Fall 2011): 4–7.

Hess, Janet Berry. *Art and Architecture in Postcolonial Africa*. Jefferson, NC: McFarland, 2006.

Janzen, John M., and Wyatt MacGaffey. *An Anthropology of Kongo Religion: Primary Texts from Lower Zaire*. Lawrence: University of Kansas Press, 1974.

Johnson, Eloise. *Richard Mayhew: Defining Moments*. Stella Jones Gallery, New Orleans, LA, October–November 2006.

Johnson, Eloise. *Richard Mayhew: Forty Acres*. Stella Jones Gallery, New Orleans, LA: October 2003.

Kramer, Hilton. "Black Art or Merely Social History?" *New York Times*, June 26, 1977.

LeFalle-Collins, Lizetta. "The Spiritual Realm of Richard Mayhew." *African American News* 13, no. 2 (2001).

LeFalle-Collins, Lizetta."The Spiritual Realm of Richard Mayhew." *American Visions* 15, no. 2 (2000).

Lindo, Nashormeh N.R. "Catharsis: A Personal Journey Back to Happy Valley." In Bridget Cooks, ed., *The Art of Richard Mayhew*. San Francisco: Museum of the African Diaspora, 1999.

Maloney, Judith. "Improvising Nature." *Research/Penn State*, March 1992.

Miro, Marsha. "A Rich Sense of Color and Composition." *Detroit Free Press*, July 21, 1989.

Momaday, N. Scott. *The Man Made of Words: Essays, Stories, Passages*. New York: St. Martin's Griffin, 1997.

Patton, Sharon. *African American Art*. Oxford: Oxford University Press, 1998.

Pinckney, Darryl. "Big Changes in Black America." *New York Review of Books* LIX, no. 9 (May 24, 2012): 35.

Price, Sally, and Richard Price. *Maroon Arts: Cultural Vitality in the African Diaspora*. Boston: Beacon Press, 1999.

Schmidt-Campbell, Mary. *Richard Mayhew: An American Abstractionist*. New York: Knopf, 2005.

Shaw, Gwendolyn Dubois. *Seeing the Unspeakable: The Art of Kara Walker*. Durham: Duke University Press, 2004.

Siegel, Jeanne. "Why Spiral?" *NKA: Journal of Contemporary African Art* 29 (Fall 2011): 78–84.

Taha, Halima. "Richard Mayhew: The Spirit of Self-Indulgence as Art." In Robert Farris Thompson, *Flash of the Spirit: African and Afro-American Art and Philosophy*. New York: Random House, 1983.

Turner, Steve. "Richard Mayhew: A Singular Vision." Steve Turner Gallery, Beverly Hills, December 2000 (Gallery Reception Announcement).

Volpe, Christopher. "The Spiritual Feeling of Space: Richard Mayhew and the Visionary Tradition," unpublished.

Wallace, Michelle. "America Black: Faith Ringgold's Black Light Series." *NKA: Journal of Contemporary African Art* 29 (Fall 2011): 50–61.

Index

Index

Index

Index